Understanding and Supporting Children
with Emotional and Behavioural Difficulties

of related interest

The ADHD Handbook
A Guide for Parents and Professionals
Alison Munden and John Arcelus
ISBN 1 85302 756 1

Attention Deficit/Hyperactivity Disorder
A Multidisciplinary Approach
Henryk Holowenko
ISBN 1 85302 741 3

Asperger's Syndrome
A Guide for Parents and Professionals
Tony Attwood
ISBN 1 85302 577 1

Violence in Children and Adolescents
Edited by Ved Varma
ISBN 1 85302 344 2

How We Feel
An Insight into the Emotional World of Teenagers
Edited by Jacki Gordon and Gillian Grant
ISBN 1 85302 439 2

Troubles of Children and Adolescents
Edited by Ved Varma
ISBN 1 85302 323 X

How and Why Children Fail
Edited by Ved Varma
ISBN 1 85302 108 3

How and Why Children Hate
Edited by Ved Varma
ISBN 1 85302 116 4

Group Work with Children and Adolescents
A Handbook
Edited by Kedar Nath Dwivedi and Ved P Varma
ISBN 1 85302 294 2

Understanding and Supporting Children with Emotional and Behavioural Difficulties

Edited by Paul Cooper

Jessica Kingsley Publishers
London and Philadelphia

First published in the United Kingdom in 1999 by
Jessica Kingsley Publishers Ltd,
116 Pentonville Road,
London N1 9JB, England
and
325 Chestnut Street,
Philadelphia PA 19106, USA.
www.jkp.com

Copyright © 1999 Jessica Kingsley Publishers

Library of Congress Cataloging in Publication Data
A CIP catalogue record for this book is available from the Library of Congress

British Library Cataloguing in Publication Data
Understanding and supporting children with emotional and behavioural difficulties
1.Behavior disorders in children 2.Problem children – Education 3.Emotional problems of children I.Cooper, Paul, 1955–
371.9'3

ISBN 1 85302-666-2 pb
ISBN 1-85302-665-4 hb

Printed and Bound in Great Britain by
Athenaeum Press, Gateshead, Tyne and Wear

Contents

Dedication

Dr Ved Varma conceived of the original idea for this book. Unfortunately, during the course of its development Ved became very ill and had to be hospitalised. When he came out of hospital he asked me to take over the editorship. Ved has certainly earned the right to take a rest from what has been a breathtakingly prolific career of publication in the field of special educational needs in childhood, and emotional and behavioural difficulties in particular. His contribution has been, and will continue to be, of enormous value. I am pleased to say that Ved is now well again, and it is to him that the final version of this book is respectfully dedicated.

Dr Paul Cooper
University of Cambridge
School of Education
May 1998

Introduction

What Do We Mean by Emotional and Behavioural Difficulties?

Children with emotional and behavioural difficulties (EBDs) present special challenges to parents, teachers and other professionals. In the school setting EBDs can be likened to other forms of special educational need, in that they interfere with the learning process. Additional particular characteristics of EBDs, however, are that they may interfere with the teaching process and also the learning of children other than those exhibiting the problems. EBDs often manifest themselves in the classroom in the form of non-cooperative or oppositional behaviour, and thus present a personal threat to the authority and sense of competence of the teacher. This threat can be a major source of stress to teachers. This can lead to circumstances which exacerbate the original difficulties, and so lock teacher and pupils into a downward spiral of failure. A particular feature, therefore, of effective school responses to EBDs is the practical recognition of the needs of teachers as well as those of students.

Although the school is often the public site for the expression of EBDs, the same problems occur, often (but not always) less publicly, in the family situation; with child and family often caught in a 24-hour cycle of conflict. Like teachers, parents too can come to see themselves as incompetent and become ashamed of their failure to cope. The child whose EBDs are the focus for these problems in turn often becomes the object of dislike and resentment to those around him or her. The low opinion that others have of the individual becomes internalised and soon the child, and those with whom he or she interacts, unwittingly cooperate to maintain and increase the EBDs.

A unifying feature of EBDs is that they are disturbing to school teachers and others who come into contact with the child exhibiting these problems. Beyond this, however, there is little evidence to suggest that the different emotional and behavioural manifestations that are given the EBDs label are related to form a single condition. EBDs is perhaps best seen as a loose collection of characteristics, some of which are located within students;

others of which are disorders of the environment in which the student operates (such as the school or the family). The third, and probably most common, category involves the interaction between personal characteristics of students and environmental factors.

The array of manifestations that might fall into any of these categories is enormous. Students' emotional difficulties may manifest themselves in terms of extreme withdrawal from social involvement, leading to social isolation within school and possibly truancy or school refusal. At another level, the student with emotional difficulties may simply be preoccupied with emotional concerns to the extent that this interferes with the learning process. Students with emotional difficulties may be involved in bullying, either as victims or perpetrators. Children with such difficulties may also engage in attention-seeking behaviours, which can involve activities that attract the positive or negative attention of others. The energy that is devoted to such behaviour is often at the expense of 'legitimate' classroom behaviour, and consequently tends to attract the negative attention of teachers in the form of reprimands and punishments. To the attention-seeking child, however, negative attention is a desirable alternative to no attention at all.

The most commonly cited forms of behavioural disturbance in classrooms take the form of unauthorised student talk, the hindrance of other pupils from working, and other forms of behaviour that interfere with teaching and learning such as the use of verbal and non-verbal interventions, as well as forms of student behaviour that directly challenge the authority of the teacher (from straightforward 'cheek' to physical assault) (DES 1989). Rarer, but more severe, manifestations include hyperactivity, bullying, problem sexual behaviour and damage to property. Less disturbing, but evidently 'disturbed', behaviours include extreme inattentiveness, socially withdrawn behaviour, and phobic and obsessive patterns of behaviour (Blau and Gullotta 1996). Of related concern is a group of problems that, whether or not they are enacted in the school environment, are often related, directly or indirectly, to dysfunctional conduct or performance in school. This group includes delinquency and substance abuse.

There can be many different causes of these difficulties: biological, psychological and social. Furthermore, the extent to which a particular manifestation can be seen as a 'difficulty' will often depend on the perspective of the observer, and as such can be seen as a product of a particular, culturally defined, way of looking at things. This cultural perspective is particularly important, because it reminds us of the possibility that behaviour that is unacceptable in one context may be not only tolerated but actually valued in a different context.

Successful intervention with emotional and behavioural problems, in the school, family and clinical setting, is often dependent on an appreciation of this complex interplay of personal and social factors. A major factor unifying the various approaches is a recognition that EBDs are often subtle (or not so subtle) forms of communication. What the child is communicating when they act out or withdraw is that something is wrong in their world and that they want or need help to sort the problem out. Ironically, this cry for help often appears to take the opposite form, and comes out as antagonism, rejection of or withdrawal from the people who are best placed to help. In these circumstances the child is sometimes pushing those around him or her to the limit of their tolerance and patience, possibly because experience has told him or her that everyone ultimately rejects them, and that it is better to get it over with now than to run the risk of forming attachments that will end in disappointment and dejection. Yet one of the child's primary needs is for attachment to, and connection with, others. Successful intervention is, therefore, always focused on creating the circumstances in which such attachments and connections can safely be made. This can be done through adjusting the child's environment, changing the ways in which significant others see and interact with the child, and through helping the child to see him or herself and others in new ways. It can also be done through the development of new social and cognitive skills.

In any event, children with EBDs often need what the people around them find most difficult to give: care, support and understanding. This is one of the central challenges presented by EBDs: to overcome what seems to some to be the commonsense approach to negative or deviant behaviour, that is, the desire to make the perpetrator suffer.

The foregoing account of the nature of EBDs is intended to represent a contemporary view of this issue which is shared by many professionals and researchers across different disciplines. The rest of this book is devoted to an expansion of some of the ideas related to this view along with consideration of some of the ways in which thinking and practice might develop in the future. The book is divided into three main parts: the first deals with the nature of EBDs, the second considers issues in the assessment of EBDs and the third and largest section looks at intervention in clinical, educational and family settings.

CHAPTER I

Educating Children with Emotional and Behavioural Difficulties
The Evolution of Current Thinking and Provision

Paul Cooper

This chapter is devoted to an exploration of the way in which current conceptualisations of emotional and behavioural difficulties have evolved, and may continue to evolve, with particular reference to the educational provision that is made for children with EBDs.

Changing perceptions of EBDs up to 1945

The history of what we now call emotional and behavioural difficulties among children and young people is a complex story. Sometimes it is harrowing and disturbing for what it tells us about the difficulties faced by young people on the rocky road to adulthood and the impediments placed in their way by the world around them. At other times it is enlightening and inspiring for what it tells us about the positive potential inherent within all children, and the ways in which this can be, and has been, brought out through the work of selfless and caring adults.

Early concerns and cultural antecedents

Clearly a history of this topic could begin almost anywhere in recorded time. Concerns about unruly and difficult children appear always to have been an aspect of the human condition. The creation myths of the Ancient Greeks centre on strife between parents and children (Guerber 1938). The first Greek deity, Chaos, was overthrown by his wife and his offspring, Erebus. Erebus married his mother and, in turn, they were overthrown by their own offspring, Aether and Hemera. These too were usurped by their creations, Uranus and Gaia. This latter pair appear to have become aware of an emergent pattern. Determined not to be victims of their own, admittedly terrifying, children, Uranus and Gaia instituted one of the first recorded preventive approaches to disruptive behaviour by taking their twelve enormous offspring – the Titans – and chaining them up at the bottom of a deep and dark abyss. So begins the long and not too happy history of the 'sin bin'. Eventually, of course, one of the Titans, Cronus, escaped the abyss, with maternal assistance, and overthrew his father. And so it went on. These early warnings about the perils of parenthood and the fear of ungrateful children are perennial themes deeply embedded in our culture.

Although English literature has often portrayed a romantic view of childhood, which has stressed the purity and innocence of the child, this literature also has its troubled and troublesome children, from Shakespeare's Goneril and Regan, who abuse and usurp their father (*King Lear*; first performed in 1605), to William Golding's ignoble prep school savages in *Lord of the Flies* (1954), who, once out of the control of adults, descend into a life a cruelty and barbarism. More recently, the cinema has produced many literal images of the child as devil, in such films as 'The Exorcist', 'Rosemary's Baby', the 'Omen' films and 'The Boys from Brazil'. In these films the superficial qualities of childish innocence are juxtaposed with intense evil. In each case the screenplays illustrate something of the implicit ambivalence that modern western society shows towards children: on the one hand idealising children and on the other demonising them. The tendency to demonise has become more overt recently, with the much publicised Jamie Bulger case (Smith 1995a) and press reports of violent and aggressive pupils who have been excluded from schools (see for example *The Guardian*, 3 September 1996; *The Times*, 19 September 1996).

1895–1945: The birth of maladjustment and the therapeutic movement

Bridgeland (1971) cites Sully's book, *Studies in Childhood*, first published in 1895, as the first systematic study of the development of childhood behaviour in England. In this book Sully identified the following three types of childhood 'deviation': 'intellectual dullness, emotional instability and deviations from acceptable moral conduct'. A year later Sully opened the first laboratory in Britain 'to be devoted exclusively to psychology and to contain an education section where students and teachers received a systematic course in child study' (Bridgeland 1971, p.49). These two events mark the birth of the psychological study of childhood deviance, or 'maladjustment'. Prior to this, children who displayed extreme or unmanageable behaviour were most likely to be classified by such medical terms as 'idiot', 'imbecile' or 'fatuous' (Bridgeland 1971, p.46). The premise of these descriptors was that these children were physiologically defective and that their maladaptive behaviour was a direct result of this. This crude biological determinism was brought into question, however, by reports of: 'children who, admitted [to schools for the training of idiot children] as being beyond help or restraint, made considerable adjustment towards normality of behaviour and educational achievement given kindly and systematic care' (Bridgeland 1971, p.46).

This led naturally to the study of social and other environmental influences on children's development and the beginnings of the discipline of educational psychology. It was at this time that Sully expressed a fundamental insight that still holds meaning today, some hundred years later: 'the normal child is one who is in adequate adjustment with his environment; the so-called abnormal child is, in the vast majority of cases, merely a maladjusted child, not a child suffering from gross pathological defect' (Bridgeland 1971, p.50). Sully believed that these 'maladjusted' children were: 'incapable of being benefited by ordinary instruction not by reason of mental defect ... but by reason of accidental circumstances, and might, with individual study and guidance, be converted into reasonably efficient and law abiding citizens' (Bridgeland 1971, p.50).

The idea that human capacities, such as moral conduct and emotional difficulties, were amenable to change through environmental manipulation represented an important development in the history of children with problems, in that it moved beyond the idea that such capacities were fixed within the child. This development established the important principle that children placed in the right circumstances can change in positive ways.

Sully and his followers were convinced that the best way to meet the needs of maladjusted children was through the provision of local facilities for assessment and guidance of parents and teachers. Soon the study of child psychology spread through British universities, and interest began to be shown in this work in teacher training institutions and some schools. Following from these developments, three psychological laboratories were set up in the first decade of the twentieth century, in Oxford, London and Liverpool, to offer advice to teachers on the management of difficult children, and in 1913 Cyril Burt was appointed the first municipal psychologist in Britain by London County Council. Burt's role was to assess the educational, training and/or treatment needs of children referred by parents or professionals; to carry out research; to advise the education committee; and to disseminate psychological information.

Of course, Sully and his colleagues did not exist in a vacuum. The nineteenth century was a great period of social reform. Sully's scientifically derived ideas about rehabilitation were echoes of the Christian moral tradition that inspired the work of pioneers with delinquent children, such as the philanthropist Mary Carpenter (Bridgeland 1971). Carpenter was particularly active in the mid-nineteenth century in challenging the ideology of punishment and retribution in relation to juvenile offenders. She set up a number of schools which were model reformatories, where corporal punishment was forbidden and discipline was maintained through 'the master's own firmness, order and kindness' (Bridgeland 1971, p.50).

As the twentieth century got underway, a fusion of these moral and scientific traditions gradually developed in the form of what we might call the 'therapeutic movement'. Very much in line with Sully's conception of maladjustment, a type of establishment began to be developed which took children who were deemed unmanageable by families, ordinary schools, the poor law and other welfare institutions. The chief characteristic of these establishments was the emphasis they placed on the rehabilitation of young people through the creation of environments which stressed care over control. That these establishments were by and large residential was no accident. They were created, often out of the vision of individuals, to be model mini-societies, where circumstances were created that gave young people experiences that led to the healing of psychic and social wounds that had been inflicted by the mainstream society of the day.

A key pioneer in this endeavour was Homer Lane, whose 'Little Commonwealth' was one such model community. Based on earlier institutions run by Lane in his native America, the 'Little Commonwealth' was founded in 1913 in Dorset, at the invitation of Lord Sandwich who donated the land on which it was built. It catered for delinquent and unmanageable young people (boys and girls) beyond school age referred by courts or directly by parents, as well as very young children. One of Lane's major contributions to this field, developed by later pioneers (notably David Wills), was the creation of a system of 'self-government', by which the young people themselves took an active part in the day-to-day management of the community, alongside, rather than under the control of, the adult members of the community. The prevailing ethos placed self-discipline above externally imposed regulation. The community strove for a family as opposed to bureaucratic atmosphere, in which personal relationships were stressed over formal relationships. Lane also dabbled in an 'amateurish' way with the then new science of psychoanalysis, in the treatment of his charges (Bridgeland 1971).

Homer Lane was, as Bridgeland (p.135) puts it, a twentieth century 'archetype', on whom later pioneers modelled their own work. A.S. Neill (1972), perhaps the most celebrated radical educationist of the twentieth century, describes Lane as the man with whom 'child oriented education began'. Drawing on the ideas of philosophical and psychological predecessors such as Rousseau, Montessori and Freud, these later pioneers developed communities founded on the healing powers of love, respect and self-regulation. Often they placed their own values and methods in explicit contrast to those of the mainstream schools of the day. A.S. Neill (Neill 1916) and George Lyward (Burn 1956) had both been teachers in mainstream schools before setting up their own private boarding schools for difficult children. Both deplored what they saw as the destructive formalism of orthodox teaching methods which, they believed, stifled children's natural curiosity and creativity, and affected children's psychological make-up in ways that were often emotionally crippling.

The particular forms which these pioneering communities took were as individualistic in style as their founders were in personality. However, they shared a commitment to what Dawson (1981) describes as four basic tenets on which the success of their work was based:

1. The extension of 'unconditional affection' to all pupils by staff

2. The encouragement of 'freedom of expression' for pupils

3. A commitment to the development of self-discipline through 'self-government' or 'shared responsibility'

4. A commitment to a psychoanalytical orientation in their work.

Of these tenets the fourth – the psychoanalytical orientation – was perhaps the weakest, in the sense that few practised formal psychoanalysis as their communities developed. This is perhaps partly due to the fact that the pioneers were practical people who soon learned that the most therapeutic aspect of their work was often the community itself. The experience of living in a supportive and caring community, where participants were acknowledged and valued for their contribution, was in itself a powerful tool in the building of self-esteem and the shaping of integrated personalities. These insights were later to be expressed with greater theoretical clarity by an American pioneer, Bruno Bettelheim, at the centre of whose particular brand of 'milieu therapy' was 'a particular social organisation, which would be the matrix within which the children might begin to develop a new life' (Bettelheim 1955, p.2).

A crucial factor in this work was the quality of the relationships that were forged between the adults and the children in their care. David Wills, a post-war pioneer, describing his own attitude to these matters, summed up a view commonly shared by many of the pre-war pioneers, when he contrasted the personal qualities he sought in teachers in his school with what he saw as the orthodox teacher persona of the day:

> I suggest that we cannot be respected if we are not known, and this is the precise contrary of the usual view – many people try to prevent the children knowing anything about them at all because they fear that if they are known they will not be respected. The man who presents himself to his class as the Teacher the Whole Teacher and Nothing But the Teacher is going exactly the wrong way about things. He has no private personal life (so far as the child knows), no hopes, no fears, never needs to eat or go to the lavatory – above all, he has no weaknesses and never makes a mistake … such people make it impossible for the children to know them. And if he is not known, fully, as a man, in the round, it is very difficult for the child to have the real kind of respect for him that I am thinking of. (Wills 1960, p.135)

Adults had to be strong, forgiving, tolerant, resilient, moral and well integrated. They had to come to relationships with children with everything to give and without being needy themselves. They had to have the wisdom to see beyond the surface rejection they often experienced at the hands of maladjusted children and see it for what it was: the expression of deep psychic wounds that could only be healed through loving relationships. In fact, the need for reliable and robust relationships was demonstrated by the maladjusted child's often single-minded determination to push and test emergent relationships to breaking point. In these circumstances only the most emotionally strong staff could survive.

The pioneers differed in their attitudes towards the place of formal education within the structure of their communities. Neill, at Summerhill, was at one extreme, making pupil participation in formal education completely optional. Lyward, at Finchden Manor, provided opportunities for pupils to engage in formal education through a system of personal tutors, with access to public examinations where this was desired by the pupil. Wills, at Bodenham Manor, provided a formal class-based system of education. For each of these pioneers, however, therapy was always considered more important than education. At best, formal academic education was seen as only one of the many aspects of community life, along with, for example, the day-to-day running and maintenance of the community, that contributed to a child's positive development. Wills (1960), for example, described Bodenham Manor School as a 'healing institution' rather than a 'school' (p.32).

It was Otto Shaw (1965) who placed the greatest emphasis on formal education at his Red Hill School, seeing it as an essential next step after the resolution of a child's psychological difficulties. Shaw's approach was based altogether more firmly on formal structures than that of many of the other pioneers, though he still adhered to the main principles of what Neill called 'child oriented education'. Red Hill was organised around a complex set of formal committees manned by staff and pupils. Here, pupils were encouraged to develop self-esteem through academic achievement as well as through the more common therapeutic measures. Formal education was compulsory and was intended to reflect the kinds of experience that children would have in a mainstream grammar school. It should be pointed out that both Shaw and Lyward, two of the most educationally oriented of the pioneers, admitted only children of high academic potential into their schools.

1945–1981: The rise of educational approaches

The dedication and, indeed, the success of these and other pioneer workers are illustrated by the fact that all of the workers named above, and many of their contemporaries, devoted their entire working lives to the development of therapeutic communities for maladjusted children and young people. All of the above named pioneers began their therapeutic work prior to the World War II and continued into the 1960s and, in the case of Wills and Neill into the 1970s, with their careers ending only with death. In some cases their working methods survived them, along with their institution. Communities that outlived their founders include Shaw's Red Hill School, Lennhoff's Shotton Hall, Wills's Bodenham Manor and, most notably, Neill's Summerhill. Along the way they spawned new generations of therapeutic carers, who carried on the work of their mentors or in turn developed their own institutions, following many of the principles laid down by the pioneers (Dawson 1981) and developing these further through such organisations as the Planned Environmental Therapy Trust and the Association of Workers for Maladjusted Children (which survives today as the Association for Workers for Children with Emotional and Behavioural Difficulties).

In many respects the fundamental principles of therapeutic child care did not change over this period (Dawson 1981). Even today we can read books by the likes of David Wills and A.S. Neill and find accounts of life with children and young people that still provide valid insights into ways of helping children with EBDs to overcome their problems. What did change over this time was the world in which these therapeutic communities were located. In post-World War II Britain, maladjusted children became a subject of interest to people other than this group of pioneers. And although for many years the 'treatment' of maladjusted children was often synonymous with residential schooling, a wide variety of philosophical orientations was adopted, some of which would have been anathema to the pioneers. In particular, in addition to therapeutic communities, schools which favoured a behaviourist approach were founded (see for example Burland 1987), where the emphasis was on the modification of pupil behaviour rather than the exploration of intra-psychic issues. A minority of schools adopted what can only be termed highly dubious authoritarian approaches. The majority of schools, however, based their approach on an eclectic blend of therapeutic and behaviourist measures that was determined by the practical needs of their pupils (Bridgeland 1971; Cole 1986).

War and the 1944 Education Act

Nineteen forty-five marks the beginning of the second major phase in the modern history of our topic. On the one hand, this phase marks the massive burgeoning of the therapeutic movement and the exponential growth of provision for 'maladjusted' children. This phase also includes important developments and changes in what came to be accepted as appropriate treatment for these children.

Two very different but equally powerful events took place in the early and mid 1940s that brought the issue of maladjustment among children to a position of high prominence. The first was World War II and the second was the 1944 (Butler) Education Act. The first event in itself must have contributed to the exacerbation of emotional and adjustment problems among children, with its insecurities, deprivations and devastating effect on the many families which became either permanently or temporarily fatherless as a direct consequence of the war. The evacuation of children and families from areas targeted by enemy bombers led to further disruption and chaos in the lives of the people concerned. Particular problems accompanied children who were evacuated from inner city areas to rural communities without their own families. A major outcome of these upheavals was a recognition of the massive scale of urban deprivation, as thousands of socially and economically deprived children suddenly came to the notice of the better-off rural people into whose care they were evacuated. Bridgeland (1971) interprets this as an unintended consciousness-raising exercise which led to welfare reforms as well as the recognition of a large-scale need for professional support for the EBDs which many of these children exhibited as a consequence of their deprivation. Other interpretations relate the 1944 Act to industry's needs for a more educated workforce (Levitas 1974).

The 1944 Education Act was one of the parcel of measures that was presented to challenge the scourge of deprivation. The extension of educational provision to almost all children up to the age of 14 inevitably brought into the schools children who found it difficult to adjust to classroom circumstances for various reasons. It was in part to address this issue that the 1945 Handicapped Pupils and Health Service Regulations were introduced. Under these regulations the term 'maladjustment', along with ten other terms referring to handicap and illness, was first used in official documentation to describe a particular group of school children for whom special educational measures were deemed appropriate. 'Maladjusted' children were defined as 'pupils who show evidence of psychological disturbance or emotional instability and who require special educational treatment in order to affect their personal, social or emotional readjustment' (quoted in Laslett 1983, p.2).

As authoritative commentators have noted (Bridgeland 1971; Laslett 1983), this was a vague and confusing definition, since the terms 'psychological disturbance' and 'emotional instability' were not further defined and, therefore, were not only difficult to differentiate from one another, but also open to a wide range of different interpretations. This flaw was at least partly offset by the fact that these regulations gave official recognition to the needs of children with adjustment and behavioural problems, and through this favoured, by implication, a therapeutic rather than a punitive approach to these problems.

Provision for these children was made largely through the existing and developing network of child guidance clinics, that had been first established in Britain before World War II, and in special schools. A small number of special classes also existed attached to mainstream schools. As has already been noted, the common pattern of special school provision for the maladjusted was residential. The relatively few private schools that had been set up prior to the war were now joined by an increasing number of other schools, some private but many state funded. Ministry of Education figures show that between 1947 and 1980 the number of state-funded residential schools rose steadily from 4, catering for a total of 94 children, to 120, catering for 4285 children. Day schools increased over the same period, from 1 school catering for 45 pupils to 90 schools catering for 3841 pupils (cited in Laslett 1983). It is interesting to note that whilst the increase in residential schools was relatively steady over this period, the rise in day schools proceeded at a much slower pace initially, but then outstripped the residential schools in rate of increase. This is illustrated by the fact that in 1955 there were ten times as many residential as day schools, by 1962 there were only four times as many residential schools, and by 1980 there were three day schools to every four residential schools (DES *Statistics of Education* 1981). This observation marks an important shift in the way in which this group of children's needs were construed and met.

This shift was characterised by a growing emphasis on the educational needs of children with problems, and a gradual rejection of what became known as the 'medical model'. The medical model approached maladjustment, like the other categories of disability, as though it were an illness of the individual. The child who was identified as maladjusted was believed to have a disturbance that required special attention to the individual, often outside the mainstream school. This understanding shaped the early work of the child guidance clinics, where psychologists and other professionals (such as psychiatric social workers) adopted a psychodynamic approach which sought to heal children's psychological dysfunctions. We have already noted that a psychodynamic orientation was preferred by many of the pioneer workers and their early successors. Furthermore, the statutory identification procedures required the central involvement of medical officers. Laslett (1983) points out that psychiatrists tended to have a disproportionate amount of influence in the identification of maladjusted children, partly because they represented a more established profession in relation to the needs of people with behavioural and emotional problems. The medical orientation, however, was giving rise to an unhelpful and false dichotomy between education and therapy. If a child was identified as being maladjusted it was almost a foregone conclusion that treatment of this condition would take precedence over the child's education and in a setting other than the child's mainstream school.

Behaviourism and 'sin bins'

The massive rise in day provision for maladjusted children, noted above, itself indicates the growing challenge to the medical pathology model, through the suggestion that children who required day placements, whilst being maladjusted to the mainstream school, were not so pervasively maladjusted as to require a totally new environment. Only a short step from this perception was the idea that the seat of some children's maladjustment resided not so much within the child as in the school and classroom environment. The idea that the educational setting itself could be made more accessible to the maladjusted child really began to take shape with the increased influence of the methods of behavioural psychology which were imported into Britain in the 1970s from the USA. This brought with it a new role for the educational psychologist, who was now a possessor of knowledge that would enable teachers to improve their skills of behaviour management within the classroom and the school, and thus teach potentially difficult children without the immediate need for the cumbersome technologies of lengthy courses of psychotherapy. The 1970s, therefore, mark the beginning of the end of the dominance of a medical perspective on maladjustment, and the development of a new educational perspective. This was accompanied by the ascendency of the educational psychologist and the School Psychological Services over the old Child Guidance Services.

It would still be many years, however, before these new behavioural approaches would come to be seen as falling within the province of mainstream classroom teachers. One of the consequences of the 'educationalisation' of maladjustment was the proliferation of a large but ultimately unknown number of small off-site units for disruptive children throughout the 1970s (Lloyd-Smith 1984). Often poorly resourced, located in unsuitable premises and existing outside the regulations which demanded statutory minimum standards in other educational establishments, these units came colloquially to be known as 'sin bins': repositories for those difficult and disruptive children who were unwanted by mainstream schools (Slee 1995). This proved to be a much cheaper option for Local Education

Authorities (LEAs) than special schooling, though it may well be the case that many children who attended these units would have been better served by special schools or other available (but more expensive) specialist interventions.

Progressive mainstream schools

Another important development to take place in the 1960s and 1970s was the creation of what might be termed the 'progressive state schools movement', which included such mainstream schools as Risinghill Comprehensive School (Berg 1968), Braehead High School (Mackenzie 1970), William Tyndale Primary School (Ellis *et al.* 1976) and Countesthorpe College (Watts 1977). These schools – often secondary, though some were primary – were run by teachers who shared the same dissatisfaction with authoritarian styles of teaching and school organisation that had been expressed by many of the 'pioneers'. A.S. Neill, in particular, was a source of theory and inspiration to this group, who sought to create mainstream school communities which were democratic and 'pupil centred'. Pupils were consulted and encouraged to participate fully in the running of their schools, sometimes through Summerhill-style group meetings. These mainstream pioneers were attempting to create communities which were democratic, caring and inclusive, and thus, often unknowingly, echoing many of the qualities of the therapeutic schools for the maladjusted. What is also important to note about this movement, however, is its political unpopularity. Fletcher, Carron and Williams (1985) chart the trouble-ridden development of these schools and their staff. The fate of many of these schools was to be closed down or renamed by the LEA, or at least to have their progressive methods modified into more traditional authoritarian approaches. Similarly, many teaching careers were stunted or ended by involvement in this endeavour. For some, the only way to pursue their educational ideals was to follow in the footsteps of the pioneers and go outside the state education system, as in the case of Philip Toogood, former head of Madeley Court School in Shropshire.

It might be argued that the popular consciousness of the time was simply not ready to accept the idea that it was socially, psychologically and educationally valuable to enable young people to be self-directing in the ways created by these schools. The realisation shared by these teachers and the pioneer workers with maladjusted children that authoritarian approaches were more likely to create deviance than cure it, and that reward, care and security are prime motivators for everyone, was not widely shared at time.

The Warnock Report, the 1981 Education Act and the rejection of the medical model

Whilst there clearly was not a widely shared desire in the UK to develop mainstream schools on the lines of the pioneer schools, there was a powerful movement in the land to improve the provision of education to disadvantaged children. Already the Plowden Report (DES 1967) had recommended the need for teaching methods in primary schools to focus more on children's individual needs as learners. The Warnock Report (DES 1978) took this concept of need a step further. The central argument of the report is that children who have physical or other disabilities (including maladjusted children) should, where possible, be educated in mainstream schools. This was based on the view that had been increasingly expressed by educational psychologists and educationists that effective teaching always involves creating circumstances that cater for the characteristics of individual children. To remove a child from mainstream schooling purely on the basis of his or her disability, without careful consideration of the impact of the disability in the learning context, was unacceptable. The report drew on evidence which showed that increasing numbers of children were being successfully educated in special classes in mainstream schools. The report made the concept of 'special educational needs' (SENs) central to the decision-making processes concerning children who had previously been termed 'handicapped', and recommended the abolition of this pathologising categorical system. Central to the report was the idea that the child's educational needs are paramount, and that placement should always be made with this as the central focus. Accompanying this was the concept of a 'continuum' of provision, which would include the whole range of possible provisions, from residential schools, to day schools, to various forms of integrated provision in mainstream schools. The report recommended the need for flexibility in placing children in the provision that they needed at any given time and the need for ease of transfer between these provisions.

In many ways the Warnock Report epitomised the anti-medical model perspective in its determination to stress the importance of the educational context over ideas of individual pathology. The 1981 Education Act, therefore, which implemented many of the key principles of the Warnock Report, marks the official abandonment of the medical model in the field of special education and the official sanctioning of the ascendency of the educational psychologist in the assessment and placement of children with SENs. Major measures of the Act included: the replacement of the categories of handicap with the single concept of 'learning difficulties'; the creation of the modern system of 'statements of special educational need', which were to be reviewed annually; and the requirement that, where practically possible (i.e. where it was seen to be compatible with the efficient deployment of resources and the effective education of other children), the child with SENs should be catered for in the mainstream school.

By 1981, therefore, many features of the political and educational climate appeared favourable to the needs of children with SENs and particularly children who, in opposition to the individual pathology implications of the term 'maladjusted', were now defined as having 'emotional and behavioural difficulties'. The new term itself, emotional and behavioural difficulties, which became the preferred term of educational psychologists and Department of Education and Science policy documents in the 1980s, was significant in that although it implied that the difficulty was experienced by the individual child, it did not imply, as 'maladjusted' had, that the fault lay within the child. A child's EBDs could be the result of unsuitable environment as well as individual pathology in a normally acceptable environment. This marked a growing acceptance of the idea that the environment was the key to EBDs and disaffection in general.

1981–1997: Environmentalism and inclusion

Changes in the incidence of EBDs

The accumulated evidence of 50 years' worth of social research throughout the world indicates that in most countries of the developed world the overall crime rate (i.e. the ratio of number of crimes committed to population size) has increased dramatically since the end of World War II. One of the most consistent and reliable research findings is that adult criminality almost always follows a developmental path that begins with childhood delinquency and/or conduct disorder of one form or another (Smith 1995).

Recorded crime represents an important aspect of EBDs but is by no means the only factor of importance. It is certainly the case that, as David Wills (1960) and many other writers in this field have observed, the difference between delinquency and other forms of behavioural difficulty is administrative rather than substantive: the difference is simply that the delinquent child has been caught and convicted whilst the other labels are often applied to children who have performed similar behaviours without technically breaching the law (e.g. if they are below the age of criminal responsibility) or without being brought to the attention of the law enforcement agencies. So, in addition to the fact that children and young people today are at greatly increased risk of committing and being prosecuted in our courts for delinquent acts than their counterparts of 40 years ago, we must consider the fact that they are also at increased risk of many other serious psycho-social problems.

If we consider broader categories of externalising dysfunctional behaviour, such as conduct disorders, oppositional defiance, drug and substance abuse, and problem sexual behaviour (including sexual assault and victimisation, as well as high-risk sexual behaviour), we find considerable cause for concern. These would appear to be problems affecting increasing numbers of children and young people (Rutter and Smith 1995).

Gender and ethnicity

When we look at the breakdown of groups and subcultures we find that males continue to dominate the crime and anti-social behaviour statistics. In the area of drug dependency, ratios of males to females vary between 2:1 and 4:1. In relation to suicidal behaviour the ratios are between 2.5 and 3 males to 1 female. In the area of depressive disorders there is a 1:1 correspondence between boys and girls up to the age of 11, after which point girls are twice as likely to be affected than boys (Smith and Rutter 1995). Furthermore, it should be pointed out that whilst females continue to account for a much smaller proportion of crime and anti-social behaviour than males (between 10 and 17% in Europe), this proportion has increased since World War II.

In terms of ethnicity, Afro-Caribbean males are substantially and distinctively over-represented in the crime statistics whilst other ethnic minorities tend to be under-represented (Smith 1995). This level of representation is reflected in the population of children in special schools and other facilities for children with EBDs in England and Wales (Cooper, Smith and Upton 1991).

The segregation of children with EBDs

In the school-age population, in spite of the rhetoric of inclusiveness, the numbers of children formally statemented as having learning difficulties due to EBDs and placed in segregated provision rose during the 1980s. This is also in spite of evidence to suggest that LEAs are educating more children with SENs other than EBDs in mainstream settings (Cole 1989).

The rise in school exclusion

In considering changes and developments that have taken place over recent years in the circumstances and conditions affecting vulnerable children, it is necessary to address the issue of school exclusion. This has become an issue of particular significance to people concerned with children with EBDs since the 1980s. An important point to be made at the outset of the discussion of exclusion is that it would be a mistake to consider the relationship between exclusion from school and the childhood psycho-social problems outlined above as a simple case of the latter causing the former. There is likely to be a much more complex relationship between these two phenomena than that, with other factors being involved.

EXCLUSION NUMBERS

Accurate figures on the national rate of school exclusion in England and Wales did not become available until the 1990s, when the National Exclusions Reporting System was set up by the government. This was established in response to a growing concern among educationists and others about a perceived increase in the numbers of children who were being excluded from schools. The official statistics confirmed these perceptions. It was shown that in 1991/92 some 3833 children and young people were permanently excluded from schools in England and Wales (DfE 1993). This represented an alarming increase of 25 per cent since 1990/91. Of the 3833, 15 per cent (600) were from the primary sector, and the remainder were from secondary schools. Academic researchers, however, have suggested that the overall figure would double if it were to include pupils who were excluded for indefinite periods (Parsons *et al.* 1994). An even larger figure would include those children who at any one time are excluded for a fixed-term period. By 1996 the figure for permanent exclusions had risen to 13,581 (Castle and Parsons 1997). This represents an increase of over 300 per cent since the 1991/92 figures.

These figures and estimates, of course, relate to formal exclusion arrangements that are sanctioned under government legislation (1986 Education Act, No. 2, and 1993 Education Act). It has been suggested by authoritative sources that these figures are an underestimate of the actual numbers of excluded pupils (Advisory Centre on Education 1992; Association of Educational Psychologists 1992). When 'informal' or 'unofficial' forms of exclusion are included it is argued that the official statistics form only 'the tip of the iceberg' (Stirling 1992). For example, in one LEA Stirling claims to have found that for every two pupils who were formally recorded by their schools as 'permanently excluded', a further 30 pupils were excluded by one or other 'unofficial' means (such as under the guise of bogus medical circumstances, through a calculated over-rigorous exertion of school rules, through collusion with parents or through 'imaginatively' used authorised absence procedures).

CHARACTERISTICS OF EXCLUDED STUDENTS

A point of particular concern is the fact that the most vulnerable and already disadvantaged children in our society are vastly over-represented among these excluded pupils. Among exclusions reported through the National Exclusions Reporting System (DfE 1992), 12.5 per cent of permanently excluded pupils had statements of SENs; Afro-Caribbean pupils were massively over-represented and there were four times as many boys as girls. Stirling (1992), in her study of a single LEA, reported 32 out of 60 residents of the authority's children's homes to be 'on either indefinite or unofficial exclusions' (p.16), with only two of these pupils being formally recorded as permanently excluded.

THE CONSEQUENCES OF EXCLUSION

The consequences of exclusion for children and young people, many of whom are already vulnerable, can be disastrous. Exclusion is almost always associated with further hindrance to already poor educational progress. Many excluded children receive only part-time education, through home tuition or attendance at a small off-site unit (OFSTED 1993). OFSTED (1993) states that excluded pupils now form the largest single category of pupils in off-site units, where recent reports (OFSTED 1995) highlight poor educational standards. Other consequences include these children being put at greater risk of being involved in criminal offences or being put in 'moral danger' (such as being drawn into prostitution) (Parsons *et al.* 1994; Stirling 1992).

WHY HAVE EXCLUSIONS INCREASED?

The causes of exclusion, as reported by schools, most often include disobedience of one kind or another and/or insolence to staff. Less common causes are physical aggression towards staff and violence or aggression towards pupils (DfE 1992). The homogeneity of cited reasons for exclusion, however, should not be taken to indicate that the problems leading to exclusion are the result of deficiencies in pupil behaviour alone. The DfE (1992) reports that 'the variation in the numbers of exclusions between individual schools seemed to be too great to be explained by the socio-economic nature of the schools' catchment areas' (p.3).

Implicated here are differences in the effectiveness of schools' policies and individual teachers' skills in dealing with potentially disruptive and otherwise difficult children (Parsons et al. 1994), an issue already highlighted to some considerable effect by the Elton Inquiry (DES 1989). Other possible factors that have been implicated include increased intolerance of children who are disruptive, or likely to be disruptive, as a result of the pressures imposed on schools by the DfEE's introduction of tables of comparative performance; local management of schools (LMS); and the pressures of the National Curriculum (Association of Metropolitan Authorities 1995; Bowe and Ball 1992; Deem et al. 1994).

As we have already noted, there is other evidence to suggest that in addition to market forces wider social changes may be associated with a measurable and marked increase in the level of psycho-social disorders in young people since 1945 (see above). It is possible, therefore, that whilst there has been an increase in stressors within schools that put greater pressure on pupils and reduce the freedom of teachers to be tolerant, it is also likely to be the case that more pupils come to school with EBDs that are, initially at least, largely the product of out-of-school influences. This is not to say that there is a simple correspondence between the increase in psycho-social disorders and EBDs in schools. As the following sections will show, research indicates that schools play a vital role in mediating the effects of externally derived problems on pupils' behaviour and school attainment (see for example Mortimore et al. 1988; Rutter et al. 1979). What is being suggested here is that the work that schools, teachers and other carers do for children with EBDs takes place within persistently deteriorating circumstances: as the knowledge, skills and practice of professionals increase, so do the challenges with which they have to cope.

Politics and legislation since 1981

The dominant theme of educational, other relevant legislation and government advice since 1981 indicates an increasing commitment to a 'market forces' model in the provision of educational services. The market analogy portrays education as a commodity that is provided by schools and other agencies in accordance with the needs and wishes of consumers (e.g. parents and employers). The theory goes that in order that the best match be made between consumer wishes and the service provided, primarily in terms of quality, it is necessary that consumers be given the maximum amount of choice between the offerings of different providers. There are many limitations to this model, both in terms of its theoretical appropriateness to education and its practical application (see Simon and Chitty 1993). One of its major flaws is the way in which it creates 'winners' and 'losers' in the market-place. For example, there are people who for social and economic reasons are less able than others to make informed choices, or to act on choices they might prefer to make. There is also a problem with the basis on which comparisons between schools can be made. The development of simplistic performance indicators which take no account of the effects of social and other factors on performance, in the form of crude comparative league tables of examination results, is misleading to say the least. Furthermore, as market forces make one school a popular destination for parents and, therefore, attract an increasing share of educational resources, so other, less favoured, schools become starved of resources and, therefore, increasingly less able to provide a good standard of service. The 'losers' in these circumstances tend to be the schools, parents and children of economically poor areas.

Associated with this view is the increasing recognition throughout this period that EBDs are best seen in interactional terms, and as largely the product of environmental influences as opposed to problems of individual pathology. This view is supported by the evidence of government reports and advice which stress the importance of whole-school policies and the classroom management skills of teachers in preventing and addressing EBDs in schools. The simple and seductive idea presented here is that the incentive to make their schools attractive to potential clients, and so 'winners' in the market-place, will encourage schools to become more effective in dealing with disruptive and difficult children. As will be suggested below, one of the effects of the market philosophy is widely believed to be an increased lack of tolerance for children with EBDs in schools and an increased incentive to exclude such pupils from mainstream educational provision.

There follows a brief review of some of the major landmarks in policy since 1981.

The 1988 Education Reform Act

This was the most radical piece of educational legislation since the 1944 Education Act. Chief among its provisions were:

1. The establishment of a government-prescribed National Curriculum for all LEA-funded schools in England and Wales, the content and examination of which were to be controlled by central government.

2. The introduction of the principle of local financial management by which school governing bodies were given increased control over many of the financial resources that had previously been managed by LEAs.

3. The establishment of open enrolment, whereby schools could admit as many pupils as the physical capacity of the buildings would allow, rather than be limited in their intake by the dictates of LEAs.

An apparently very positive aspect of this Act was the emphasis it placed on the concept of the 'entitlement' of all children to the full range of the National Curriculum. Provision was also made for modification or 'disapplication' of the curriculum where it was felt that the demands of the curriculum were inappropriate to individual children, such as those with SENs.

Unfortunately, in spite of the inclusive rhetoric underpinning the Education Reform Act, it has been seen to have negative consequences for many vulnerable children. Some of the factors that have been implicated in the rise in exclusion rates, such as LMS, have been mentioned above. There is also evidence to suggest that in some circumstances the National Curriculum has been perceived by teachers as constraining them in their choice of teaching strategies, and that a major casualty here has been those very teaching strategies which are often most appropriate to the needs of children with EBDs (Cooper and McIntyre 1996).

The 1989 Children Act

The Children Act is an important landmark which, together with educatio.. legislation, led to profound changes in the legal basis of the relationship between children and adults. This Act is consistent with a trend towards children being seen as a minority group with their own rights. The emphasis shifts from one of adults having rights over children to adults having responsibilities of care towards children. This shift has important implications for adults in the caring professions working with children with EBDs, not least of which has been the need to take account of the child's perspective when decisions are made about his or her living circumstances and other issues relating to care and welfare.

These very positive developments have gone some considerable way towards protecting children and young people from the kind of atrocities some children were seen to be subjected to in a number of highly publicised cases of physical and sexual abuse perpetuated by their families and so-called professional carers. On the other hand, some disquiet has been expressed over the ways in which the increase in children's legal powers and status may in some circumstances limit the abilities of legitimate carers (both professional and familial) to exercise a properly caring role, such as when a child or young person chooses to place themselves in potentially harmful circumstances through the exercise of their legal rights (Davie, Upton and Varma 1996).

Having said this, there are many ways in which the extension of children's rights under this Act have brought the legal framework closer to the humanistic ideals of many of the pioneer workers with 'maladjusted' children (see above). This would appear to be at least one area where the consumer–provider model has had a beneficial effect on the lives of children with difficulties.

The 1989 Elton Report

The Elton Report (DES 1989) on 'discipline in schools' is an interesting and important document. The report was called for by the government on the basis of a spate of lurid stories in the tabloid press which depicted a crisis of pupil violence and thuggery in schools, much of it allegedly directed against teachers. In addition to gathering information from experts and other interested parties, the committee of inquiry commissioned the largest survey of teachers' perceptions of, and attitudes towards, school and classroom behavioural problems ever carried out in England and Wales. The committee's report came to the unremarkable conclusion that press reports had been exaggerated. Their evidence showed that violent behaviour was relatively rare in schools, but that there was a significant problem of persistent indiscipline of a mild but educationally disruptive nature. Key problems identified by teachers were:

- pupils talking out of turn
- calculated idleness and work avoidance by pupils
- pupils who hindered other pupils in their work
- pupils who were not punctual
- pupils who made unnecessary non-verbal noises.

Behavioural problems were considered to be:

- largely the product of environmental influences
- largely equated with acting-out behaviour
- most often synonymous with indiscipline rather than serious EBDs.

The report stressed the idea that these problems were largely the product of environmental influences within the schools and that solutions would most readily be sought in:

- improved school effectiveness (development of whole-school policies, etc.)
- improved teacher effectiveness (classroom management, communication skills).

Since its publication the Elton Report has proved highly influential in helping to shape the espoused policies of schools and teachers for dealing with problem behaviour. It has been instrumental in introducing important values and insights that had been known for many years by EBDs specialists to a wider audience of teachers. It has helped to bring behavioural methods into the classrooms of mainstream teachers throughout the country. However, in the context of the present discussion, it represents a missed opportunity. By focusing on the majority concerns of the majority of teachers surveyed, the committee merely confirmed the point that had been known by many people for a long time: that extreme forms of anti-social behaviour are almost always bound to be less prevalent than milder forms of such behaviour. For example, because the incidence of violence against teachers was among the least commonly identified problems experienced by teachers on a regular basis, this problem is hardly addressed at all within the document. The review of research presented in previous sections of this chapter would support the view that had the committee considered these issues longitudinally then it would very likely have uncovered an increase in all levels of disruptive and anti-social behaviour. This might then have been a cue to consider the relationship between the different levels of disruption, and to recognise the need to develop strategies that would address the whole range of EBDs in schools, rather than simply concentrating on the mildest manifestations of the problem.

It is being suggested here, therefore, that an unintended and undesirable legacy of the Elton Report has been to create an artificial division between what might be termed mildly disruptive behaviour or 'indiscipline' and the more severe 'EBDs', which is compounded by other government advice (see below). By not addressing the most severe problems likely to be encountered in schools, the Elton Report adds weight to the arguments of those who would (and clearly continue to) deny inclusive education to children with EBDs.

The 1993 Education Act and the 1994 SENs Code of Practice

These instruments extended the radical agenda of the 1988 Education Reform Act. In particular, part III of the 1993 Act related to SENs, and replaced the 1981 Education Act as the main authority on the law relating to SENs. Important measures in this Act included:

- Excessive delays in the statementing process, which had left some children in the limbo of an interminable (though inactive) assessment stage, were to be prevented through the introduction of statutory time limits on the various stages of the assessment process.

- Parental consultation was made a more prominent feature in decision-making processes surrounding the education of children with SEN.

- SENs tribunals were to be set up to hear claims questioning the appropriateness of LEA decisions regarding the education of children with SEN.

- The introduction of the non-statutory Code of Practice on the Identification and Assessment of Special Educational Needs, which

provides guidance to LEAs (and governing bodies of other
non-LEA schools) on their duties under the 1993 Act (part III).

The Code of Practice offers guidance and advice on the following key issues
(see Harris 1995):

- the need for early identification of children with SEN
- the central role of the mainstream school in providing for the
  needs of children with SEN
- the need for clear procedures for the identification, assessment and
  monitoring of SEN
- the need for clear procedures to ensure adherence to time limits,
  inter-agency cooperation, and the taking into account of parents'
  and children's wishes;
- the need for clarity and precision in the drafting of statements of
  SEN.

Central to the Code of Practice is a five stage model of assessment of SEN.
The first two stages of the model are entirely school based; stage three
involves the introduction of agencies outside the school into the process, and
stages four and five are carried out by the school and the LEA, with stage five
involving formal statementing. A key principle is that a child's SENs should
be met with the minimum degree of disruption to his or her normal
educational experience. The higher the stage of assessment the greater the
departure from standard mainstream provision.

Other important measures in the 1993 Education Act, particularly in
relation to the education of children with EBDs include:

- The abolition of the category of indefinite exclusion from school
  and the introduction of a maximum 15 day limit on school
  exclusion in any one term.
- The creation of a legal basis for LEAs to establish a new type of
  'school' known as a Pupil Referral Unit, the purpose of which is
  'to provide full-time or part-time education for pupils of
  compulsory school age who, by reason of illness, exclusion from
  school or otherwise, may not receive suitable education unless
  arrangements are made for them' (Harris 1995, p.41).

1994 DfE circulars on 'pupils with problems'

In 1994 the DfE produced six circulars for schools, offering advice on the education and management of children with SENs in the light of recent legislation. Colloquially known as the 'six pack', this body of information provides considerable insight into the government's ideological orientation towards SENs in general. The two circulars of particular concern here are 'Pupil Behaviour and Discipline' (8/94) and 'The Education of Children with Emotional and Behavioural Difficulties' (9/94).

'Pupil Behaviour and Discipline' builds on the recommendations of the Elton Report (see above) and highlights evidence of good practice drawn from reports by Her Majesty's Inspectorate. It sees good behaviour and discipline as essential to effective teaching and learning. The need to ensure pupil success in school is seen as a necessary prerequisite of good behaviour. Important aspects of this circular include emphases on the following:

- The development of whole-school policies on behaviour and discipline, underpinned by rules of conduct developed by staff in consultation with parents and pupils, which provide pupils with clear boundaries of acceptable behaviour.

- The encouragement of positive behaviour, as well as developing coherent and consistent policies for dealing with rule breaking.

- The development of a moral code within schools that is conducive to an atmosphere of respect for others, through provisions within the formal curriculum and religious education and through the more informal social aspects of school life, such as teacher–pupil relationships.

- Effective teaching, which involves provision of differentiated learning experiences according to pupil needs and effective classroom management.

- Encouragement of positive behaviour through the use of formal rewards and other forms of positive reinforcement.

The circular also made reference to particular problems that might arise and that required prompt action. These problems were: truancy, bullying, racial harassment and sexually inappropriate behaviour.

'The Education of Children with Emotional and Behavioural Difficulties' echoes many of the points raised in the discipline circular. Importantly, however, it provides a particular view of the parameters of EBDs:

> ... emotional and behavioural difficulties lie on a continuum between ... those that are challenging but within expected bounds and those which are indicative of serious mental illness.

> Emotional and behavioural difficulties range from social maladaptation to abnormal emotional stresses... They become apparent through withdrawn, depressive, aggressive or self injurious tendencies. (para. 4)

It would be overly generous to describe this statement as a 'definition'. It is important, however, in that it echoes the distinction implied in the Elton Report between different orders of behavioural difficulty. Interestingly, however, there seems to be little distinction drawn between the *causes* of EBDs and *causes* of indiscipline:

> Emotional and behavioural difficulties are frequently engendered in the first place, or exacerbated by, the environment in its broadest sense, including the school's, teachers' or peers' responses to the child's actions. The classroom in particular is a complex environment which has a major effect on the behaviour of both teachers and pupils. There is a substantial body of evidence which shows that schools in general have a significant effect on children's behaviour. (para. 8)

1997 'Excellence for all Children': Meeting Special Educational Needs

At the time of writing, the proposals contained in the DfE's 'Excellence for All Children' represent ideas for discussion, and as such do not have the status of the other documents reviewed in this section. Having said this, the *aspirations* presented here, in relation to the education of children with EBDs, are very encouraging. It might even be argued that the new Labour government, elected in 1997, has brought with it an approach to EBDs that at last begins to fall into step with the best professional and academic thinking on the topic.

The importance of EBDs is highlighted by the fact that one of the eight chapters of the document is devoted specifically to issues of EBDs. No other category of SENs is singled out in this way. Furthermore, the document takes the important step of acknowledging the link between school exclusion and EBDs (para. 8.1). The implications of this somewhat belated acknowledgement are that the unhelpful distinctions between indiscipline and EBDs, which are prominent in many government publications on the topic, begin to be undermined. Similarly, the idea that children's problems in schools are invariably the result of poor management (in the classroom or in the school as a whole) comes into question. By recognising the fact that EBDs in schools may be the product of a wide range of factors – some within and some without the school – the way becomes open for the development of more comprehensive approaches which go beyond simple classroom management strategies, and to recognise the need for such approaches to be placed within a broader national and LEA-wide support structure.

At the time of writing we have yet to see, however, if this promise turns into practice.

Theoretical orientations towards the education of children with EBDs

The dominant educational ideology, in relation to SENs, which develops throughout this period is that of 'inclusive education'. This approach is consistent with the legislation to a large degree in that it focuses on the characteristics of effective teaching and effective school organisation, and concomitant issues in the professional development of teachers and the promotion of school improvement (see Ainscow 1984). Fundamental to this approach are the following principles:

- all children, including those who have SENs, have a right to education in mainstream schools.

- mainstream schools can cater for the needs of children with SENs if they develop appropriate management policies and if individual teachers develop appropriate skills.

- the teaching skills required for the education of children with SENs are often the same as those required for all children, regardless of their disabilities or difficulties.

In order to trace the origins of this viewpoint, we must go back to the pre-1981 era.

Laslett (1983) describes the growing influence of behavioural psychology in the treatment of 'maladjusted' children and the way in which this gradually replaced the individual pathology model. The extent of this move towards the behavioural model is illustrated in the overt influence of behaviourism in the recommendations of the Elton Report and circular 8/94. Throughout the period of the 1980s the principles of behavioural theory became central to the theory and practice of effective approaches to dealing with behavioural problems in young people. This is evident not only in the writings of academic educational psychologists (see for example Wheldall 1987; Wheldall and Merritt 1984), but also in practitioners' accounts of their own practice, as illustrated in a recent collection of papers by practitioners on their approaches to dealing with children with EBDs in a variety of educational settings (Cooper 1995).

Another important development from behavioural psychology is the literature on classroom management (see for example McManus 1989; Smith and Laslett 1993). Such texts have proven to be highly popular with teachers and have contributed greatly to the idea that many behavioural problems in the classroom can be averted by effective contingency planning based on behavioural theory. The extension of these principles beyond behavioural control to the realm of classroom learning has also taken place (see for example Wheldall 1987; Wheldall and Glynn 1989), and this has been influential in the inclusive schools movement.

Behavioural psychology provides a major underpinning to the legislation and practice relating to SENs and EBDs in schools, and particularly in relation to ideas of 'effective teaching' and 'effective behaviour management'. At the administrative level, what has come to be known as 'school effectiveness' research and the 'school improvement' literature have had an equally important impact, which is also reflected in government advice and legislation. Seminal research studies in the UK by Rutter *et al.* (1979), Reynolds and Sullivan (1979) and, more recently, Mortimore *et al.* (1988) and Smith and Tomlinson (1989) have demonstrated through increasingly sophisticated statistical analyses important differences between schools in terms of the educational and behavioural outcomes of their students that cannot be accounted for in terms of catchment area or other intake variables. These and other studies, both here and abroad (see for example Purkey and Smith 1983), increasingly point to within-schools factors as being responsible for these differences. The precise characteristics of effective schools vary, but there are some common factors, such as: the leadership style of the head teacher, the establishment of clear whole-school policies and goals, an emphasis on academic achievement, a positive approach to problem behaviour and good staff–pupil relationships (Charlton and David 1990). More recent research efforts have been directed towards identifying the means by which such effectiveness can be achieved (see for example Cooper 1993a).

More deeply embedded influences on recent thinking about EBDs issues lie in sociological sources. Young's (1971) collection of papers heralding 'new directions' in the sociology of education led to a departure from the economic determinism that characterised much of the earlier sociology of education, and a move towards a recognition of the role that individuals (e.g. teachers and pupils) play in the construction of their own social realities. This impetus gave rise to a diverse collection of studies of the micro-world of the school, with particular reference to ways in which teachers and pupils in schools interact to create the circumstances which determine pupil success and failure. Pupil deviance and academic low achievement were particular targets for these researchers (see for example Cooper 1993a; Davies 1984; Ford, Mongon and Whalen 1982; Hargreaves, Hester and Mellor 1975; Keddie, 1971; Lawrence, Steed and Young 1982; Schostak, 1982; Sharp and Green, 1975; Tattum, 1982). Repeatedly, these studies revealed a picture in which deviant identities were constructed by the social arrangements in particular schools. On the positive side, these studies suggested together that deviance and disaffection in school would diminish or be prevented from occurring where pupils were encouraged to see themselves as valued and active participants in their school communities. In this way this work was complementary to the school effectiveness literature, and in some cases (see for example Cooper 1993a) drew directly on school effectiveness sources.

An important aspect of this sociological thrust was the growing attention this gave to school pupils as important participants in the social world of the school, with their own distinctive viewpoints and sets of interests. This in turn was related to a growing interest in what has been termed 'the sociology of childhood' (Franklin 1986; James and Prout 1990). Writers in this field set about exploring the world through the eyes of children, and through their work highlighted the plight of children as a disenfranchised minority group in society (Cooper 1993b). Elements of this theoretical perspective are clearly evident in the Children Act, as well as more recent publications which address the need to consult and empower children as a means of protecting and furthering their rights (Davie et al. 1996).

A further theoretical strand which can be traced from the period surveyed in Laslett's original study concerns that of humanistic psychology. This is perhaps most marked by the role of counselling in schools. Concerns noted by Laslett about the emphasis placed by behaviourism on the control of children's behaviour have been echoed by many writers and educators throughout the period in which behaviourism has held sway in Western education. The need first recognised by the pioneer workers with 'maladjusted' children to engage with children's emotional interiors in a non-judgemental and therapeutic manner has been a consistent theme running alongside the development of behavioural approaches in schools (see for example Bovair and McGlaughlin 1993; Cronk 1987; Hamblin 1974). This theme is further developed in the ecosystemic approach to EBDs which, derived from systemic family therapy, draws on humanistic and behavioural psychology as well as social systems theory to create ways of construing and intervening in problem situations that take account of the full range of psychological, emotional and social influences that may be relevant (Cooper and Upton 1990).

The commonality of insight shared by the pioneer workers with maladjusted children and modern theorists working from academic sociological and psychological perspectives (particularly the humanistic and systemic) is striking. It could be suggested that it has taken almost 50 years of state education for educationists to recognise what the pioneer workers knew before World War II, namely that psychological disturbance and disaffection have much to do with the kinds of social relationship and environment that people experience, and that psychological health and social responsibility will grow in a caring and nurturing environment, just as they will decline in a dehumanising environment. In many ways the history of the changing perceptions of 'maladjustment' and EBDs can be seen as the gradual dissemination of this view to the point where it begins to be a central influence in mainstream legislation and the thinking of committed professionals.

In recognising the great progress that has been made, however, we must be careful not to become complacent. We have explored the ways in which perceptions have changed and indicated some of the ways in which social and political conditions have also changed. The remaining chapters of this book deal in detail with current thinking and practice with regard to understanding and supporting children and young people with EBDs.

CHAPTER 2

Emotional and Behavioural Difficulties and Adolescence

Paul Cooper

Introduction

This chapter is concerned with EBDs during the adolescent years. Adolescence is taken to be that period which covers the age range of 12 to 18. This is an important period in relation to the topic of EBDs, because, as we shall see, it is during these years that individuals are at greatest risk of experiencing EBDs of one kind or another. Furthermore, individuals are more likely to experience EBDs in later life if they have experienced them in their childhood and adolescence. The chapter begins by charting the nature of adolescence, as a developmental concept. It then goes on to explore the range and extent of EBDs in adolescence. Finally, consideration is given to some of the socio-cultural influences that may help to make the adolescent years so risk laden.

The nature of adolescence

Adolescence means different things depending on the perspective from which we address it. However, if we begin with the simplest definition of adolescence as a chronological stage which exists between childhood and adulthood and occupies roughly the ages of 12 to 18, we can begin to make some fairly uncontroversial statements about the nature of this developmental zone. First, this phase is marked by important biological developments. Adolescence is distinguished from childhood by the advent of puberty. The early part of adolescence is marked by the process of development to full sexual maturity. Second, the transition to full adult status goes beyond the period of physical development, and the second half of adolescence is devoted to the social transition towards adult ways of behaving. Third, this is a period where difficulties of a social, behavioural and emotional nature are most likely to occur. This is not to say that most adolescents experience emotional and/or behavioural difficulties. There is, however, a good deal of research data to show that more problems of a psycho-social nature occur in this age group than in any other (Rutter and Smith 1995).

There are a number of theoretical positions that can be called upon to account for the mechanisms which operate to produce this concentration of psycho-social problems in adolescence. These include two main groups of theories. The first set of theories includes those which emphasise the effects of innate factors particular to the constitutional make-up of individuals, such as theories of temperament and biologically based individual difference. The second set of theories includes those which emphasise the power of environment and experience to shape an individual's behaviour and ways of perceiving the world. These include:

- behavioural theories
- psychodynamic theories
- cognitive theories
- systems theories
- socio-cultural theories.

The value of these different approaches in helping us to understand the problem of adolescent EBDs will be explored later in this chapter. Before approaching this analysis, however, it is necessary to explain in more detail the precise nature of the EBDs experienced by adolescents.

The increase in juvenile delinquency since 1945

Every generation seems to complain about the unruliness of young people and that 'children are much less well behaved now than they used to be'. It is often argued that this view is based on faulty recollection or the natural human desire to see the past through rose-tinted spectacles. It was noted in Chapter 1 that the international crime rate has dramatically increased since World War II. It was also stated that research evidence consistently points to a link between adult delinquency and childhood behavioural problems.

With a few exceptions, notably Japan, the overall rate of recorded offences throughout the world has increased since 1945 by at least a factor of 2 and at most a factor of 27. For most countries the increase has been by a factor of between 2 and 6, with England and Wales experiencing an increase by a factor of 5.5 (Smith 1995). Up to 1981 the increase in international crime rates followed a steady progression, with the rate of rise increasing after 1981 (Smith 1995). The crimes which have witnessed the most substantial increases include theft of motor vehicles, breaking and entering, and serious physical assault, including sexual offences but excluding murder (Rutter and Smith 1995).

These rates encompass all recorded crimes for all age groups. When the figures are broken down by age it is shown that the majority of offences are committed by 'teenagers and young adults in their twenties' (Rutter and Smith 1995, p.405), with the statistics showing an 'apparent rise in the prevalence of crime up to the age of 14 or 15' (Rutter and Smith 1995, p.423). This relationship between age and prevalence of criminal behaviour is considered 'the most basic fact of criminology' (Rutter and Smith 1995, p.421). The further significance of this fact is that whilst many people who commit crimes cease to do so in adulthood, one of the strongest predictors of adult criminal careers is childhood delinquency (Farrington 1995). This makes the issue of childhood offending a major focus for the prevention of nearly all crime.

In considering developments since 1981, post-war crime figures for the conviction of young offenders reached a peak in 1985 in England and Wales, rising sharply between the late 1970s and mid 1980s. They then decreased up to the end of the 1980s (Smith 1995). This does not diminish the fact that overall there was an approximately ten-fold increase in the incidence of crime committed by children and young people between 1951 and 1990. Furthermore, there are strong arguments to suggest that the apparent decline in reported crime is an artefact of changes in policy and judicial practice, rather than a change in juvenile behaviour, with courts making greater use of cautioning for juveniles from the mid-1980s onwards (Farrington 1995).

For a more reliable account of changes in the experience of children and young people over the period with which this book is concerned, we must refer to data on a wider range of psycho-social and behavioural problems.

The rise in other psycho-social problems since 1945

In addition to criminality, the last 50 years have seen a dramatic increase in psycho-social problems among adolescents and young adults. These include formally diagnosed problems such as conduct disorder and oppositional deficient disorder, as well as problem sexual behaviour, drug and substance abuse. Along with these disruptive externalising problems there has also been a rise in internalising problems such as depression and other emotional problems.

Conduct disorders and oppositional defiance disorder

Conduct disorders refer to 'those persistent behaviours in which adolescents engage that violate the basic rights of others and/or the norms of society' (Blau 1996, p.62). Oppositional defiant disorder, as defined by the American Psychiatric Association (APA 1994) represents many similar characteristics of conduct disorders but in 'a lesser more socially acceptable form' (Blau 1996, p.63). Smith (1995) provides a more catholic definition of conduct disorders which appears to encompass both conduct disorders and oppositional defiant disorders as defined by the APA. Included under this heading are such behaviours as '... disruptive aggression such as teasing, quarelsomeness, lying, malicious mischief and fire-setting, stealing, truancy, staying out late at night, running away from home and gang activities' (Smith 1995, p.423).

Research studies find a high degree of continuity between conduct disorders in childhood and later criminality, with, for example, one study showing that between 70 and 90 per cent of young adults arrested for violent offences had been rated as highly aggressive in early adolescence (Smith 1995). In the general child and adolescent population, prevalence rates are estimated at between 2 and 16 per cent (Blau 1996).

Drug and substance abuse

Studies of per capita alcohol consumption in the UK indicate a near 100 per cent increase between 1950 and 1990 (Silbereisen, Robins and Rutter 1995). In young people (15–19-year-olds), longitudinal studies show a fairly unchanging pattern of daily and weekly drinking throughout the 1980s, with between 2 and 7 per cent of adolescent males and half that number of females being rated as 'heavy drinkers' (i.e. consuming the equivalent of 25 pints of beer per week for males). US surveys identify a much higher proportion of heavy drinkers among young people (41% in 1982 and 32% in 1990), but they employ a much lower threshold of consumption (five or more drinks in a row at least once in the previous two weeks) (Silbereisen et al. 1995).

The apparent significant decline in US consumption and the negligible decline in UK consumption should be considered in the context of the massive increase in the consumption of illicit drugs by young people between the 1950s and 1970s. Overall rates for drug abuse and dependency for the UK in the late 1980s were calculated at 13.5 per cent for 18- to 29-year-olds, 6.7 per cent for 30- to 44-year-olds and 0.8 per cent for 45- to 64-year-olds. The ratio of males to females in the statistics for the youngest age groups varies between 2 and 4:1 (Silbereisen *et al.* 1995). The US claims 'the highest rate of adolescent drug abuse among the world's industrialised nations', and there are indications that substance abuse is increasing in the early adolescent population (Baugher-Palmer and Liddle 1996, p.114). Smith and Rutter (1995) conclude, on the basis of a wide ranging survey of available evidence: '…Interpol statistics for eight European countries show substantial increases in drug-related deaths since 1980. A range of British data suggests a continuing increase in drug use in the 1980s' (p.774).

International studies repeatedly show a high correlation between adolescent drug abuse and anti-social and criminal behaviour, as well as health problems, poor performance in school work, reduced life opportunities, emotional dysfunction and relationship problems (Baugher-Palmer and Liddle 1996; Rutter and Smith 1995).

Emotional and other problems

The evidence presented above indicates that there are good reasons to believe that there have been significant increases in the measured behaviour of young people since World War II in terms of criminal and anti-social activity. In addition to these, what we might term 'externalising' or 'acting-out' problems appear to be less visible, but equally destructive, problems affecting the emotional and psychological well-being of young people in the second half of the twentieth century. These problems include increasing levels of depressive illness and suicidal behaviour among young people (Diekstra, Kienhorst and de Wilde 1995), and increasing levels of problem sexual behaviour, including sexual victimisation and the perpetration of sexual assault (Terre and Burkhart 1996).

These psycho-social problems taken together suggest that life has become increasingly difficult for children and young people in Western society. Since World War II the proportion of people experiencing and exhibiting psycho-social problems in this age group has increased to a larger extent than it has for any other age group. This research indicates that this increase will ultimately translate into increased levels of these problems in the adult population, even when we allow for the effects of maturation in reducing the incidence of these problems.

Gender and ethnicity

As we saw in Chapter 1, males outnumber females considerably in many of these areas of concern, including criminal and anti-social behaviour, drug and substance abuse, and suicidal behaviour. Girls only outstrip boys in the area of depressive disorders during adolescence. Having said that, the overall rate of increase in the female crime rate has been greater than that among males since World War II. In terms of ethnicity, the evidence points to Afro-Caribbean males being at greatest risk of criminality and social exclusion.

Segregation and exclusion from school

As was noted in Chapter 1, recent years have seen a dramatic increase in the number of children excluded from mainstream schools in England and Wales, mainly because of aggressive and anti-social conduct. Although the increase in numbers affects all age groups, the largest group of excluded pupils is composed of adolescents, and of these the vast majority are boys. Added to this is the fact that the proportion of children being placed in off-site provision for pupils with EBDs has remained virtually unchanged over the last 20 years.

These facts further support the two basic lines of argument in this chapter:

1. that adolescence is a period of particular difficulty in terms of the risk of EBDs

2. that the risk factors have increased measurably for succeeding generations of adolescents. Attention will now be turned to asking why this state of affairs prevails.

Why is adolescence such a high-risk stage?

At the beginning of this chapter a number of different theoretical positions were mentioned that could help us to understand how and why adolescent EBDs occur. In the following sections these positions are briefly discussed.

Theories of temperament and biologically-based individual difference

Temperament is a concept, favoured by some psychologists and psychiatrists (Berger 1985), to account for what might be termed 'personality differences' among people. It is suggested that traits, such as extroversion, introversion, sociability, emotionality (i.e. neuroticism), fastidiousness and malleability can be demonstrated to be, for many people, stable over time and likely to have a strong genetic basis. In relation to childhood and adolescent behavioural problems, there is a powerful body of research which suggests that there is often a genetic aspect to Attention Deficit/Hyperactivity Disorder (AD/HD) and Hyperkinetic Disorder (see Chapter 1) (Comings 1990). Other researchers, in turn, have shown that there is a consistent relationship between the core features of the AD/HD diagnostic criteria, particularly hyperactivity and inattentiveness, and juvenile delinquency (Farrington 1990; Rutter and Giller 1983). This is not to say, as some have suggested (see for example Moir and Jessel 1995), that these problems are 'caused' solely by genetic factors. What it does suggest, however, is that some people may be born with a greater susceptibility than others to behave in ways that may lead them into anti-social and/or criminal activity. One of the suggested possible mechanisms associating AD/HD with anti-social behaviour is that the learning and cognitive processing problems that flow from this condition may make it more difficult for children with AD/HD to internalise social and moral rules if they are communicated through oral language (Barkley 1990). One possible means of overcoming this problem is to seek to teach rules to children with this disorder through more activity-based methods (Cooper and Ideus 1996).

Evidence for the biological basis of anxiety or depressive disorders suggests only limited support for the idea of genetic predisposition (Graham 1991; Mills 1996). There is stronger evidence that neurochemical abnormalities may play a role in adult depression (Graham 1991). In adolescence an association has been observed between postpubertal hormonal changes and depressive feeling in boys, as well as irritability and depression in pre-menstrual adolescent girls (Graham and Rutter 1985).

Behavioural theory

Behavioural theory, or learning theory as it is sometimes known, is one of the most powerful theoretical tools we have for understanding the way behaviour is shaped by experience. A fundamental tenet of behavioural theory is that almost all human (and animal) behaviour is learned (Berger

1985) in response to positive or negative reinforcers which, respectively, encourage and discourage the repetition of the behaviours to which they are applied. Other important behavioural concepts identified by Berger include 'habituation', in which the repetition of a stimulus ceases to produce the initial response over time, and 'sensitisation', in which a 'noxious' stimulus produces a response that increases in intensity over time, though the stimulus itself does not increase in intensity. A further important behavioural concept is that of modelling, whereby the individual imitates the behaviour of others when either they receive direct personal reinforcement from the model or they observe the model receiving reinforcement. In relation to adolescent EBDs, behavioural theory could be taken to imply that adolescence is a period when either response patterns change, for example as a result of habituation, or when patterns of reinforcement change, so that, for example, behaviours that were previously reinforced are now not reinforced, or different behaviours become the target of reinforcement. A third possibility is that the source of reinforcement or choice of model changes, for example, from parents to peers. What is clear from numerous studies of adolescent deviance is that children who develop deviant identities during this period (particularly in the school setting) often receive positive reinforcement from their peers combined with an aversive experience in the school situation (see for example Cooper 1993a; Hargreaves 1967; Rosser and Harré 1976).

Psychodynamic theory

Psychodynamic theory is extremely useful in helping us to make sense of the idea, suggested in the previous section, that something changes in the psychic world of the individual at adolescence, both in terms of the adolescent's view of him/herself, and in terms of the way that others view the individual when they reach this particular life stage. The basis of the psychodynamic approach is that any individual's current intra-psychic experience is most effectively understood with reference to their early childhood experiences and mental processes (Dare 1985). There are various theories about the precise ways in which this approach can be applied to the adolescent phase of development, some of which shed light directly on the issue of dysfunctional behaviour that is directly related to this phase. Central to most psychodynamic theories, such as those proposed by S. Freud, A. Freud, E. Erikson, M. Mahler and D. Winnicott (see Dare 1985), is the idea that the passage to psychological maturity is marked by a series of intra-psychic conflicts which have to be resolved for healthy development to take place. These conflicts initially revolve around anxieties relating to survival needs in early infancy and the need for attachment to the mother or other primary carer at this time. Later conflicts tend to be concerned with the need to escape these early dependencies and develop an individual identity.

Erikson in particular identifies adolescence as a period of crisis, where the task is to sort out and establish an individual identity that is distinct from that which may have been established in the pre-adolescent phase. Such theories can help to account for the feelings of strangeness and self-consciousness that are often characteristic of the adolescent. The stress engendered by these feelings, along with fear and uncertainty about the future, may be associated with adolescent moodiness and depression. Similarly, the need to individuate from adults may take the form, for some people, of a need to reject the moral values and codes of conduct proposed by adults in favour of alternative, peer-oriented values. This process may well be exacerbated when interaction with adults is unrewarding or aversive, such as when a child is failing in school or experiences parental criticism. Overly protective or domineering adults may, in these circumstances, encourage feelings of guilt and worthlessness in their adolescent charges and encourage them to repress these natural feelings. Psychodynamic interventions that attempt to deal with or prevent dysfunctional feelings and behaviour include creating circumstances which encourage the individual to articulate and confront the conflicts which they are experiencing. In addition to formal psychotherapy, some forms of counselling, such as Rogers's (1951) 'person-centred approach', are valuable in this regard. Central to these approaches is the principle of acceptance, whereby the individual is encouraged to acknowledge and accept their feelings as legitimate.

Cognitive theory

Theories of cognitive development help us to understand the ways in which human beings' mental schemes for comprehending the world around them change over time. Piaget's seminal theory of children's intellectual development identifies a series of stages through which children's ways of knowing develop. Each stage is a move further away from an egocentric and idiosyncratic form of comprehension, and a move towards abstract, objective and rational ways of perceiving (Hobson 1985). Early adolescence, the period between 12 and 15 years, is the stage of 'formal operations' when the highest level of abstract, generalisable thought becomes possible. Along with this come powers of abstract thought and moral reasoning. The work of

Vygotsky suggests that these powers of reasoning are heavily dependent on the socio-cultural context (Hundiede 1985). This suggests that reasoning is not simply an abstract process, but rather that the reasoning function operates by drawing on specific experiences and the context of these experiences. Reasoning is learned through the experience of interacting with others in real-life situations. It is difficult, therefore, to dissociate the affective from the purely cognitive when examining an individual's reasoning process. This point has been demonstrated very clearly in a number of research studies which have sought to examine adolescents' perceptions of the world. In particular, studies of deviant, disruptive and disturbed adolescents often reveal a capacity to account for deviant behaviour as a reasonable and rational response to aversive circumstances (Cooper 1993a; Rosser and Harré 1976; Tattum 1982). What is distinctive about the adolescent phase in this respect is the sense of autonomy that accompanies powers of independent reasoning. The sense of indignant injustice that often characterises adolescent defiance can be accounted for in these terms. This highlights the value of democratic and incorporative strategies in preventing and dealing with disruption in schools (see for example Reynolds and Sullivan 1979), and the importance of self-government and shared responsibility as practised by the pioneer workers with maladjusted children (see Chapter 1). These approaches acknowledge and utilise the adolescent's powers of abstract thought, argument and decision making, whilst oppressive and authoritarian approaches suppress these qualities, allowing them only to operate as a form of resistance.

Systems theory

Systems theory has come increasingly to the fore in recent years, and is seen to offer powerful insight into the influences on individual and group functioning (Cooper and Upton 1990). One way of thinking about systems theory is as an amalgam of behavioural, psychodynamic and sociological perspectives. The central point in systems theory, when it is applied to social systems, is that individuals never exist in a vacuum; their perceptions and behaviour are heavily influenced by, and act as an influence on, the behaviour and perceptions of all others with whom they interact. Human beings organise themselves into groups in order to meet a variety of needs (for example: families, work groups, peer groups, schools, etc.). These groupings can be seen as social systems. A characteristic of systems is that they function with the purpose of maintaining their own survival. Sometimes the survival of the group is maintained at the expense of an individual within that group, as in the case of a 'scapegoat' or the 'class clown' or what family therapists refer to as 'the symptomatic individual' in a dysfunctional family. In these circumstances, systemic solidarity and harmony (homoeostasis) are secured by using an individual as a focus for negative feelings and fears. This helps to distract other members of the group from other conflicts and disharmonies that may put the whole group at risk. A common family systems example of this is the situation where a child's behavioural problems are unwittingly exacerbated by parents' needs for distraction from their own marital difficulties: so long as they are preoccupied with their child's problems they do not have time to address their own, possibly more painful, conflict; so they resist solutions to the child's problems. Systemic approaches to problem solving, therefore, tend to focus on contextual factors surrounding the symptomatic individual, and to ask questions about the purpose that the problem behaviour may be serving for others in the system or in related sub-systems.

Socio-cultural theory

The above theoretical explanations help us to understand something of the complexity of individual psychology. However, they tell us little about why these problems may have come to affect increasing numbers of young people over time. The search for obvious causes of the increase in psycho-social disorders has not produced any clear-cut answers (Rutter and Smith 1995). For example, the idea that there is a direct causal relationship between psycho-social disorders and socio-economic deprivation is not borne out by Rutter and Smith's analysis. Whilst there is a connection between these factors, their longitudinal survey shows that the period of greatest increase in the disorders coincided with a dramatic improvement in living standards. Rutter and Smith suggest that the influences producing these worsening outcomes are more complex, pointing to a range of circumstances which have made life increasingly difficult for children and young people in the second half of the twentieth century. It is to a consideration of some of these issues that we now turn.

As was shown in the first chapter of this book, the second half of the twentieth century has seen major changes in the ways in which society and the law view children and young people. Although it is true to say that these recent developments follow from a tradition that stretches back into the previous century and beyond, the most recent of these developments makes a fundamental difference to the very nature of childhood. Thus whilst earlier efforts to ensure the welfare of children focused on issues of protection, or the securement of certain welfare rights, the most recent developments in this area, such as the Children Act (1989), have stressed the importance of children's own perspectives on their needs, conditions and grievances (Davie, Upton and Varma 1996; Hendrick 1987). The crucial shift has been from child as passive recipient of the protection of adults, to child in partnership with adults for the securement of children's rights. The major change here is in the authority relationships which exist between children and adults. The child's right to speak for him or herself, rather than to be spoken for by adults, creates a new political and social status for children. An inevitable accompaniment to this new status, however, is the creation of new vulnerabilities.

As children and young people become identified as a distinctive group in society, with its own culture(s), its own grievances and its own political issues, so they become more exposed in certain ways. An example of this is the way in which advertisers increasingly target youth and children directly, rather than via their parents. Similarly, there is now a wide range of printed and other media that is directed at children and young people. The point being made here is that as children and young people become an increasingly distinct group in society, so they increasingly inhabit a social world that is separated from that of adults. The positive side of this is that it is likely to encourage self-determination and make children less vulnerable to negative adult influence, such as physical and emotional abuse. The downside is that it may also make them less likely to profit from positive adult influence, such as the wisdom and perspective gained through life experience. Rutter and Smith (1995) suggest that this increasing cultural isolation of youth from other groups in society may make them more vulnerable than earlier generations to psycho-social disorders.

Other problems may relate to the frustrations of youth. Never before have children and young people been made so aware, through the mass media, of the possibilities of material and other forms of success in society. Rutter and Smith suggest, however, that along with such promise often comes disappointment: the glittering prizes are not as readily available as they appear. This means that dissatisfaction with one's life and circumstances may come earlier in the life cycle than for previous generations.

These aspects particular to the condition of youth and childhood in the twentieth century have also to be considered in the wider context of social conditions. The second half of the twentieth century has seen dramatic increases in economic security, in the decades immediately following World War II, followed by a complete reversal of this trend in the 1980s and 1990s. As children and young people become a recognisable and separate group, so the structures that have traditionally supported personal and social development, such as employment and careers, are disappearing. Likewise, the huge increase in divorce and family break-up are further undermining the national sense of security. It is increasingly difficult for young people to identify, with any conviction, a positive future for themselves. This of course creates further problems for caring professionals to work constructively with them, since our education system is still very much rooted in a notion of preparation and progression that belongs to industrial, as opposed to post-industrial, societies.

What we are left with, then, is a picture of youth as being increasingly isolated in a decaying and often hostile social world. Although many of these problems were in evidence before the 1980s, it was during this period that they became most evident. The harshness of this period is perhaps best summed up by quotations from two prime ministers who have presided over Britain and Northern Ireland since 1979. The first quote is from Margaret Thatcher, who is reported to have said: 'there is no such thing as society; there are only individuals' (cited in Davies and Lloyd-Smith 1996). The second is from John Major, who said, with reference to the rise in youth crime and as a comment on the use of therapeutic as opposed to punitive methods of dealing with offenders: 'we should learn to condemn a little more, and understand a little less' (Party Political Broadcast, 20 January 1993). It might be argued that these uncaring and ill-founded statements are not reflected in much of the policy and practice that have developed over recent years. What these statements illustrate, however, is something of the enormous challenge that faces those who seek to work for children with EBDs.

Conclusion

There are no simple solutions to the problems of adolescent EBDs. As with EBDs in general, multi-dimensional causes require multi-modal interventions. There is a role for schools and teachers in educating young people in ways that help them to have a positive sense of self. Young people also need to be educated to make choices and to understand the ways in which they can influence the world in which they live. There needs to be continuity between the routine approaches to social and learning functions of schooling, and approaches to issues of EBDs. This requires school communities that place a high value on student participation. It requires approaches to classroom teaching that begin with and value the view of the world that pupils bring with them. This is all part of the need to recognise the fact that adolescence is indeed a world of its own. The only way to understand this world is through the eyes of those who inhabit it. Of course, this is not simply the job of school teachers. Teachers need to work alongside counsellors, social workers, psychologists, the medical profession and other professionals to prevent and deal with the kinds of problem that have been outlined above. Of paramount importance is the need to be aware of the vast array of influences on EBDs during this stage of development, and the need to work in partnership with young people to deal with these difficulties.

CHAPTER 3

Sex Differences, Gender Issues and Emotional and Behavioural Difficulties

Pam Maras and Paul Cooper

S deserved more help than he got, he was a quiet boy who got forgotten in favour of the rowdy ones. (Maras and Hall 1996, p.62)

Overview

The above quotation is from the mother of a boy described as experiencing emotional and behavioural difficulties. Though short, it illustrates one of a number of tensions in relation to boys (and girls) who experience EBDs. In this chapter we consider some of these tensions. We begin by considering trends in the numbers of boys and girls who experience psycho-social disorders before focusing on two related questions: why so few girls, why so many boys? We draw on feminist, social developmental, social psychological and educational explanations for sex differences, gender issues and EBDs. We conclude by suggesting conceptual and practical ways forward at both institutional and curricular levels. We construe EBDs as an umbrella term encompassing a wide range of difficulties and needs, including problems which manifest themselves solely in either emotional or behavioural terms and problems which have both emotional *and* behavioural dimensions (Cooper 1996a; Maras and Redmayne 1997).

Sex differences and the prevalence of EBDs

EBDs are most commonly described within a range of psycho-social diagnoses, of which, it has been suggested, there has been a rise in the identification in young people over the last decade, both in the UK and in

North America (Blau and Gullotta 1996; Rutter and Smith 1995). Within this increase, substantially more boys than girls have been identified as displaying seriously problematic behaviour whilst girls have been described as experiencing more depressive disorders (Blau and Gullotta 1996). In terms of outcome behaviours, estimates of illegal drug dependency range from a boy to girl ratio of 2 to 4:1. In contrast, although depressive disorders have been shown to be equally attributed to younger, primary-aged, boys *and* girls; over 11 years of age more girls than boys are identified, rising to a ratio of 2:1, adult women to men. Similar sex-differentiated trends have been shown in relation to crime and conduct disorder, with significantly more boys than girls being identified, although the difference between the two is becoming less (Rutter and Smith 1995).

This general picture is reflected in the distribution of girls and boys in EBDs special schools. Cooper, Upton and Smith (1991) found a male to female ratio of 6:1 in a survey of EBDs provision in England and Wales; and OFSTED, in its first 12 inspections of Pupil Referral Units, identified a boy:girl ratio of 3:1 (OFSTED 1995). One of the most visible outcomes of EBDs is exclusion from school. Findings from the studies already cited reflect earlier DfE permanent exclusion figures that showed that four boys to one girl are excluded from school (DfE 1992). There is some evidence that children diagnosed with Attention Deficit/Hyperactivity Disorder (AD/HD) are mainly boys (see for example Brown 1990; Graham 1989; Rutter 1989); however, when looked at more closely, identified boys mainly represent a hyperactive subtype of the phenomenon. When numbers of children with less 'well presented' Attention Deficit Disorder (i.e. without hyperactivity) are considered, it is more likely that girls are represented in this group to the same degree as boys (Hinshaw 1994).

More recently, similar findings were identified in research in a Local Education Authority (LEA) in southern England (Maras and Hall 1996). Exclusion and Special Educational Needs (SEN) data made available by the LEA did not unequivocally support the commonly held view that the numbers of pupils who experience EBDs or that are excluded are significantly increasing. However, the researchers were able to speculate with confidence that the profile of identified pupils was changing, particularly in the case of secondary-aged pupils. Furthermore, the extent and degree of annual trends appeared to be directly related to the LEA area, sex and age of excluded pupils. In line with national and international trends, significantly more boys than girls were described as experiencing EBDs and behavioural problems only, whilst there was a clear trend towards emotional difficulties being attributed proportionally more to girls than boys. Overall numbers of both boys and girls increased in line with progression through National Curriculum (NC) school years; proportionally more boys than girls were reported as having additional (mostly learning) needs, though the overall number of pupils with additional SENs reduced in line with progression through NC school years (Maras and Hall 1996).

In addition, data from one area within the LEA indicated that proportional differences *between* girls and boys identified as experiencing emotional and/or behavioural difficulties have fallen in younger (5–10 years) and older (15–18 years) children, whilst in the middle age range (11–15 years) behavioural difficulties were still attributed significantly more than emotional difficulties to boys. It is interesting to note that this middle age range is critical in terms of adolescent emotional and social development (Maras and Hall 1996). It is also important to bear in mind the arbitrary nature of both decisions about children who experience EBDs and the consequences of such decisions, which can involve identified children taking either a discipline or SENs route or, indeed, a combination of both courses (Maras and Redmayne 1996). Current work (Lovey and Cooper 1997) is drawing attention to the very real effect that schools can have on such outcomes.

In terms of the way these anomalies have been viewed, some commentators have focused on within-child factors (see for example Erikson 1950) and some have considered external environmental factors (see for example Slee 1995). Still others have taken account of potential interactions between the two (see for example Farrington 1987; Rutter 1975; Rutter and Giller 1983). In addressing these issues, we refer to social developmental theories of children's recognition and acceptance of sex differences, sex-typed behaviour and peer relations; social psychological theories of attribution and volition; and more recent feminist and critical views on the conceptualisation and consequential scripts available to teachers and students in their daily interactions. We introduce these different theories not just as an academic exercise, but because we believe they do, and should, inform everyday practice. We also take the view that individual- and group-based perceptions are central to the impact of sex differences and gender issues on EBDs.

Sex roles, peer relations and EBDs

Developmental work on behaviour and gender issues can be broadly seen as taking two related routes. Some research has considered aspects of sex-role identity, particularly the recognition of norms and conformity to gender-based roles. Other work has looked at the impact of sex-role development and behaviour on peer relations. Both of these perspectives relate to, and are seen in parallel with, not just social and emotional development but also the acquisition of cognitive skills and ability. As a general rule, the development of cognitive, social and emotional awareness and skills starts in early childhood, is gradually consolidated between the ages of 5 and 12 years, is tested in the turbulence of adolescence and is generally developed by the late teens. At the same time as children are developing physical strength, social skills and cognitive maturity, they are also acquiring self-image. However, they are not developing in isolation; whilst this is going on they are interacting with others: first parents and families and then peers assume increasing importance within the milieu of the child's developmental progress. Peer groups change in their size, sex composition and importance, and the ability to interact with peers can be affected by many factors, including social and family background, ability and who is making the judgement. In addition, the effectiveness of children's peer relations has been shown to be directly related to their skill in following accepted social rules and norms (Dunn and McGuire 1992) and ability to negotiate meaning from them. Conforming to the norms of these sometimes competing groups requires a whole range of interpersonal skills, and acceptance by peers assumes increasing importance as children get older. Acceptance (or not) by peers can be influenced by a number of factors, including similarity and proximity; it can also be influenced by a child's capacity to recognise and conform to sex-typed behaviours – research suggests that boys and girls who fail to do this have problems (Puttallaz and Wasserman 1990).

Interactions with parents, families and teachers are also important for children's social development, and can affect children's behaviour and may be different for girls and boys. Mednick, Gabrielli and Hutchings (1984) investigated the relationships between court convictions of adopted children and those of their genetic and adoptive parents. The authors found that there was a tendency for genetic fathers and sons to be recidivists whilst adoptive fathers were at most one-time offenders (see also Maras and Masser 1996). Similarly, research has shown that girls' and boys' views of teachers differ; girls show concern for interpersonal relationships and inclusiveness and boys focus on teacher control and use of punishment (Jules and Kutnick, in press). These last findings highlight important social aspects of boys' and girls' development and school experience. As noted earlier, social and emotional development takes place along with cognitive and physical development. As such, most social developmental research utilises models founded in traditional work on cognitive development. This is problematic in terms of both depth of analysis and outcomes for both boys and girls; because of their individualist nature, traditional models of cognition tend to miss the very social core of the problems they are addressing. In order to address such past deficits, researchers would do well to adopt a relational approach (Kutnick 1988) that considers any action (including that resulting in, or caused by, EBDs) to be based on interpersonal principles, in contrast to the predominantly operant and individualistic nature of the behavioural and cognitive approaches (Maras and Kutnick 1996). Research in progress has shown that when such a truly social developmental approach is adopted, differences between boys and girls can be better accounted for and identified, and are invariably associated with both individual- and group-based factors of children's social interactions, with both girls and boys adopting gender-based social strategies.

Such findings reflect research that has looked at the formation and running of groups in schools (see for example Bennett and Dunne 1992; Galton and Williamson 1992), much of which has been atheoretical and based on the pedagogy of the classroom rather than the social psychological processes underlying group and intergroup relations. Social psychological research on delinquency, a phenomenon often related to EBDs, has taken an intergroup approach (see for example Abrams, Simpson and Hogg 1987; Emler and Reicher 1995) and reflect findings from sociological research on anti-school subcultures (see for example Ball 1981; Hargreaves 1967) with findings that suggest that in many instances membership of groups, be they delinquent, EBDs or whatever, has an important psychological impact on the feelings of self-worth and self-esteem of young people. Such findings are rarely taken into account in research on EBDs. Similarly, little research considered the attitudes and feelings of pupils participating in group and individualised intervention strategies (Maras and Kutnick 1996), despite the fact that both are employed every day in classrooms, and research suggests that girls and boys work differently in group and individual situations.

Perception, attribution, volition and EBDs

As noted above, children's ability to interact with others is affected by their developmental maturity and ability to recognise and respond appropriately to social cues that occur in interactions with others (Asher and Coie 1990). Research has indicated that such interactions are differentially affected by children's sex, sex-role development and gender identity. Traditional social developmental theories that take this line most often locate EBDs firmly within the arena of individual children's competence. However, it is clear that other people also have an impact on, and are impacted by, children's behaviour. The way EBDs are manifested and perceived by both pupils who experience them and others who describe them is obviously an important area of concern.

There is strong evidence documenting sex-differentiated manifestations and perceptions directly linked to the 'E' (emotion) and 'B' (behaviour) in EBDs, with the former being seen in the experience of girls and the latter in the more explicit 'acting-out' behaviour of boys (Rutter 1975; Rutter, Tizard and Whitmore 1970). Simple explanations for this are encompassed in the literature on attribution and are compounded by the impact of expectations and attributions commonly made in respect of girls' social behaviour, suggesting that girls are perceived, socialised and subsequently treated differently from boys. With girls, ways of expressing their difficulties (i.e. internally and in a non-disruptive manner) are seen as more legitimate by parents and teachers, with the potential consequence that girls who experience EBDs may be in danger of being neglected because they 'don't act out'. Conversely, the tendency for boys to be over-represented in the 'B' component of EBDs may result in the neglect of their emotional needs and consequent psychological well-being, as suggested in work that shows a rise in adolescent male suicide (Rutter and Smith 1995).

The impact of how we see others is affected by our perceptions of self, and there is evidence that suggests that children's self-perceptions are gender based (see for example Archer 1992; Erikson 1968; Gilligan 1982; Hill 1993). Research has looked at social and psychological aspects of the self-perception of 77 11-year-old boys and girls from EBDs and mainstream schools (Maras and Hall 1996). The study, conducted by Sara Piggott, utilised Harter's (1985) measure, which is designed to tap four factors seen as subdivisions of children's self-perception: social acceptance, physical appearance, behavioural conduct and (global) self-worth. Although there may have been differences between the degree of problems encountered by the boys and girls who participated in the study, which were not measured by the study, there were a number of interesting and significant trends and differences in the pupils' self-perceptions:

1.   All the mainstream children perceived themselves as significantly more socially acceptable than the children from the EBDs schools.

2.   Girls from the EBDs schools rated themselves as less socially acceptable than any of the other groups.

3.   Overall, girls rated themselves as significantly less physically attractive than any of the other three groups; in contrast, boys from the EBDs school rated themselves as more physically attractive than any of the other groups.

4.   Boys from the EBDs school rated themselves as significantly lower than any of the other groups in terms of their behavioural conduct, and mainstream girls rated themselves as significantly higher than any of the other groups in terms of their behavioural conduct.

5.   Although mean scores for global self-worth were broadly similar for each group, girls from the EBDs school rated themselves significantly lower on the global self-worth measures than the other three groups.

Findings from this study offer some insight into sex differences and differences between pupils who are in mainstream and EBDs schools. Previous research findings have shown that the self-esteem of boys with EBDs is lower than that of their peers; however, the label EBDs, the sense of social identity obtained from it, and a degree of cultural preference for anti-establishment status conferred by EBDs status and provision may actually enhance boys' expressions of self-esteem (Tajfel and Turner 1979). On the other hand, the girls' attendance to personal appearance may have been related to the disproportionate number of girls who experience eating disorders (Lask and Bryant-Waugh 1992), an area which incidentally mirrors the sex-biased prevalence of EBDs. Although the authors were unable to say conclusively that their findings were a consequence of experiencing EBDs, rather than being related to being in mainstream versus segregated provision, they do add weight to evidence from qualitative work that indicates that children's self-perception can be both predictive and indicative of EBDs (Maras and Hall 1996). This view is supported by research by Harter (1990) among others, who shows the same findings for children experiencing EBDs in both inclusive and segregated contexts.

Whether increases in self-esteem at this level realistically reflect boys' actual feelings and sense of personal worth is not so clear; indeed, it may be the case that the ethos of EBDs provision may have the effect of socialising 'delinquent' boys to quash feelings of low self-esteem, since the expression of such feelings may be counter, or culturally, unacceptable within the context of behaviourally based provision that is founded on obedience to authority. Qualitative work with boys in EBDs schools found that boys commonly claimed to feel shame, guilt and low self-worth (Cooper 1993a). In the same vein, ongoing work with pupils who have left a residential EBDs school has found that, although most of the respondents were positive about their experience at the school, a significant number also indicated that they would not wish their own children to experience special segregated provision (Maras and Hall 1996).

Children's self-perceptions can have an impact on attribution and attributional style, both of which are deemed to be artefacts of individuals' social information processing (Dodge 1993). Personal–emotional needs and socialising influences are thought to be influential in helping an individual attend to features such as others' intent, social norms, rules and threats, which can then be acted upon in terms of the individual's emotional needs and goals, moral acceptability and/or anticipated consequences, finally, enactment, where the selected response is transformed into behaviour (Crick and Ladd 1991). In work that utilises this position, the term EBDs is often used interchangeably with 'conduct disorder', a main element of which is aggression, and is generally focused on boys (see for example Dodge 1993). However, authors do make the general conclusion that both aggressive and depressed children display processing biases and deficits at all stages of processing and in numerous types of social situations (Dodge 1993, p.563), suggesting that they do attend to both girls and emotion – facts that are not immediately obvious in reported research findings which focus mainly on boys' biases in evaluating and acting on information in an aggressive manner. Indeed, it has generally been hypothesised that chronically aggressive boys enact responses without sufficient prior evaluation and see aggression more positively than other children – that is, they see aggression as less morally 'bad' (Deluty 1983) and more 'friendly' than do their peers (Crick and Ladd 1991 – see Deluty (1981) for further examples). In addition, aggressive boys have been found to be less competent in selecting appropriate behavioural responses that depend on procedural knowledge of rules and sequential associations than other children. For example, 'a boy who represents a peer bumping into him as an instance of peer threat might associate this threat with expectations of future harm and might apply a rule of response access that leads to the generation of aggressive retaliation as a possible response' (Dodge 1993, p.574).

Dodge (1993) posits that early experiences of physical abuse, exposure to aggressive models and insecure attachment relationships may lead a child to develop memory structures of the world as a hostile place; a world that subsequently requires coercive behaviour to achieve desired outcomes. If this is indeed the case, how do such situations explain the sex-differentiated prevalence of EBDs? We should, of course, first note that from a pragmatic point of view, most studies in this area have been conducted with boys; this could, of course, be because it is boys who are identified and *vice versa* – a 'catch 22' situation that hinders work in this area. Also, it may be that boys' and girls' responses to early childhood experiences do in fact differ. For example, Hetherington, Cox and Cox (1979) looked at children from middle-class families in which the mother was awarded custody following a divorce. The children were found to have a number of identifiable characteristics; their play and social interaction was less mature socially and intellectually (a characteristic that continued into the second year for boys) and they tended to display more negative reactions (including dependency, attention seeking and aggressiveness). In addition, the 'divorced' children were initially more anxious, guilty and apathetic than other children – an effect that was also found to remain for boys. Two years later, some of the boys in the study were found to be unpopular with other boys, having difficulty gaining access to play groups and spending more time playing with girls and younger children than their peers. Six years after the divorce, boys were found to be somewhat more aggressive and rather less socially competent than other boys of their age. The girls' adjustment appeared to depend on the then current marital status of their mother (Hetherington, Cox and Cox 1981).

Despite this evidence, the mere presence of one of these events in a child's life does not necessarily predispose a child to 'contrast' EBDs; it may be the permanence of the psychological trauma for the child that results in the emergence of EBDs, or rather the label of EBDs being applied to the child (Maras and Masser 1996). For example, if we take the finding of Hetherington *et al.* (1979) that some boys who had suffered a parental divorce were found to be unpopular with other boys, Rabiner and Gordon (1993) found that peer-rejected boys (specifically submissive rejected boys) 'cared less about sustaining interactions with boys' and aggressive rejected boys (aggressiveness being a negative reaction displayed by 'divorced' boys) 'cared less about peers' feelings' (Hetherington *et al.* 1979). Rejection and withdrawal from peers or the mere demonstration of behavioural difficulties may be sufficient for a child to be noted by their teacher as being 'different' from the norm (Brodzinsky *et al.* 1984; Guidubaldi *et al.* 1986; Hetherington *et al.* 1979). Teachers' perceptions and subsequent attributions of cause and responsibility of girls' and boys' behaviour have been found to be related to the sex of children identified.

Many factors may influence teachers' perceptions of what constitutes 'problem behaviour', not least, perhaps, the teacher's personal characteristics, school experience and/or classroom management techniques. In addition, gender is often correlated with teachers' expectations about the acceptability (or not) of certain, particularly aggressive, behaviours. Ledingham *et al.* (1982) found that agreement between different types of observers of behaviour generally increased when the observers were considering a high-magnitude behaviour (such as aggression). As such, teachers may not 'notice' or refer to behaviour of a low magnitude, which may be more typical of girls, and there is now convincing evidence that such actions and attributions can have reinforcing effect on girls' and boys' subsequent behaviour (see for example Babad, Bernieri and Rosenthal 1989; Safran and Safran 1987).

Morality, values and EBDs

The theories described so far allude to differing degrees to internal (to the child) features as a basis of EBDs. In contrast, there is a growing literature that depicts gender issues in terms of illegitimate masculine power built on (notions of) male domination and oppression of females (see for example Carrigan, Connell and Lee 1987). One outcome of such views is that women are empowered, and emergent feminist views are related to societal changes that value traditional feminist traits and values more than male ones (Miedzian 1991). It has been suggested that these changes in values (and consequentially accepted morality) may be having a counter-effect on the scripts available to boys, whose emerging sense of self may become inextricably linked with incompetence and moral inferiority (Cooper 1996b). It has been suggested that this situation may be particularly damaging to boys with SENs, who often start from a point of low self-esteem and poor self-image by virtue of their relative failure to perform as well as their peers in a Judeo-Christian culture in which traditionally defined female traits are becoming increasingly highly valued (Cooper 1996b).

These counter-explanations to developing critical and feminist perspectives are problematic for three main reasons. First, from a practical viewpoint they misinterpret the intent (though, perhaps not the effects) of key theorists and may in fact reflect current uncertainty about, rather than common understanding of, the status and 'pecking order' of current morality and values. Though challenging the dominance of patriarchy in relation to traditional views, few feminist theorists have in fact laid claim to be superiority of what they have identified as previously unheard or under-rated relationally based traits. Rather, they placed them on the agenda and show the genderised nature of moral and other reasoning and its development (Gilligan 1982).

Second, views about the superiority of feminist traits are not reflected in common understanding. Indeed, at a practical level rarely a day goes by without media comment about, and undue attention to, the relative competence or alleged superiority of either men or women – a point aptly illustrated by media attention whilst we are writing to the suggested links between the size of women's brains reducing in the latter stages of pregnancy and accompanying jokes and ribaldry.

Third, if in fact the counter-position to current critical views were 'true', this would illustrate well the very position central to feminist thinking in the area. For indeed, that low-achieving boys are affected by their failure to attain traditionally masculine ideas about competence is contradictory, such views being posited in a patriarchal system of competition rather than cooperation; a situation that is particularly tenuous given suggestions that girls and women are generally more group (collectively) oriented than boys and men (Bacon 1966). Furthermore, as Segal (1997) points out in the preface to the new edition of her seminal book *Slow Motion*

> Of course it is only particular groups of men in society who will occupy positions of public power and influence. But this is precisely what secures rather than undermines the hierarchical structuring of gender ... Despite forceful feminist critique, despite all the documented upheavals or 'crisis tendencies' in men's lives (as women gain greater independence and control over their own), the forces securing 'men' in power have only been dented, rather than substantially dismantled. (Segal 1997)

Notwithstanding these last points, there are nevertheless still practical problems and contradictions in thinking in this area. Many of these are centred on commonly held traditional notions of gender as dichotomous with two clear and homogeneous groups (men and women). Mac an Ghail (1995) points out that sex/gender identity and traditional sex-role theories are inadequate in explaining '...the complex social and psychological processes involved in the development of gendered subjectivity that are underpinned by institutional and wider material powers'. In terms of the outcome and inadequacy of conceptualisations, as Arnot suggests, 'The simplicity of the portrayal of the process of learning and gender formation, its formation, its assumptions about the nature of stereotyping, its somewhat negative view of girls as victims had all but contributed to the creation of particular school based strategies' (Arnot 1991, p.453). The over-simplicity alluded to by Arnot is mainly founded in the inadequate conceptions of gender identity along with the notion that identities are in some way fixed entities rather than, as Hall suggests, '...a production, which is never complete, always in process, and always constituted within, not outside representation' (Hall 1990, p.222). So how can we remedy over-simplistic conceptualisations and consolidate and value differing perceptions? One way is to attempt to move away from one-dimensional pendulum definitions of gender and EBDs. Both gender and EBDs are generally conceptualised as homogeneous phenomena that are rarely considered in relation to learning and curriculum, which in themselves are biased and ethnocentric (Maras with Archer 1997).

EBDs, gender issues and levels of action: towards synthesis

To sum up, significantly more boys than girls are identified as experiencing emotional and behavioural difficulties, and within the spectrum of EBDs there is convincing evidence that behavioural difficulties are attributed more to boys and emotional (including depressive disorders) to girls. Before we conclude this chapter, it is useful to take stock of the terms and expressions commonly used when discussing EBDs and gender issues. In this chapter we have drawn on notions of value and morality in relation to gendered behaviours, actions and the scripts available to describe them; it is not uncommon for terms such as under- and over-representation to be used when talking about the number of girls and boys described as experiencing EBDs. One does not have to ponder too hard about these points to recognise a tension that begs a plethora of questions about the nature of EBDs as they are generally construed within the context of SENs. The concept of SENs implies meeting needs; however, needs are often not met (Maras 1995) or are based on gendered preconceptions and identification, particularly since much of the emphasis is on disruptive behaviour and as such on teachers' perceived needs (Maras 1996). The growing interest in AD/HD has at least allowed parents a helpful mechanism whereby the focus is moved back to children's learning, other difficulties and associated needs (Cooper 1997). As such, it allows disruptive children the same opportunities as any pupil experiencing difficulties in school in terms of entitlement to have their needs recognised and to delivery of a fully differentiated curriculum in order to enhance learning and maintain and extend knowledge.

A further tension concerns the perceived distinctiveness of EBDs and concepts such as gender as discrete entities. It is impossible to write about gender, in education or in any other context, as if gender were a discrete phenomenon unrelated to other facets of identity. It is also important that identification and provision are not considered as single homogeneous ideas (Maras with Archer 1997). Indeed, research has shown that 'the impact of gender issues is qualitatively different for girls and young women from perceived minority ethnic groups and for disabled girls and women than for other girls and young women' (Maras with Archer 1997, p.268). It is not useful to look at gender, EBDs or any other construct unless linked to social consequences, personal experiences and ambiguity underlying surrounding myths: gender, EBDs and other aspects of identity should be conceptualised as multiple, overlapping categories in relation to learning. If such an approach is not adopted, the outlook is gloomy, for, as Mirza (1992, p.10) highlighted in her work on black girls in school, 'marginalisation of the gender issue is a consequence of the political undercurrents that have shaped research on race and education', as indeed they have shaped research and policy on SENs.

So how can we look at curricula which are traditionally ethnocentric, class and gender based (King 1991; Nicholson 1980)? First, curricula should take account of cultural diversity that encompasses not just behaviour, ability and gender but all differences *and also similarities*: that moves towards valuing diversity. A good starting point would be to listen to the stories of students' school experiences (Cooper 1993a; Cooper and McIntyre 1996). Similarly, we must look at curricula from both the individual child's point of view and the historical context; as Illich so aptly pointed out nearly 20 years ago: 'The result of the curriculum production process looks like any other modern staple. It is a bundle of planned meanings, a package of values, a commodity whose 'balanced appeal' makes it marketable to a sufficiently large number to justify the cost of production' (Illich 1973, p.46).

Given our proposition that individuals' perceptions of EBDs are based in part on their ideological positions, we cannot of course preclude the notion that researchers' perceptions, and consequently research questions, may be similarly biased and thus reflected in published work. How can educators take on board the impact of their own prejudices and recognise and value difference? It is all very well to aim at such aspirations from an academic stance, to lay down positions from a theoretical view, but what can teachers do and how can their valuable knowledge be integrated into provision? As a foundation, policy and practice that take on board diversity – rather than just paying lip service to it – are needed, as are curricula that encompass awareness of diversity, recognition and respect for cultural, religious and other traditions, and including gender issues and understanding of both female and male culture and values.

In taking this multi-faceted approach, schools and teachers would do well to re-appraise the types of gendered 'scripts' they utilise and that are made available to pupils at both the pedagogical and curricular levels. Roles, scripts, school and classroom ethos should promote and value community, inclusion, tolerance and freedom of expression as a means of enhancing social and self-esteem. Curricula should include, re-appraise and value humanities subjects as equal and complementary to technology and science subjects, which have increasingly assumed more importance in day-to-day school life. We also need to ask whether we need a concept of gender in education. Curricula subjects are not intrinsically valued, values are imposed both implicitly and explicitly, as are behaviours.

The ideas we propose expose potential tensions between equal opportunities and explanations for sexual divisions that propose more radical anti-sexist perspectives as a means of reducing inequality (Weiner 1992). In order to allay problems of past research, policy and practice, some commentators on gender issues in education have drawn on the work of Foucault in an attempt to deconstruct existing theory and account for power positions of teachers (see for example Walkerdine 1990). Others have criticised the dualism inherent in notions of individuals living outside society and society as something different and separate from the individuals within it (Henriques et al. 1984; Slee 1995).

Unfortunately, few have conceptualised EBDs as multi-faceted and dynamic, founded within, interacting with and informing gender issues within a current social context that in fact offers little hope for young people (Maras with Archer 1997). This point is reflected in Clive Wilkinson's moving account of young people who have dropped out of, or have been dropped by, society (Wilkinson 1995). Schools are not separate but a part of society; as Mehan points out, 'Schools are not black boxes through which students pass on their way to predetermined slots in the capitalist order; they have a vibrant life, composed of processes and practices that respond to competing demands that often unwittingly contribute to inequality' (Mehan 1992, p.1). Finally, what of the way forward? What first steps can schools and teachers – for that is what we are talking of here – take to design and implement policy that incorporates notions of value and diversity, and recognises and takes account of the contextual nature of inequality (Maras with Archer 1997)? This can only be done when gender, along with race, disability, ability and behavioural norms in education, are conceptualised in an egalitarian way that allows for both difference and equivalence. Such an approach is unlikely to be adopted at the present time, given differing conceptualisations of both the problems of gender and other inequalities and the task of educators in addressing them.

CHAPTER 4

Cultural Issues in Child and Adolescent Psychiatry

Harry Zeitlin and Rafik Refaat

Introduction

There are very few communities today which have uniform culture. Population movement has resulted in mixtures of national origins, varying cultures and disparate appearance. Minority groups are often, but by no means always, the result of relatively recent immigration. Theories and political views about race, ethnicity and culture are all very interesting and it is hopeful that today we can discuss such things more openly than in the past, but in practice what should we do to help families from different cultures? This chapter will look at some aspects of culture that are relevant to clinical practice and at the means of working with children and families from different cultural backgrounds.

Terminology

The terms race, ethnicity and culture are too often used without regard to any precision of meaning. Race as a biological term, like the term 'species', implies a fundamental genetic separateness. There is no justification for this in fact. Any genetic differences do not result in reduced fertility of mixed offspring, the biological sign of species difference. Ethnicity is also a rather vague term that at times is used for physical differences, national heritage, religion or other cultural determinants. Here the terms national heritage, religion and culture will be used in preference. Whilst the term race is misleading, the term racism is used to indicate a social attitude and does not indicate anything about the person subject to it. Guidelines for the classification of ethnicity have been proposed and include 'Relevant genetically determined polymorphism, Self assigned ethnicity, Observer assigned ethnicity, Country or area of birth, Years in country of residence and Religion' (McKenzie and Crowcroft 1996). For these purposes the most important will be the self-assigned ethnicity.

The child in context

To gain an understanding of children it is necessary to see them in context, both with their environment and with their development. A useful model is to consider the child as being at the centre of a series of systems: the family, a child-oriented system including peer groups and school, and lastly the society in which they live (Figure 4.1). The relationship between the child and those systems is an important perspective. The child is affected by each, not only in terms of cultural style and protection, but also in terms of pathogenic influence. Whether the child is within each of these environments is also relevant, as both cultural influences and protection are changed. There may be dissonance between the child and the parental culture, between the parental culture and the majority social culture, and indeed between each of these and the social system around the child and family. All have to operate within the laws of the land. Children without families or outside a peer group or school have additional difficulty and are more vulnerable to adverse influence.

A different context to consider is that of the child's development. Problems relating to development, including parental expectations, are common to all, but it may be more difficult to evaluate developmental status where there are language problems and where behaviour is modified by culture. The degree of independence may, for example, be very different for children of the same age in families of European, Asian or West Indian heritage.

Relevant issues

Genetic differences in vulnerability

There are major difficulties in assessing differences in incidence and types of disorder in immigrant and minority groups (Bird 1996). Most of the evidence indicates that all cultural groups suffer from the same range of problems in similar proportions. Higher rates of drug and substance abuse have been reported in children of minority groups but this appears to relate more to the higher rates of poverty (a social rather than genetic factor). The relationship of poverty to disorder is itself complex, being at least in part related to parenting style and relationship with the mother rather than genetic ethnicity (McLeod and Shanahan 1993). Anorexia nervosa is said to be rare in people of Afro-Caribbean origin and in cultures which have little contact with Western society but again this may be attributable to cultural influence rather than genetically determined vulnerability (Apter and Shah 1994). Afro-Caribbean origin is reported as being linked to differences in the nature and incidence of psychotic disorders, but how this might apply to children and teenagers is not yet determined (Van-Os *et al.* 1996).

Impact of a move to a different majority culture

A move of home is a major event, and when that involves a change of country to a different majority culture the effects, apart from stress, can be very varied and extreme. Some of the factors operating include:

- disorientation due to the move from familiar to strange
- loss of friends and extended family
- language change
- adaptation to new social demands
- suspicion of neighbours who are different
- being subject to xenophobia from the host society
- racism, abuse and aggression
- difficulty in obtaining work
- poverty.

Curiously, whilst it is very evident that all of these, particularly racism, have undesirable effects, there has been little study of the nature of the effects on children. When families which have moved to a new cultural environment present to a clinical service, it is important to understand their special needs as families in transition as well as some of the perceptions and misperceptions that take place between the immigrant family and the host culture. There is usually a natural fear of the unknown, manifest in a wariness of strangers and a suspiciousness, often merited, of those of the majority culture. Their reactive behaviour may vary considerably, determined in part by the nature or perceived nature of the new culture and partly by their own motives for moving. Some may stick rigidly to their own culture, even to the extent of resisting learning a new language, whilst others may strive to outdo the host culture in their behaviour.

Understanding the culture of the person in front of you

One school of thought is that each professional team should have a member who is from the same culture as the family being seen. In some circumstances that may be an advantage, as in areas where there is a large number of recent immigrants from a single country that has a relatively uniform culture. However, there are difficulties with this. First, it is most important that professionals are employed because of their expertise rather than their private culture. Second, it is hazardous to assume that the culture of the professional will be the same as that of the client just because their heritage is from the same part of the world. A successful professional born in the UK may have a very different culture to an impoverished recent immigrant, even if they are both of Asian origin.

Case study

D is 15 but first came here when she was 13, when she developed a severe acute psychosis. Her family were of Asian origin but had been living in East Africa. She was very ill and remained in hospital for some time. Her family announced that they were going on a trip, previously arranged. They said that D would want them to go. It was thought at first to be an uncaring attitude; however when pressed about the holiday they were initially cautious but went on to explain that they are Muslim and this was a pilgrimage to Mecca. When D recovered she agreed that they should have gone and subsequently the whole family went again, but together as a caring close family.

It is more important for any professional to develop the skills to help their client to share something of their own culture with them. That requires initially an openness of mind, rather than reliance on generalised stereotypes. The professional has also to create the situation in which that is possible. A sole interest in the problem precludes this. For any family seeking help there should be the following:

- a statement of the reason for referral
- a request for information about the child and family (apart from any systematic search for pathogenicity)
- an acknowledgement of the special cultural setting and invitation to speak more of it
- a recognition with the family of special implications of the child's problem within their cultural framework.

Professional stereotyping and prejudices

There is a danger of professionals imposing their own prejudices and stereotypes on to the problem in various ways. We have to recognise that some professionals carry with them their own socially determined prejudices, but it is more likely that stereotypes derive from unfamiliarity and a fear of offending. Unfortunately, almost as much prejudice may stem from a drive for political correctness, when the qualities of the individual may be overlooked in favour of an ethnically correct solution. Training in awareness of the need to consider cultural and national characteristics helps, but should not remove the ability to see and listen to the real needs of the child.

Case study

One fostered child complained that her social worker only thought about being black whereas her real problem was that she was raised as a Christian and her foster parents were not. A different black child who had been adopted by a white family complained that no one had ever talked of her physical difference. Her adoptive parents said that no professional had ever been prepared to talk about it openly except in the context of whether the child should be with them.

Cultural differences in acceptance of treatment

There is evidence that different parts of the community access services to very different extents. Why this is so is not always clear. Whilst the anxieties of the family may play a large part, the attitudes of the referrer may well contribute, as well as the overall lack of knowledge of cultural differences. As an example, risk factors for repeated self-harm are now documented from research, but whether different risk factors are more important in some cultural groups than others is not known. Targeting services to those with the wrong risk factors in effect reduces service access, and research into such cultural differences is needed.

There are various reasons why some families will see referral to a child mental health service as shameful or demeaning. It can be a well-entrenched part of the culture concerned, and indeed stigma is not alien to Western culture. The reason may, however, be more 'accidental' and where the country of origin had scant mental health resources only the most severely ill people would be taken to them, perhaps being held in control by several family members. Referral was, therefore, only for the mad. Changing this perception may take time but it is time well spent. An attempt should be made to seek terms of reference that can be understood by the family in explaining the sort of work carried out by the professional. Even the most detailed and illustrated explanations may be misunderstood or not assimilated, and patience is needed, though with care to avoid being patronising.

Problems of within-family cultural dissonance

Parent–child cultural differences include children who adopt different eating customs, dress or religion from their parents. Teenagers choosing a partner from a different culture is a common problem for children and parents. The differences are often more subtle, however. No matter how observant of traditional ways, children of immigrants from other countries and cultures will have a different experience from their parents simply because they have moved to a different setting. The child may wish to be observant of the parent culture but cannot do it in the way that their parents experienced in a different country.

Case study

AK is a boy of 15 who is the oldest of four. The family attended in crisis when their argumentative but usually conforming child went out with friends and got drunk. The boy had struggled academically since he went to secondary school. When seen he had a moderately severe depression. His family had come from an Arabic country four years ago. Any parent might have been concerned about their child getting drunk but it was against these parents' religion and they saw it as a rejection of themselves. They constantly felt that he did not continue

Case study continued
their customs and traditions, often reprimanding him for that. For them the eldest son was of paramount importance and his difficulty with learning had caused great distress, even though their next child, who was born in England, was bright and progressing well. AK was in fact quite able but was more affected by the move and change of language than they thought. He was also desperate to succeed as the first born, and under-performed because of constant fear of failure. Treatment of his depression, and enabling his father to give him some responsibility at home and to give praise for the way that he did carry out his religious and cultural ways, improved their relationship, made the boy more observant in his religion and resulted in better school performance.

Heritage and culture as part of identity

A normal process for children in their teens is one of a move to independence and separation. Though often seen as rebellion and breaking parent–child relationships, it is normally a change rather than destruction of relationship. The child, the developing person, moves to establishing an identity profile of his or her own but more often than not relying heavily on their family experience. Identity is now understood as being a composite of various domains, including gender, occupation, religion, hobbies, special skills and personal attributes. Aspects of personality may be chosen or assigned by others, and each attribute may be seen as having positive or negative connotations. The nature of personal identity is of central importance to the development and persistence of disturbed behaviour.

Clearly, many aspects of identity formation are related to characteristics of minority groups. Physical appearance, being black, Chinese, Mediterranean; dress, wearing a sari, turban, skull cap; religious affiliation, going to a church, mosque or synagogue, would all be part of identity domains. Culture is relevant in the life experience of the child and also as part of their heritage. For many children there are several different cultural components to their heritage, for each of which they may have pride without having to adopt wholly.

Unfortunately, physical appearance and religious affiliation may be the basis of prejudice and racism. That implies the attribution of a negative connotation to potential identity domains that should be strongly positive for the individual. The task of the therapist is to enable the young person to be in a position to evaluate the physical or cultural characteristic free from the socially assigned connotation associated with prejudice. 'Ego-enhancing treatment', identifying and endorsing those fundamental characteristics that are relatively culture free, temperamental attributes, and personal skills and interests, facilitate this and is work that can be done with the child or with the family.

Children of mixed parentage

There is an increasing number of children who are described as 'mixed race', usually implying one Afro-Caribbean parent and one Caucasian, though in reality parental cultural mixes may be of many different varieties. For the children there are difficulties in confusion over identity and self-concept. There is a tendency for such children to be officially 'classified' as being of the minority group, though there is little evidence to indicate this as being best for them. Indeed, forced allocation to a minority group can have a depressing effect on self-esteem. Having both parents together and supportive is known to help. For all families, preparation for parenthood and work to reconcile potentially splitting differences is of importance, but even more so for mixed partnerships. Openness and free discussion of the different cultural origins with freedom to accept both parts of their heritage, as well as membership of mixed groups, is also of use.

Working with children and families

All families will be part of a culture and it would be rare to sit down with a family and child for assessment where they were of identical culture to oneself. Working with children who have emotional and behavioural problems and their families should present an essentially similar task, no matter which culture they are from. However, where the culture is relatively more different to the majority culture, they are likely to experience special problems and the tasks are, if anything, clearer.

Assessment

STATUS OF THE INTERVIEWER

The perceived status of the professional is always important. He or she has to be approachable but also of sufficient status to give confidence in their expertise. It may be difficult to evaluate the reaction in some groups as, for example, Chinese families may take a non-judgmental approach to reflect lack of interest. Come what may, there are often misunderstandings about the professional but an immigrant may have no idea what sort of person they are talking to at all. Careful explanation should always be given. An attempt should be made to understand what matters to the parents and accord appropriate status and respect.

> *Case study*
> A very quiet woman told of her concerns about her child and listened to advice, but became progressively more silent until, for the last part of the session, she said nothing. She missed the next appointment but came to a third offered by letter. When asked about her obvious unhappiness towards the end of the first interview, she said that it had nothing to do with the child or advice, but why had she been put to sit in the lowest chair in the room?

WHO AND WHERE

It is first necessary to determine who to see with whom and where. For the most part it is best to be guided by the family themselves. Some may wish to have present a large part of the family, including grandparents, aunts and uncles. In others, parents, at least in the first instance, wish to tell of their concerns and perhaps themselves, by themselves. Culture makes major differences to family structure and systems, and sensitivity to the functioning of the family facilitates therapy. The father in Greek families differs in role greatly from that of Irish families. The dominant role in the former may require the therapist to defer to the paternal authority in order to gain his compliance. In Irish families the father is a far more shadowy figure and the maternal line is the one that tends to hold the family focus.

Forcing a family to do what they do not wish to do is not a good start. A home visit can be the most effective way of lowering anxieties, as home may be the only place they feel is their own territory.

Case study

An Irish girl had gone to England, become involved in drugs, had two children by different fathers and was now HIV positive. The two children were taken into care but the maternal grandmother in Ireland was seeking to become the children's carer. A home visit was made at the grandmother's request and when visited the main living room was crowded with all of her adult children, their partners and various, more distant, relatives. They already knew all that the grandmother had to tell, but more importantly they would all be involved in supporting the children if they were returned. The interview was complicated as everyone had something to say, but it gave an excellent view of the family structure and functioning.

MAKING SAFE

It is always the task of the clinician to make it safe for children and families to talk to both the clinician and each other. For both the parents and the children, knowing something about the person other than the problem enables the work to start without an immediate attribution of pathology.

Getting an account of the person's culture raises anxieties. Some may not refer to the subject at all, relying on their own stereotyped images of what they imagine to be the culture concerned. At the other extreme, it is unhelpful to assume that all that is important about a person is that they are 'black' or 'Arab' or 'Chinese'. For parents who have come because of concern over a problem in a child, listening to their worries first is probably the best way round. Having heard of the complaint and the child's development, 'Could you tell me more about yourselves?' may be a useful non-directive opener. Showing interest in the person's occupation or general account of themselves prepares the way for asking about differences between themselves and the majority culture. The professional may be afraid either of offending or of appearing ignorant, but in practice explaining that you do not know enough about the person's culture and asking directly and openly for help is far less open to misinterpretation than a silence about what is clearly an important part of the person's life. It is most important that the professional can open the subject with comfort and without embarrassment.

ACCEPTING ANGER

Many children with emotional and behavioural problems are either angry or avoiding being angry, and the same applies to their parents. Their anger, if not directed towards each other, is likely to be directed towards the interviewer, partly because he or she is there and partly because they are the safest person to be angry with. Acknowledging and accepting such anger is part of the work of a mental health professional.

Case study
The father is from Nigeria. He is a short man with a tall elegant wife, also from Nigeria. In Africa he worked as an engineer but had only been able to find work in the UK sewing garments. The 12-year-old son had been disruptive in class and an initial assessment with the boy and mother had only suggested that there was considerable parental disharmony. The father had eventually been persuaded to attend but had presented as an angry, defensive man who was abrupt to the point of being offensive. He shook the proffered hand on arrival with surprise and at first contributed little. Eventually he referred to his job here and said that it was not like his real work at home. He was told that his anger was understandable and with encouragement he expanded on his expertise in engineering. He became less defensive and in the absence of the child told of his feelings of inferiority and that he was rejected and subject to racial discrimination whereas his wife, because of her beauty, was accepted. There had been frequent rows, to which the child had been exposed. A key part of therapy was assisting the father to see how important it was to model for the boy non-aggressive ways of resolving interpersonal difficulties that arose at school.

INTERPRETER OR NOT?

Where families have limited use of English (or whatever the majority language) the best means of communication becomes an issue. Use of language is always a slightly tricky matter. It is important to understand the concerns of the client but also to be realistic in sharing their problems. An interpreter may or may not give the true meaning of what is said. However, the family has to cope with the society that they live in, usually without the help of a professional interpreter. It is therefore for the most part better to use the family resources for communication except perhaps during the initial assessment and maybe on the odd occasion to clarify specific points and to establish how confusion should be dealt with. Children acquire language more easily than adults, and to be granted the role of helping in this way can actually reduce family tensions.

Whilst it is not possible in this context to explore in detail each form of therapy, some of the steps essential to working with families from cultural groups may be summarised as follows:

- welcoming and explaining to the child and family
- listening to their concerns
- understanding the person/family as well as the problem
- making it safe for all to speak openly
- accepting anger
- defining the problem
- prescribing solutions to fit the person in their culture.

RAISING THE SUBJECT OF PREJUDICE

Children are subject to teasing for all manner of reasons. Prejudice may be only one and it should not be assumed that distress in a child from teasing is solely due to racism. Nonetheless, children who are more easily identified as 'different' will be at significant risk of some form of social prejudice, and particularly for 'black' children this unfortunately occurs frequently. Children can usually tell adults that they are being bullied or teased but they find it difficult to speak of the content, so that for some time there is a risk either of ignoring racist attacks or of the professional incorrectly assuming a racist content when there is none. Once the child is aware that you see them and are interested in them as 'real' people, an opening to refer to prejudice and racism may be offered among other possible reasons as to why young people become distressed or are teased. The next step is to afford the opportunity for the child to explain safely. Drawings may help with some children but whatever medium for communication is used patience is required. One child described a psychiatrist as someone who doesn't wait for you to answer a question before asking the next one.

INTERVIEWING CHILDREN

All children are likely to be defensive on their first contact, so making it safe for the child to speak of his or her problems remains an essential first step. The child may or may not perceive that there are issues specially relevant because of his or her family culture. Always introduce yourself, ask what you should call the young person and explain what your job is. Check briefly that you agree on the reason for attending and then say, 'tell me about yourself apart from any problems'. It is in instructive to be as non-directive as you can, at least at first. More often than not children will not put their special culture or heritage first, but will refer to the same aspects as any child, such as their age, school and interests in a sport or music. The child may need some prompting, such as 'what do you like to do?', 'what do you like at school?', 'tell me about your family'. Take an interest in what the child says and do not be afraid to show enthusiasm over something that they like and you know about or share as an interest. Ask older children about their ambitions. Play back to them the picture that you have of them as a person, but make sure that it is as positive as possible.

Once you have established that you recognise them as a person other than in terms of a problem, or indeed an 'ethnic group', problem areas become easier to bring into the open. If the parents have already indicated that there are issues about race or culture, it now becomes possible to ask more directly about them. If asked a direct question about their heritage most children will say that they are proud of it, even if it has been a source of argument with the parents. Asking a child to explain about his or her national or religious customs to you puts the child in a position of strength over your ignorance and can help their confidence.

Case study

An Iraqi family had been living in the UK for four years. Their teenage daughter appeared to be rebelling against them. When seen with her parents she remained sullen and silent. Seen alone and encouraged to talk of herself, she spoke of liking pop music and going out with friends. She said that she argued about religion and tradition with her parents, but when asked directly about whether she was proud of her origins she bristled and unhesitatingly said that she was. She really argued because she felt that her parents were too protective of her.

Conclusions

There are lessons to be learned from working with children and families from minority groups that can be applied to all families. Many of the seemingly special issues associated with helping children with emotional and behavioural disturbance when they are from families with a minority culture should in any case be taken into account with all families. The culture of that child and family should always be an important factor. We are more aware of appearance and culture when the differences are greater but a wide range of physical attributes, from obesity to having red hair, can be the source of teasing and hostility. The ability of the therapist to feel at ease when discussing these issues is of paramount importance in helping the child and family to do the same. In summary:

- be aware of the need to consider the particular culture of the child and parents

- practise discussing cultural issues without embarrassment

- give respect to the parents and child

- listen to them

- be interested in them apart from their problem and special culture

- try to be aware of your own prejudices and stereotypes

- try to take their culture into account in finding solutions.

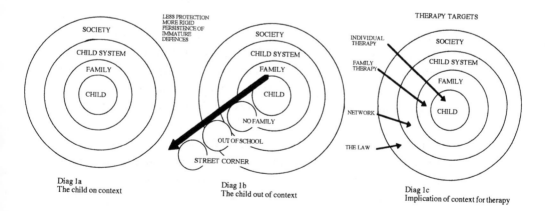

Figure 4.1 The Child in Context

CHAPTER 5

The Assessment of Children with Emotional and Behavioural Difficulties
Psychometrics and Beyond

David Jones and Melanie Jones

Introduction

It must be recognised at the outset that psychometric assessment remains a controversial topic. There is a strong lobby against testing, both within the ranks of educational theorists and in the public at large. What do tests actually measure? Much has been written about test validity. At a practical level the concept of predictive validity is important. It refers to how well a test result predicts performance or behaviour in other situations. An intelligence test with good predictive validity is able to reflect performance in situations involving problem-solving or reasoning ability. Similarly, an anxiety scale should reflect how a child is likely to feel in real-life social situations which might be expected to cause unease. A questionnaire or rating scale completed by a parent or teacher, on the basis of past experience of interacting with a child, is expected to be predictive of the child's behaviour in the future. The great majority of tests used in psychometric assessment do have satisfactory predictive validity when used with subject groups which are similar to those used to establish the normative data for the tests.

Often there is greater controversy surrounding the construct validity of a test. This concept refers to the extent to which a test can be said to measure an underlying theoretical construct. The debate over the value of testing has often really been about the status of the theoretical constructs, in particular the concept of intelligence. Whilst the number of psychologists has probably at last become greater than the number of definitions of intelligence in the literature, rousing claims and counterclaims are still to be found in recent psychology journals. For example, Howe (1990) in *The Psychologist*, the house journal of the British Psychological Society, poses the question 'Does intelligence exist?' and asserts that there is insufficient evidence to support the existence of a construct able to provide an explanation for individual differences. Nettlebeck (1990), in the same journal, responds with a strongly worded article entitled 'Intelligence does exist'. The ghosts of older debates about nature versus nurture, the genetics of intelligence, racial differences and whether intelligence is a single or multi-factor construct are still very much a presence in our test cupboards. With hindsight, it seems that in the past over-enthusiastic use of intelligence tests resulted in children from under-privileged backgrounds, and from minority cultures, being wrongly labelled as below average in ability. The influences of cultural and socio-economic factors on test performance were as well known 20 years ago as they are today, and yet psychometric assessment came close to losing its credibility both in the United States and in Britain.

Psychometric assessment has come a long way since the early years of the twentieth century, when Binet introduced a battery of tests to help identify children having difficulty in responding to the demands of the Paris school system. The various revisions of the Stanford–Binet Scales came to dominate intelligence testing for over half a century and introduced greater sophistication into standardisation procedures (Terman and Merrill 1960). Unfortunately, testing in schools increasingly came to be construed as a means of segregating children with difficulties or identifying the academic high-fliers for special treatment. Fashions change quickly in education, and the segregation of children who were in various ways troublesome to the system has been superseded by a deliberate policy of mainstreaming. Since tests are no longer a central requirement for labelling and classification, it has become possible to adopt a more constructive view towards assessment. Slowly there has been a reconciliation and a recognition that in both the educational and clinical domains psychometrics offers a valuable set of procedures for identifying learning difficulties and special educational needs. The legacy from the early test movement is that there are potential merits in interpreting a child's current level of performance by reference to a normative sample of other children of the same chronological age. Nevertheless, there is a reduced emphasis on global estimates of intelligence (IQ) and more reflection on the profile of different scores and attainments.

The case for including psychometric assessment in the assessment of children and adolescents with emotional and behavioural difficulties is compelling. Cognitive difficulties rarely occur without some degree of emotional disturbance or lowering of self-esteem. Similarly, emotional difficulties frequently result in varying degrees of impairment in motivation and concentration, which in turn influence both cognitive abilities and academic attainment. The careful use of psychometric assessment offers the psychologist an opportunity to attempt to unravel the complexity of the interactions between cognitive and emotional difficulties. The task presents a formidable challenge. Reliance on a linear model of causality for disturbance in either domain is far too simplistic in all but a few cases. There must always be a willingness on the part of the psychologist to widen the assessment to include personality characteristics, whilst recognising that such measures may have lower statistical reliability than measures of cognitive functioning. It is also important to learn how parents, teachers and others, including the peer group, perceive the child. Often the interpretation will need to include direct observation and a considerable degree of expert intuition.

Taking a wider perspective of intelligence and personality

For many years the choice of model in personality theory was between a multi-trait interpretation (Cattell 1973) and a two-factor model (Eysenck 1970). Cattell identified 15 source traits to account for personality characteristics of adults and a separate intelligence factor. The Eysenck model advocates a simpler structural interpretation of personality. The two major dimensions were labelled the Normal–Neuroticism dimension, which largely reflects differences in anxiety, and the Extroversion–Introversion dimension, which reflects differences in sociability and persistence. Later the P-Scale, or Toughmindedness, was added as a third dimension of personality (Eysenck and Eysenck 1975). In the Eysenck model, both learning ability and performance on cognitive tasks are influenced by an individual's level of anxiety and degree of extraversion.

A more recent speculative, but revolutionary, view of personality suggests that it should be construed in terms of five broad factors, which have quickly come to be known as the Big Five (Digman 1990; Goldberg 1993; Hampson 1995). Unfortunately, direct measurement of the factors is not a straightforward procedure. The factors are identified as:

1. Extroversion (or Surgency), which includes traits such as extroverted–introverted, talkative–quiet and bold–timid.

2. Agreeableness, which is largely based on characteristics such as agreeable–disagreeable, kind–unkind and selfish–unselfish.

3. Conscientiousness, which reflects traits such as organised–disorganised, hardworking–lazy, reliable–unreliable, thorough–careless and practical–impractical.

4. Neuroticism (or Emotional Stability), based on traits such as stable–unstable, calm–angry, relaxed–tense and unemotional–emotional.

5. Openness to Experience (or Culture, or Intellect). This complex factor includes the concept of intelligence, together with level of sophistication, creativity, curiosity and cognitive style in problem-solving situations.

To date, the model lacks the sound basis of the measurable factors which can be claimed for Cattell's Institute for Personality and Ability Testing (IPAT) questionnaires for assessing the personality of adolescents and children. For example, the Children's Personality Questionnaire (CPQ; Porter and Cattell 1963) measures 14 source traits, including intelligence, for children aged 8 to 12 years. Nevertheless, the 'Big Five' model has an intuitive level of appeal in its labelling and degree of complexity. It is important to know whether or not children appear agreeable to their peer group and to adults. More will be said about sociometry later in this chapter.

It is not necessary to become committed to a particular model of personality to perceive the value of extending an assessment of a child with complex behavioural difficulties to include normative data on a range of personality characteristics and some aspects of social functioning. Providing each of the measures has adequate validity and reliability, and there is an awareness of the variations in the quality of the normative data for the different measures, a valuable profile can be assembled for each child. Assessment at this level will always be the art of the possible. Any profile will be a partial picture of current functioning constrained by the time limits on data collection and the willingness of the child to cooperate.

Beginning the assessment

The starting point for any assessment is the referral. Who seems to be the most worried by the child's behaviour? What does the referrer hope to get back? A psychometric assessment is, by necessity, a lengthy procedure, and should neither be commissioned, nor undertaken, needlessly. In the case of emotionally and behaviourally disturbed children it is almost always preferable to begin by assessing whether the child has general or specific learning difficulties. A satisfactory degree of rapport must be established between the child and the psychologist before testing begins. This can usually be achieved by an age-appropriate discussion about why the child thinks he or she has been asked to be seen, and who they feel has concerns about them. It is important to emphasise that the motivation of everyone involved is to help, and not to criticise. Similarly, before beginning any cognitive or attainment tests, it should be stressed to the child that however well he or she performs there will often be some difficult items. Knowing that they will be tested to the limits of their ability helps make failure on difficult items acceptable. With careful management most children experience the assessment as stimulating and not threatening.

Unless there is a recent set of test records available, the assessment should begin with an evaluation of intellectual abilities. In the case of school-aged children, there is now a good choice of intelligence tests. It is usually worthwhile to begin with the most recent battery of tests with good standardisation data. Currently, for those aged over 6 and under 17 years this is the Wechsler Intelligence Scale for Children – Third Edition UK (WISC-III.UK; Wechsler 1992). It is worth reflecting on Wechsler's view of intelligence as an aggregate rather than a particular ability. He defined intelligence as the 'capacity of an individual to act purposefully, to think rationally and to deal effectively with his or her environment' (Wechsler 1944, p.3). The sub-tests are organised into separate Verbal and Performance Scales, each of which yields an IQ score. Both scales can be combined to produce a Full Scale IQ, which is the best estimate of global intelligence. The Verbal Scale comprises five sub-tests: Information, which measures general knowledge:

- Similarities, which is a test of verbal reasoning
- Arithmetic, which is a test of mental arithmetic
- Vocabulary, which tests the child's ability to define words

- Comprehension, which tests the child's understanding of social rules and concepts
- Digit Span is an additional Verbal sub-test which can be used to assess short-term memory, although the score is not used in the calculation of the IQ.

The Performance Scale also comprises five sub-tests:

- Picture Completion identifies the ability to detect missing parts of pictures of objects or scenes
- Coding is a self-paced task involving the child drawing in the appropriate symbol to match a shape in the case of younger children and digits for older children
- Picture Arrangement requires the child to re-arrange sets of pictures to express a meaningful story
- Block Design is a constructional task involving the manipulation of cubes to match two-dimensional patterns
- Object Assembly involves a jigsaw-type task requiring the assembly of pieces into common objects.

Two additional Performance tasks are available: Symbol Search and Mazes.

It is recognised that different combinations of sub-tests provide valuable additional information on cognitive functioning. A Standard Score can be calculated for Verbal Comprehension based on Information, Similarities, Vocabulary and Comprehension. Similarly, there is a Standard Score for Perceptual Organisation based on Picture Completion, Picture Arrangement, Block Design and Object Assembly. There is a Freedom from Distractibility Standard Score based on Arithmetic and Digit Span, and a Processing Speed Index based on Coding and Symbol Search.

Intellectual assessment is likely to take at least an hour, and depending on the findings a decision will be taken on whether to proceed to an assessment of literacy skills (see below). Children with emotional and behavioural difficulties will sometimes refuse to cooperate, or even to give verbal responses. Patient attempts to engage them by measuring receptive vocabulary may reveal whether there are communication difficulties or extreme negative behaviour. Since cognitive assessment depends upon evaluating potential, there is little to be gained from attempts at coercion.

Recognising learning difficulties

The Education Act 1981 defines learning difficulty in a child operationally as 'a significantly greater difficulty in learning than the majority of children of his age' (DES 1981, p.3). Earlier classification systems had tended to recommend special schools for children with intelligence test scores more than two standard deviations below the mean for their age group. In IQ terms this was a cut-off score in the region of 70. If, on assessment, a child obtains a WISC-III. UK Full Scale IQ below 70, then there is a likelihood of moderate learning difficulties, but the profile of sub-test scores should be carefully evaluated. If there are indications from school reports, or the medical history, that functioning has deteriorated, then the possibility of lack of stimulation in the home environment, or even emotional abuse, has to be considered. It is certainly important to determine whether English is the main language spoken in the home. The results on the Verbal and Performance Scales should be considered separately. The Test Manual provides tables indicating the statistical significance of differences between IQ scores. Generally, differences of 8 points or more may be important. If only the Verbal Scale IQ is below 70, reasons for the discrepancy need to be considered. Lack of stimulation in the home environment, deafness or specific learning difficulty may provide an explanation.

Recognising specific learning difficulties

Often children with emotional and behavioural difficulties will be reported to be underachieving in one or more areas of schoolwork, even though their overall abilities have been judged to be at least within the average range. In this group the most frequently reported problem is difficulties in reading and/or spelling. Rather like intelligence, the concept of dyslexia has been around for a long time, but its use as an explanatory concept has not been universally accepted in educational circles. In the past a child was considered to be dyslexic if he or she was of at least average intelligence but performance on reading tests was of the order of two years below that expected for the child's chronological age. Many preferred to use the label 'specific reading difficulty' for this problem.

Clearly, children with dyslexia are at a severe disadvantage in many classroom situations, experiencing difficulties in reading from the board and following written instructions, and being limited by finding it difficult to use textbooks for independent study and revision. Also, they receive frequent criticism for the poor standard of their written work. Not surprisingly, some children with dyslexia or specific literacy difficulties develop poor self-esteem and sometimes avoid the experience of repeated failure by acting-out or challenging behaviour in the classroom.

The relatively new Wechsler Objective Reading Dimensions (WORD) (Rust, Golumbok and Trickey 1993) provide an effective method for the assessment of literacy skills. The Basic Reading Scale assesses the child's ability to read single printed words aloud. The Spelling Scale assesses spelling of single words which are read aloud and then repeated in a sentence. Finally, the Reading Comprehension Scale measures the child's under-standing of short written passages of text. All three scales have been standardised to give scores which are based on age group means of 100 and so are directly comparable with the WISC IQ scores. Test age equivalents are also provided for each scale.

More detailed assessment of number skills can be carried out using the Wechsler Objective Numerical Dimensions. There are separate scales for Mathematics Reasoning and Numerical Operations, and a Composite can be calculated. The standard scores for each of the three measures can be compared directly with IQ scores and the WORD standard scores.

Attention Deficit/Hyperactivity Disorder

Many children with emotional and behavioural difficulties are labelled as hyperactive by their teachers or parents, and considered to be unable to concentrate. Both major classification systems of psychiatric disorders, DSM IV (American Psychiatric Association 1994) and ICD 10 (International Classification of Diseases, World Health Organisation 1992), recognise a condition characterised by short attention span and impulsivity. Unfortunately, restless and impulsive behaviour also characterises many children with conduct disorder. Differential diagnosis between the two conditions is difficult. Often children with Attention Deficit/Hyperactivity Disorder are perceived as underachieving at school, failing to concentrate appropriately in lessons, and lacking in regard for the property and feelings of others.

Psychometric assessment does have a part to play, particularly when decisions are to be taken about whether to put the child on a trial of stimulant medication such as Ritalin (methylphenidate). The WISC sub-test profile does not provide a reliable diagnosis. Some authorities have suggested that a pattern of relatively low scores on Arithmetic, Comprehension, Information and Digit Span (the ACID combination) is characteristic, but the evidence is not compelling. The Freedom from Distractibility Index (based on Arithmetic and Digit Span) can reflect attention span, but often concentration can be sustained for the short periods involved to complete the tests and in the relatively novel experience of the testing environment. The Matching Familiar Figures Test (Kagan 1966) measures the extent to which a child is reflective (in the sense of being slow and accurate) or impulsive (in the sense of being fast and inaccurate) in responses to test stimuli. The test consists of 12 items, and in each case the child is shown a picture of a familiar object and then asked to identify it from a set of 6 choices. Maze tests have also been found to provide a useful means of studying organising and planning response strategies.

Detecting specific language impairment

Specific language impairment (SLI) is a relatively rare condition. If the condition is not diagnosed and appropriate educational support provided, the children concerned may well be subject to emotional distress. These children provide an example of the importance of adequate cognitive assessment for all children with suspected communication difficulties or unexplained abnormalities in behaviour patterns. Children with SLI are identified using a range of verbal and non-verbal tests. They are typically assessed as having SLI if their language skills are well below those expected for their age but their performance on non-verbal tasks is within the normal range. Measures of non-verbal ability may be obtained from WISC III.UK Performance sub-tests, such as Block Design.

Assessing children's language skills is complex, since there are many different facets to language (e.g. vocabulary, morphology, grammar) which must all be tested separately when attempting to identify the particular problems that SLI children have with language. Several standardised tests are commonly used. The British Picture Vocabulary Scale (BPVS; Dunn *et al.* 1982) may be used to test comprehension, and the Test of Word Finding (TWF; German 1986) provides an estimate of a child's single-word vocabulary. In the BPVS, the child must indicate which of four pictures represents the single word spoken by the tester. The TWF consists of several sub-tests; these include picture naming (the child sees drawings depicting both nouns and verbs), category naming (the child sees a picture of a group of objects), naming by completing a sentence spoken by the tester, and description naming (the child finds the name for an object implied by three attributes).

The Test for Reception of Grammar may be used to assess a child's comprehension of sentences; the child must select the picture that best matches the sentence spoken by the tester (Bishop 1989). The Grammatical Closure sub-test of the Illinois Test of Psycholinguistic Abilities focuses more specifically on morphology (Kirk, McCarthy and Kirk 1968). In this sentence completion task, the child is required to provide a morphologically marked word, such as the plural, reflexive, past tense or a preposition.

Although the tests listed above are useful for identifying children with SLI, they are not sensitive enough to be able to probe for the particular problems that SLI children have with language. Consequently, tests specially designed to assess the parts of grammar with which SLI children are thought to have difficulty are currently being used by researchers. For example, van der Lely has designed two such tests. The first is the Test of Active and Passive Sentences, which uses a picture choice task to assess whether a child understands full and short passive sentences (van der Lely 1996). The second, the Advanced Syntactic Test of Pronominal Reference tests whether a child can assign reference to pronouns (e.g. him, her) and reflexive anaphors (e.g. himself, herself) (van der Lely 1997). The task is to say 'Yes' or 'No', depending on whether the sentence (containing the pronoun or anaphor) matches the picture. These tests have not been standardised, so they can only be used for exploratory purposes at the present time. However, it seems likely that future classifications of SLI children will have to be linguistically based and highly specific in order to capture the intricate nature of their problems with language.

The group of children currently classified as having SLI is highly heterogeneous. Furthermore, there remains some disagreement about whether there is a language-specific (modular deficit) or a more general auditory–perceptual impairment.

Assessing anxiety and other personality traits

Anxiety questionnaires for children tend to consist of a series of items which describe how the child feels about the self, about interactions with others and about being in specific situations. Sometimes there is an attempt to control for response bias towards agreeing or disagreeing with statements by a careful balancing of the wording of the items. Many anxiety questionnaires include a 'lie scale', consisting of items designed to detect when a child is attempting to fake responses to present the self in a good light. However, sometimes a high score on a lie scale is a reflection of social immaturity rather than an intention to deceive. A detailed review of the wide choice of anxiety questionnaires and other instruments for assessing anxiety can be found in Jones (1997). A brief consideration of some of the more widely used measures is given below.

The Revised Children's Manifest Anxiety Scale (RCMAS), devised by Reynolds and associates, is one of the more widely used questionnaires in clinical research studies (Reynolds and Richmond 1978; Reynolds and Paget 1981). The theoretical background is of interest since the RCMAS is derived from the Manifest Anxiety Scale (Taylor 1953), which in turn was based on items selected from the Minnesota Multiphasic Personality Inventory. The RCMAS is a measure of general anxiety and should be regarded as a trait measure. It does not identify the specific situations in which children experience anxiety. Examples of items in the RCMAS are 'I worry about what my parents will say to me' and 'I worry about what other people think about me'. In all, the scale contains 37 items including a short lie scale.

The Junior version of the Eysenck Personality Questionnaire (JEPQ) is often used to measure the personality characteristics of children in Britain (Eysenck and Eysenck 1975). Anxiety is assessed on the Neuroticism (or Emotionality) dimension. As with the RCMAS, this is a trait measure of anxiety. An advantage of the JEPQ is that it has a second major dimension labelled Extroversion–introversion, which provides insight into the child's feelings about social interactions and stimulation. The questionnaire is intended for use with children in the age range 7 to 16 years and has separate norms for boys and girls. In addition, the Toughmindedness (P-Scale) provides an estimate of some of the more unpleasant aspects of personality characteristics. Norms are available for the age range 7 to 15 years. The means suggest an increase in anxiety with age for girls, but little change for boys.

Cattell and his associates have developed a series of multi-trait measures, of which the best known is the 16PF for adults. As mentioned earlier, the *Children's Personality Questionnaire* CPQ measures 14 source traits, including intelligence, for children aged 8 to 12 years (Porter and Cattell 1963). Two forms of the test are available, and administration of both forms is recommended for clinical use. It can be a daunting task for children with poor motivation or a short attention span, as each form can take up to 50 minutes to complete. Questions in the CPQ are in a forced-choice form, such as 'Do you have many friends or just a few good friends?' Cattell considers that the test estimates the level of free-floating, manifest anxiety, which may be influenced by long-term and situational variables. Versions of the IPAT scales are available for both younger and older children.

The Child Anxiety Scale is a useful, quick screening test for anxiety level for children in the age range 5 to 12 years (Gillis 1980). The test has 20 items which are read out to individuals or small groups of children. Each item is clearly identified on the record form by a drawing, for example of a butterfly or a spoon, to minimise the chance of mistakes in entering the responses.

The State-Trait Anxiety Inventory for Children (STAIC) consists of two separate self-report scales, one to measure state-anxiety (A-State) and one to measure trait-anxiety (A-Trait) (Spielberger *et al.* 1970). The A-State scale investigates how children are feeling at the time they are actually taking the test. There are 20 items, and for each statement the child is required to choose from three boxes; for example, 'I feel ... very frightened', 'frightened' or 'not frightened'. For half of the items the 'very' box indicates the presence of anxiety and for other items it indicates the absence of anxiety, as in 'I feel ... "very satisfied"'. The A-Trait scale has 20 statements requiring responses in terms of how the child generally feels; for example, for the statement 'I feel unhappy' there is a choice from 'hardly ever', 'sometimes' and 'often'. The STAIC is intended for children aged 9 to 12 years. Adolescents can be given the State-Trait Anxiety Inventory, which is the adult version (Spielberger, Gorsuch and Lushene 1970).

Several tests attempt to measure the construct of test anxiety. It sometimes emerges that children who appear quite challenging in the classroom situation are anxious about taking tests. Other children, who may be coping quite well academically, still experience enormous anxiety at the thought of tests and examinations. In extreme cases the anxiety leads to absenteeism and escalates into school refusal. The Test Anxiety Scale for Children (TASC) consists of 30 items, for example 'When the teacher says that she is going to find out how much you have learned, does your heart beat faster?' (Sarason *et al.* 1960). Children who respond positively to 10 to 15 items are considered moderately test anxious and those who score more than 15 are classified as highly test anxious. The School Anxiety Scale includes many of the TASC items but is a longer test, having 74 items in all (Phillips 1978). Both test anxiety scales appear to have a similar multi-factorial structure, providing possible measures of fear of assertiveness and self-expression, test anxiety, lack of confidence in meeting the expectations of others, and physiological reactivity to low levels of stress.

Assessing depression

Recent evidence suggests that depression in children and adolescents is perhaps more common than we used to think. The pattern of symptoms can be variable. The features of the syndrome are typically an inability to obtain pleasure from activities which would normally be pleasurable, lowered levels of self-esteem, increased self-blame, social withdrawal, low energy levels, feelings of agitation and, in extreme cases, suicidal ideation. In addition, loss of appetite and sleeping difficulties are not uncommon features. Many children with emotional and behavioural difficulties will show some of these characteristics on an intermittent basis and it is important to consider whether an underlying depression is causal in their disturbed behaviour patterns. Encouraging the child and parents to keep a diary record of mood changes and the duration of periods of feeling low can provide important data for the assessment.

Several scales are available to measure depression in children. The Children's Depression Scale (CDS) consists of 66 statements to be rated by the child (Lang and Tisher 1978). In addition to an overall depression score, there are measures of different ways in which children might show their depression and also a Pleasure and Enjoyment Scale. Further information can be obtained from administration of the CDS–Parents Questionnaire. The Children's Depression Inventory is a children's version of the widely used Beck Depression Inventory (Kovacs 1980–81). It consists of 27 items which require children to choose one of several alternative statements to best describe themselves for the past two weeks. The symptoms covered include feelings of sadness, ideas relating to suicide and self-injury, and patterns of eating and sleeping. There remains some uncertainty as to whether depression scales of this sort adequately distinguish between general emotional disturbance and specific depression. A further test which can be used when the depression appears to extend to feelings about the future is the Hopelessness Scale for Children (Kazdin, Rodgers and Colbus 1986). On this test, children are required to choose between 'true' and 'false' for 17 statements, mostly about how things will be in the future.

Projective testing

Whilst projective tests provide insight into unconscious processes and emotions, many psychologists take the view that it is difficult to establish their validity. Test administration is generally a fairly lengthy procedure, and interpretation of the child's responses requires special training and acceptance of a psychodynamic model. An evaluation of projective techniques that could be used with children with emotional disturbance is beyond the scope of this chapter. Instead, the Object Relations Test will be cited as an example of a technique which is used with adolescents. The stimulus material consists of 13 cards arranged in three series, each depicting a scene involving one person, two people, three people and a group. There is a progression across the series from hazy pictures to more realism. The subject's task is to tell the story associated with each picture. Interpretation of anxieties includes attention to perceived threat and feelings of loss.

Parent rating scales

There will always need to be an element of clinical judgement in the degree of reliance placed on rating scales completed by parents. The Child Behavior Checklist (CBCL) has been widely used in the USA and, to a lesser extent, in Britain (Achenbach and Edelbrock 1983). It consists of 113 items and includes scales providing measures of social competence in activities, social behaviour and school behaviour. The main section provides scores on nine scales measuring specific childhood diagnostic categories. Depression, somatic complaints, social withdrawal, aggression and delinquency are perhaps the most relevant for the assessment of behaviours related to anxiety. Two higher-order factor scales provide information on Internalising and Externalising.

A shorter multidimensional rating scale for completion by parents which has grown in popularity is the Connors Parent Symptom Questionnaire (PSQ; Goyette, Connors and Ulrich 1978). The 48-item version of the PSQ includes a short anxiety scale and a measure of psychosomatic problems as well as hyperactivity–impulsivity and conduct problems. Rutter and colleagues have devised a brief rating scale to be completed by parents to identify behaviour problems in school-age children which has been standardised in Britain (Rutter, Tizard and Whitmore 1970). For younger children, a suitable rating scale for completion by parents is the Pre-School Behaviour Checklist (McGuire and Richman 1986).

Teacher rating scales

The Connors Teacher Rating Scale has been widely used to help identify children with Attention Deficit/Hyperactivity Disorder, although it provides measures of other behaviour characteristics, including anxiety (Goyette *et al.* 1978). Similarly, the Rutter (B2) Rating Scale for teachers is an easily completed screening measure of a range of difficulties experienced by children, including anxiety (Elander and Rutter 1996; Rutter *et al.* 1970).

The Bristol Social Adjustment Guides, particularly the Child in School Guide, have been used widely as a checklist to be completed by teachers mainly to provide an index of maladjustment in the school setting (Stott 1974). Several behavioural characteristics are assessed, but the focus is on ways children show over-reacting and under-reacting behaviours in their everyday school activities and interactions with teachers and peers.

Sociometry

Children with emotional and behavioural disturbances are frequently unpopular with their peer groups. Sociometry provides a range of techniques to establish how children in a school class or some other social group rate each other (Hughes 1988; Williams and Gilmour 1994). The most frequently used technique is peer nomination, which requires each child in a class or social group to choose several children (typically three) according to given criteria. For example, positive criteria are statements such as 'pick the boy you like the most' and 'would like to play with', and the negative criteria might be 'pick the boy you like the least' and 'would not like to play with'. Combining the positive nomination scores from the group provides an estimate of popularity and peer acceptance, and combining negative nomination scores gives an indication of degree of rejection. It is possible to construct a measure of a child's social impact on the group by summing the positive and negative nominations. Sub-groups which can be identified include 'neglected children', who are those with relatively few positive and negative nominations, and 'controversial children', who are those with a high social impact who are liked most by some children and liked least by others (Coie, Dodge and Coppotelli 1982; Newcomb, Bukowski and Pattee 1993). Reasons given by children for social rejection of their peers often focus on aggressive behaviour. There are strong ethical reasons for insisting on the exercise of great care in the setting up of situations in which children are required to rate each other, whether for popularity or even for traits such as aggressiveness. In extreme cases, where exclusion from a school is under consideration, it may be justifiable to include an assessment of the perceived effect of the troublesome child on the peer group. There is evidence that aggressive, socially rejected children with behavioural difficulties are at risk of developing conduct disorders. Children who are socially withdrawn and do not show disruptive behaviour are at risk of bullying and in some cases may develop later emotional disturbances. When sociometry is not a practical option, a Loneliness Scale (Asher, Hymel and Renshaw 1984) can be used to gain an impression of social relationships.

Concluding comments

Where the balance of evidence indicates that either specific or more general cognitive difficulties are involved, it is important to interpret the information to the school system in a way which will make it possible to address the child's special educational needs. If the school has initiated the request for assessment this should not present difficulties. Nevertheless, recommendations for individual remedial support for children put pressure on scarce resources and the suggested plan of action must be realistic and achievable. Early referral provides an opportunity for intervention before the child has developed an entrenched sense of failure and has lost motivation to cooperate. When the psychometric assessment eliminates significant cognitive or attainment difficulties it is still important to be aware of the child's ability and personality profile when designing and implementing an intervention programme in the school or clinic.

CHAPTER 6

The Psychiatric Examination/Interview

Vimod Kumar

Introduction

In psychiatric examination, interview with the child and family is the main instrument in gathering information, making the diagnosis and formulation, and establishing the therapeutic relationship and its management. Child and Adolescent Psychiatrists are medically trained doctors with experience in adult psychiatry who have specialised in working with children and adolescents. Most of them work in community-based services but some are based in hospital settings and are responsible for running day and inpatient units. They are part of a multi-disciplinary team which may involve various other disciplines such as nursing, psychology, social work, psychotherapists, art therapists and teachers. For the purposes of description, assessment and treatment are considered separately but in practice both are ongoing processes, constantly updated in view of the information available. Assessment involves gathering information and exploring specific areas further, to make sense and formulate the nature of the problem and the need for further information, investigations, tests (psychological and biological) and plan management of the referred problem. Assessment is an active two-way process between clinician and child and family. The process is influenced by the assessor's formal training, context of assessment and specific needs for management or treatment.

Emotional disorders or problems relate to the child's difficulty in areas of emotions, that is, anxiety, fear and depression and so on; and behaviour disorders or problems relate to difficulties in the areas of conduct or behaviour of the child, that is, aggression, stealing, lying and so on. Generally speaking, emotional disorders are internalised problems and the child suffers more than society, whereas in conduct or behaviour disorders the child's behaviour causes problems and disturbance more within family or society and may not be seen as a problem by the child. Various studies have found the prevalence rate of emotional and behavioural disorders to be between 5 and 25 per cent. Up to the age of 11, boys, and after that girls, have a higher rate of disorders and rates are higher in urban than in rural areas (Offord and Flemming 1991; Rutter 1989; Rutter et al. 1975). Although one in five children may show symptoms of emotional or behavioural disorders, the majority of them are not referred to specialised services for assessment or treatment.

Psychiatric examination involving a psychiatrist may form part of his or her general work within the team or may require using their particular skills in cases requiring assessment of mental state or, physical and developmental problems. Most psychiatrists have an obligation to provide assessment for psychiatric emergencies, such as overdoses, self-mutilation or acute psychotic disturbances. In addition, assessment may be needed for specific purposes by other agencies, such as social services for child care proceedings, parents or solicitors in contact/custody disputes, and courts in criminal proceedings. In this chapter the main emphasis is on assessment as a general part of work within the team, rather than assessment for special purposes which requires looking at particular areas in more detail. In addition to interviews, the assessment process may involve physical examination and tests, as well as psychological tests and questionnaires.

Referral and context of assessment

Most child and adolescent psychology/psychiatric services have a defined protocol for referral to their service. This varies from accepting referrals from mainly health care professionals (i.e. GPs and other consultants) to open referral systems, including acceptance of self-referrals. Referrals may be initiated by the child and family themselves or by other agencies. If families are involved in referral, kept informed and feel part of the referral system, they are more likely to be motivated to attend. Once a referral has been accepted, the child and family are informed of the referral and whether an appointment has been offered or they have been put on the waiting list. At the same time, consent from child, parent or guardian may be obtained to seek information from other services, especially school. If the child is 16 or over the letter should be addressed to the child.

Most child psychiatric services see children in rooms large enough to accommodate the whole family. Toys and drawing materials should be available, and if possible the same room should be used in subsequent interviews. When offering the appointment it is useful to provide information on the nature of the service and its likely duration. It is also important to be clear about who is invited for the interview; this would depend upon the nature of the problem and the reason for the referral. Although in the majority of cases the whole family would be invited for assessment, in some cases it may not be advisable or possible to have the whole family and this could be negotiated before offering the initial appointment. Although there are no rigid guidelines it is generally preferable that the family is seen in the first interview, which can then be supplemented by interviews with certain members of the family and interviews with the referred child. However, if adolescents, especially if they are 16 or older, express a wish to be seen first or without their family, this should be respected. In this chapter, interview with family, parents and the child are dealt with under separate headings. As the majority of emotional and behavioural problems in children are multi-factorial in nature, assessment may be required either in more than one setting and/or information may be required from diverse sources to make an accurate assessment of the problem. Although most assessments would be carried out in a clinic setting, some may take place at other sites, that is, in hospital (hospitalised children and overdoses), family settings (especially in care and custody disputes), residential settings (children's homes and penal institutions) and school. Although one is observing and assessing in all settings, different types of information are highlighted through different interview techniques. In any interview situation, one should be sensitive and encourage the child and family to express problems and feelings in their own time and words. Specific and probing questions are asked to explore the areas mentioned by the family first, before covering other areas not mentioned by the family. One should try to make the child and family feel at ease and should involve them as much as possible in the formulation of the problem and subsequent management.

The family interview

It is generally felt that if the family is interviewed first, rather than the individual, it is easier to involve the family in subsequent assessment or therapy; hence it is important to see the family first. There are exceptions to the above rule. For example, in cases where a family member is a sexual abuse perpetrator (unless the interview is to assess chances of rehabilitation after acknowledgement by the perpetrator) or there is a likelihood of violence from the family member. The family interview may not be possible during psychiatric emergencies or other crises, or where the adolescent (especially if 16 years or older) expresses a wish to be seen alone. In most interviews with families two therapists are involved, and if the assessment is for family therapy then a one-way mirror may be used or the session video-taped. For this, prior consent should be obtained, preferably in writing. The room should be large enough to accommodate the family comfortably. The chairs should be in a circle so that all members can see each other without any obstructions. There should be some material for play and drawing; preferably not noisy and messy play. It is preferable to have a blackboard for drawing genograms. Like all interviews, the family interview has three main phases: introduction, main interview and ending. The length of the interview depends upon its purpose. If the interview is for family therapy assessment, most interviews would be one and a half hours' duration, which may involve a break, especially if there are people observing or supervising the session. Jenkins (1994, pp.69–70) suggests a short diagnostic family interview which takes only 10 to 15 minutes and can provide considerable information on various areas of family functioning. In family interviews the focus is on the entire family, and hence all members are involved in discussion, interaction and problem solving.

The first stage of the family interview starts with greetings and introductions. This is also called the social stage (Hayley 1976). It involves the therapists introducing themselves to the family and in turn being introduced to all family members. It is important to greet all family members and to spend some time with each one. Family members are asked general non-threatening social questions about their name, age, occupation, school, hobbies, and so on. An effort should be made to come to the level of the member at both a verbal and non-verbal level. If for any reason there are absent members, then one should ask about them and the reason for their non-attendance. It is important to clarify how people like to be addressed.

During the main phase of the interview, other than gathering factual information about the problem areas, one is also looking at the structure of the family (hierarchy, boundaries, alliances), communication (verbal and non-verbal communication, beliefs, attitudes), feelings (general mood, feelings towards each other, themselves and society), and problem-solving skills. One is also looking at the developmental processes of the family

(family life cycle, changes manoeuvred and past coping skills). One is looking at areas of both weakness and strength.

One of the best and simplest ways of gathering information and involving the family is through a genogram. Detailed information about genograms and their use is provided by McGoldrick and Gerson (1985). In short, various symbols are used to define people's relationships and people are placed in order of hierarchy, as outlined in Figure 6.1. Genograms provide information as well as facilitating family interaction. They help children to learn more about their family and extended family. They also help them to become engaged in consultation. They give information on how the family has negotiated the first-order changes (from one life cycle to another life cycle, that is, from being a couple to parents with a child) and second-order changes (changes required in the same life cycle).

During the family interview one still has to keep the focus on the problem, so it is useful to discuss the problem, its history and various coping strategies employed in its resolution. This will clarify problem areas and the family members' involvement in the difficulties; their perception of the problem as well as that of the member of the family who has been referred. Specific techniques are employed in questioning which facilitate interaction and reveal relationships between family members. These include interactional questioning, circular questioning and family sculpt. Interactional questions relate to asking family members questions about their actions; for example, what do you/another family member do when the problem presents and how is it responded to by another family member? Carry on with their actions until they have finished with the problem area: what does John do when he is being annoyed by his younger brother, Paul? What does Paul do? What does father or mother do? How does John respond to Paul/mother/father, and so on? Circular questioning pertains to asking one family member to describe the interaction or relationship between two other family members and repeating a similar process with other family members (Palazzoli *et al.* 1980); that is, asking Paul about the parents' actions with each other or with John when John is angry. Family sculpt is a technique involving all family members being placed in a given space by one family member (as perceived or wished by that member) and encouraging people to express their views and feelings in that situation. More detailed use of this technique is described by Hearn and Lawrence (1985). It is also important to facilitate the expression of feelings by the family.

(a) The following symbols are used to describe people and their relationships:

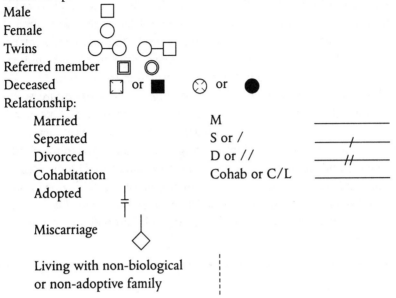

(b) Example

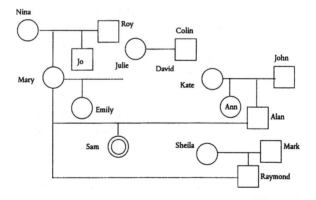

Sam is the five-year-old referred member of the family. She is living with her seven-year-old half-sister, her mother (who has a history of depression) and her mother's cohabitee. She has regular contact with her natural father (who has a history of anti-social activities), who is an only child and is living with his parents.

Figure 6.1 A genogram

It is important for the therapist to express some of their own feelings and encourage other family members to do the same. In family interviews, clinicians are generally more active than in other forms of interview and are seen as part of the system. For this reason it is helpful to be observed by a fellow team member or to view the session if it has been video-taped. The amount of factual information gathered varies in the first family interview session, and in most cases additional interviews with parents and children are needed to supplement the information obtained in the session.

Most family sessions end with clarifying the aims for future sessions, including the expectations of various family members. This involves feedback on the problem area, discussing possible factors underlining its initiation and maintenance, highlighting positive strengths in the child and the family, and looking at ways of improving weaknesses. The emphasis is on change and the role family members can play in solving difficulties, both the problem referred and others discussed in the sessions. The session is normally ended by organising future appointments and who will attend these appointments.

Case study

John is eight years old, the older of two children, and was referred for problems of hyperactivity and aggression both at home and at school. During the family session, his parents acknowledged that they were working long hours, and were unable to communicate with each other about the children or to support each other about various stresses upon them. They admitted having problems in their relationship. His mother admitted taking out her stress by picking on the minor misbehaviours of the children, especially with John, who played up more and got attention only when naughty. Father admitted having a soft spot for John and giving in to him, even though it caused problems with his relationship with his wife. He empathised with John as he had been of similar temperament in his childhood and felt that John would grow out of his problems. John's brother, Paul didn't feel that John was as bad because he did play with him. He complained that John hit him when he lost. John said that he only hits because Paul gets carried away when he wins and comes very close to his face and teases him. John and Mum were upset and tearful in the session, whereas Paul did not express much of his feelings. One of the ways of looking at family functioning would be that John was triangulated in parental conflict and was serving a useful function in maintaining the family homoeostasis.

The parental interview

Parents can provide detailed and relevant factual information about the child and the relationships between themselves and other family members. The parent or parents should be interviewed separately from the child if they express a wish to be seen separately, where it is felt that they may be more open to discuss their relationships if seen separately, and in cases of contact and custody disputes. It is well recognised that child-sensitive interviewing of parents can provide reliable and valid information on the child's problems, and marriage and family relationships (Graham and Rutter 1968; Quinton, Rutter and Rowlands 1976). In 1981 Professors Rutter and Cox, with their colleagues, published a study on psychiatric interview techniques and concluded that parents, when encouraged to report freely, were able to give significant information about the problem and their family but that systematic questioning was superior to free reporting. They found that more feelings were expressed if the therapist was less talkative, asked more open questions, expressed feelings, empathised, and asked direct questions about feelings and emotions. Although a number of questionnaires, semi-structured interview schedules and structured interview schedules exist, these are all likely to be used in research rather than in ordinary day-to-day clinic settings. Interviewing both parents gives an opportunity to assess parental relationships in more detail. Most of the factual information about the child's problem and development can be obtained at this interview. The relevant areas to be covered are listed in Appendix 1. One should spend significant amount of time on the problem area; that is, its nature, severity, duration, and initiation, and reaction and coping by the child, family and other systems (i.e. school and peer group). Relevant areas should be covered thoroughly, along with coping mechanisms and the relationships and feelings of the child and family, and should cover both weaknesses and strengths.

The process of interview is similar to the family interview. The parent is made comfortable and at ease by asking more general questions before moving to the problem areas. While talking about problem areas, non-directive questions with specific probes are used. Parents are encouraged to explain everything in their own way and are not rushed. The therapist tries to keep parents to the task, guiding them when needed and avoiding too many repetitions (i.e. we have covered this area before and I have a reasonably good idea about it and shall welcome your thoughts on ... – bringing them back to the area to be explored further). The therapist has a 'map' of the area to be covered and is gentle in guiding the parents to cover it. 'Snapshots' and examples of behaviour are asked about along with the reactions and feelings of the people involved.

An interview with parent(s) gives an opportunity to assess a parent's own development, health, parenting skills and emotional health in more detail. This is highly significant in cases where parents have suffered from mental illness and in cases requiring assessment of a parent's parenting abilities.

The child/adolescent interview

The purpose of interviewing the child/adolescent is many fold. In addition to gathering information, especially about the child's emotional state, it helps to form a relationship with the child/adolescent. In some cases a particular type of assessment is carried out individually with the child to look at their suitability for a particular form of treatment. Regardless of the nature and purpose of the interview, one should explain, as well as ascertain from the child, the understanding and purpose of the interview. Clinicians should be sensitive to the child's developmental level and communicate at their level, both in verbal and non-verbal communication. The younger the child, the more the need for play material. Also, with younger children it may take time before they can be interviewed on their own and it may be necessary for them first to be seen with their parents a number of times. Generally speaking, children can provide accurate factual information, but the quantity is a lot less with younger children, who are generally better able to provide specific rather than general details of events and their contexts. However, children are better able to give information on their own emotional state and anti-social activities than their parents. As with adults, it is better to ask open-ended questions, that is, asking them what they felt or did when they were faced with a particular event. This gives them the option of talking a lot more than with a closed question, where the answer could be either yes or no. An interview with a child involves more planning, especially if play material is required. It is best to have a set amount of material rather than a room full of toys and so on, which may be very distracting to the child. Adolescents can be interviewed in the same way as adults and probably will not require any play material.

The interview with the child is similar to any other interview and has an introduction, main interview and an ending. The introduction involves introducing oneself and trying to put the child at ease by asking general social questions. Even if one has already been introduced, one should still try talking about general issues first before approaching the main part of the interview. During this phase clinicians should clarify the nature and purpose of the interview and should ask the child/adolescent about their understanding of the interview. Issues of confidentiality should be discussed and any misunderstandings clarified before proceeding with the main interview.

Although the main purpose of the interview is to gather information about the child's understanding of problems and their feelings around various issues, one has to be extremely patient to obtain good information from the child. The clinician has to be guided by the child and should remain sensitive to the way the child is responding rather than bombarding them with questions. Children's wishes should be respected and, where possible, confrontation or pressure avoided. It is better to start talking about areas not related to the problem. While talking about problem areas, one should try to be non-judgemental. Children should be asked to describe an event rather than just to admit whether an event happened or not; that is, rather than asking whether they hit someone or not, it would be better to ask what was happening at the time and who was doing what, followed by what they and the other person did and so on, until that particular event is completed. Once issues around one particular area or problem have been explored, one could move on to other areas, that is, from one behaviour or emotion to another behaviour or emotional area. In the main interview, one tries to explore behaviour, emotions and thinking processes. Once an event or problem is mentioned, then one can explore its frequency, duration and the people involved as well as how it was resolved.

In the interview one covers not only areas related to the child's own personal life, but also the child's relationships within the family, school and peer groups. Even with unmotivated or very reticent children, persistence can lead to rapport-building. If one is getting little or no information, one may use leading or closed questions to start some communication with the child/adolescent. An interview with a child involves observing their physical and emotional state, speech, social interaction, thinking process, level of play, self-esteem and fantasy life. Full mental state examination, especially in suspected cases of mental illness, is carried out, covering the areas outlined in Appendix 2.

Physical examinations

Most Child and Adolescent Psychiatrists, especially those working in busy outpatient clinics, do not perform routine physical examinations, whereas in the hospital setting, especially for inpatients, physical examination is performed as routine. In the majority of cases, physical examination is carried out by general practitioners or paediatricians, who also carry out any relevant investigations. In the wake of increased referrals for Attention Deficit Disorder, many psychiatrists request another health professional to monitor the height and weight of these children on a regular basis, while others do this themselves. Gabel and Hsu (1986) studied adolescent psychiatric inpatients and found that routine tests did not add to the original diagnosis or find significant physical disorders. Physical examination is warranted in children and adolescents with eating disorders, with developmental delay and with psychosomatic presentations. If one notices a bruise or injury on a child one must at least make a note of naked-eye examination of the injury, even if a full physical examination is to be carried out later. Physical examination is a significant part of assessment in cases of abuse and neglect, and should be conducted by an experienced paediatrician.

Psychological tests

Most psychological tests are given by clinical psychologists who have been trained in administering and interpreting tests. As there are numerous tests available, formal psychological testing need only be done if it is felt that it would enhance or add to the information already available. These tests also bring objectivity and measurements to the problem. It is important to highlight the reason for asking for psychological tests and the area which should be covered. More routine neuropsychological assessments are carried out in children/adolescents involved in head injuries. A list of commonly used psychological tests and questionnaires is given in Appendix 3.

Formulation

Formulation is a way of summarising one's findings and collating all relevant positive information and important negative information. It includes brief demographic data, the history of the presenting problem and any other relevant problem areas. It describes significant features from family, personal and developmental history. It includes pre-morbid personality and various coping strategies used by the child and their family. It describes the child's relationship with their family and society. It includes mental state examination and the results of any examinations or tests which were done. A formal diagnosis using ICD 10 or DSM IV is included, along with future plans for further investigation, information gathering and management, which may include more than one form of treatment, for example, medication and family, marital and individual therapies. It includes comments on prognosis. Formulation is constantly updated in view of the further information available.

Case study

Carol is 15 years old, the younger of two children living with their parents, and was referred by her GP because of symptoms of school refusal and depression. She was seen with her family and individually. She was described as a sensitive girl who, six months previously, started to present with symptoms of anxiety and panic, following some teasing by her peer group at school. She started to miss odd days of school, with physical symptoms of not feeling well, feeling dizzy, stomach ache and headaches. Gradually her symptoms and school attendance became worse, and she became withdrawn, unhappy and tearful. She was not going out of the house, not sleeping or eating well and had lost half a stone in weight. She was very pessimistic about her future and had suicidal thoughts. Her parents were concerned about the change in Carol's personality from being an outgoing to a withdrawn, anxious and insecure person.

There is a family history of depression in Carol's maternal grandmother. In family sessions, Carol's family were cohesive and did not show any significant disturbances in communication, relationships or hierarchy. On mental state examination Carol was pleasant and cooperative but appeared depressed (subjectively and objectively). She was preoccupied with thoughts of worthlessness and was very pessimistic about her future. She did not have psychotic symptomatology and was well oriented in time, place and person.

School reports confirmed that she had been a very likeable, popular girl who suddenly changed into a withdrawn, lethargic and listless girl with very little interaction with her peer group. She was not being subjected to any behavioural problems at school. There were no significant stresses or changes within the family. She was not physically examined and no biological or psychological tests were carried out.

Carol is suffering from a depressive illness. She is of normal intelligence, with no developmental delay, medical illness or psychosocial stressors. She will benefit from antidepressant medication, individual cognitive behaviour therapy, family counselling, liaison with her school and regular mental state examination. Her prognosis for recovery from this episode is good, but there may be further recurrences in future.

Appendix I: History taking

1. Referred problems

Find out their nature, frequency; where they occur, with whom, what makes them appear, what makes them worse and what makes them better? How are they dealt with by the child, family and other people?

The same process is repeated with any other problem areas mentioned.

2. Other areas

a. Physical symptoms
    i.e. hearing, vision, aches and pains, clumsiness, fainting or fits. Physical symptoms of anxiety, i.e. palpitations, breathlessness.
b. Other emotional symptoms
    i.e. unhappiness, sadness, depression, anxiousness, fearfulness, etc.
c. Other behavioural difficulties
    i.e. aggression, lying, stealing, biting, destruction, etc.
d. Habits and other problems
    i.e. problems with eating, sleeping, bedwetting, soiling, overactivity, rocking, head banging and other comfort-seeking activities.
e. Relationship problems
    i.e. with family members, peers and authority figures.

3. School

School attendance, behaviour in lessons and at playtime.

4. Developmental history

Any problems in development, i.e. motor, emotional, speech, social, physical and sexual development.

5. Personal history

i.e. any difficulties during mother's pregnancy, at birth, and attachment problems. Temperament as an infant and as a toddler. Any separations.

6. Past history

History of medical illness and hospitalisations. History of any emotional and behavioural problems and any help sought. History of any anti-social activities and their outcome.

7. Family history

History of medical problems, past and present, in the family (mainly blood relatives). History of emotional, psychiatric or anti-social problems. Parental relationship, parent–child and sibling relationships. Outside activities and support. Family stresses.

Appendix 2: Mental State Examination

1. General appearance and attitude

In general appearance note the state of presentation, i.e. clothing, looks, nourishment and any sign of injuries or scars. Notice any asymmetry, that is facial asymmetry which maybe a sign of neurological problems, or prominent features (e.g. excessively tall or small for age; mannerisms etc.). Take note of the attitude of the child towards the clinician, other people and problems mentioned. The degree of trust and rapport established is noted.

2. Speech

Rate, flow, content of speech and articulation, as well as any delay in development of speech or difficulties in comprehension or expression of language are noted.

3. Activity level

Level of motor activity (high or low). Abnormality, i.e. tics, coordination.

4. Play

Level of play, i.e. individual, parallel play and symbolic play. Main content of play.

5. Mood

Predominant mood, i.e. depression, anxiety, fearfulness and specific mood in relation to content of speech, as well as any abnormality in mood (i.e. lability or inappropriate affect).

6. Bodily functions

Appetite, sleep and sphincter controls.

7. Thought process

Expression of thoughts as well as content. Abnormality in form or content is a significant feature in psychosis.

8. Perceptual disturbances

Any abnormality in perceptual disturbance, i.e. hallucination (true or pseudo-hallucination).

9. Orientation

Orientation in time, place and person. Level of consciousness.

10. General knowledge, intelligence and learning

Appropriateness to age.

11. Temperamental traits

Carefree or worrier, introverted or extroverted, generally happy, irritable or miserable etc.

12. Insight into difficulties and problems

Level of awareness of their problems, attitude to referral and need to solve the difficulties.

13. Physical/neurological examination

A brief physical examination or neurological examination may be included. This would include height, weight, circumference of head, skin colour and abnormalities, asymmetry or abnormalities of head, facial features, eye, chest, abdomen and limbs. Chest and abdomen examination involves feeling abnormalities, percussion and auscultation, enlargement of normal organs or presence of abnormal growths. Naked-eye examination of genitalia (wherever possible) and detailed examination are only done in cases of sexual abuse (by experienced clinician).

Neurological examination would involve looking at tone, posture and reflexes, as well as ability to move limbs symmetrically. Both fine and gross motor coordination are tested. If there are focal signs then a detailed examination could be done by an experienced clinician (paediatrician/ neurologist).

ICD 10

1. Clinical syndrome
2. Developmental delay
3. Intellectual function
4. Medical conditions
5. Abnormal psycho-social situations.

DSM IV

1. Clinical syndrome
2. Developmental and personality disorders
3. Physical disorders and conditions
4. Severity of psycho-social stressors
5. Global assessment of functioning.

Appendix 3: Psychological tests and questionnaires

There are numerous psychological tests and questionnaires which can be used in children and adolescents as well as families. The following is a short list of tests and questionnaires commonly used.

1. Questionnaires

*   Rutters A and B Scales for parents and teachers
*   Connors Parent and Teacher Rating Scales
*   Child behaviour checklist
*   Behaviour screening questionnaire.

2. Intelligence tests

*   Wechsler Intelligence Scale for Children – Revised
*   British Ability Scale
*   The Goodenough–Harris D. Drawing Test ('Draw a Man' Test).

3. Developmental tests

*   Denver Developmental Screening Test
*   Griffiths Mental Developmental Scale
*   Bayley Scales of Infant Development.

4. Education attainment tests

- Neales Analysis of Reading Ability
- Schonell Graded Word Spelling Test
- Schonell Graded Word Reading Test
- The Wide Range Achievement Test.

5. Personality tests/social adjustment

- Rorschach's test
- Children's Appreception Test
- Vineland Social Maturity Scale
- Bristol Social Adjustment Guides.

6. Tests with parents and family

- Parental Stress Index
- The Bow–Anthony Family Relation Test.

CHAPTER 7

Cognitive, Behavioural and Systemic Approaches to Coping with Emotional and Behavioural Difficulties in Children

David Jones

Introduction

Emotionally and behaviourally disturbed children form a heterogeneous group. Children rarely make direct requests for help themselves, but often the disturbed behaviour is a signal of past or ongoing distress. By the time others have reacted the difficult behaviour is well established, even though the original problems for the child may no longer be in evidence. The choice of intervention to help the child cope with his or her difficulties, and to reduce the detrimental effects they may have on others, is dependent on both the nature of the disturbance and what the individual child and family are prepared to accept. Any intervention needs to begin with a comprehensive behavioural analysis, although situations frequently arise where opportunities for direct baseline observations are not possible. For example, many referrals involve recent acts of aggression towards other children in school or challenging behaviour towards teachers, and there is a request for urgent action to prevent exclusion.

The referral itself is an important starting point in the intervention process, although it can be surprising how often it is not an accurate source of information about the problem behaviour. In some cases the referral may constitute a specific request for cognitive or behavioural therapy, but more frequently the appropriateness of this choice of intervention is decided in an evaluation of the referral by a multi-disciplinary child mental health team.

The range of approaches for helping troubled children which now come within the ambit of cognitive and behavioural psychotherapy has increased considerably in recent years. A brief overview of the evolution of this therapeutic discipline will help show how methods based on different theoretical perspectives have a logical coherence.

Learning theory and social learning theory

Behaviour therapy with children has a long history and is based on the application of the principles of learning theory and the scientific methodology of experimental psychology to the treatment of disordered behaviour. Initially, constructs such as thoughts and feelings were not considered of particular relevance to the task of changing behaviour patterns. The emphasis was on measurement, both in the establishment of a baseline and in the careful monitoring of progress. Each intervention was a scientific experiment. Fundamental to the approach is the view that the learning of both normal and abnormal behaviour can be interpreted in terms of the principles of classical and operant conditioning and the laws of reinforcement.

It is worth emphasising again that the learning theory view of disturbed behaviour in children is that it lies on a continuum with normal behaviour. This is in contrast to the early medical model that construed atypical or troublesome behaviour as reflecting an underlying illness. The rivalry between the two positions has largely been replaced by collaboration. Generally, behaviour therapists recognise that the classification of disorders facilitates treatment planning. Applications of the principles of learning theory to achieve behaviour modification remain a necessary part of intervention, whatever label is given to the condition.

Behaviour therapy seeks to replace abnormal or difficult behaviour with more acceptable behaviour patterns. The key to intervention is an understanding of the child's environment and of past reinforcement history. The individual develops in an environment which includes parents or other caretakers, perhaps siblings, a wider family group and an ever increasing social network as the child gets older. It is necessary to understand the patterns of significant interaction in the family, and often others will need to be persuaded to change the ways they affect and respond to the child. The quality of the physical environment is also seen as a potent influence on the child's behaviour and expectations. With increasing age, the school, teachers and peer group become a major feature of the environment.

Critics of early developments in behaviour therapy claimed that the approach was too mechanistic and did not take sufficient account of the complexities of human relationships. This derives from a misunderstanding of a school of psychotherapy which has been theory driven and has always sought to take account of individual differences in both inherited characteristics and life experiences. The child is not seen as merely a passive recipient of experiences which will shape behaviour and expectations. Individual differences in temperament and reactivity are obvious from birth onwards. Some babies quickly acquire reputations for being difficult, irritable or unresponsive (Thomas and Chess 1977). Both the temperament and physical appearance of the young child influence the ways in which others react towards them. The child often unwittingly, and sometimes purposefully, modifies the social environment in which he or she develops. Development is better understood as a series of spiralling social transactions rather than a sequence of interactions (Sameroff and Chandler 1975).

From early in their development, behavioural methods were extended to take account of some of the principles of social learning theory. This wider model addressed a range of psychodynamic concepts in learning theory terms. It was recognised that social approval and mastery over aspects of the environment might function as secondary reinforcers. The emphasis shifted to include an understanding of how children become socialised and learn the rules and values of the family and the culture. Experimental studies of normal children showed that not only direct experiences, but also vicarious learning through observation of others, influence behaviour. The child observes that parents and others appear to have control over many aspects of the environment and desired rewards. Becoming more like these seemingly powerful others becomes a source of reinforcement for the child. By this reasoning, social learning theory provides a powerful explanation for the development of imitative behaviour.

It has also been demonstrated that some aggressive and deviant behaviour in children is likely to be based on observational learning. A single exposure, or 'one trial learning', may be sufficient to bring about the incorporation of new behaviours into a child's repertoire. Experimental studies have shown that even exposure to aggression on film and television may serve to mediate aggressive behaviour in children (Bandura 1986). Unfortunately, studies of exposure to models performing pro-social behaviours indicate that they have a less powerful influence on child observers than models who are seen to yield to temptation and appear to break rules to gain rewards. It would be wrong to over-generalise from experimental studies, but there is sufficient evidence to advise caution in allowing children to view gratuitous violence. Further evidence indicates that fears and phobias may sometimes be acquired without direct contact with the anxiety-provoking situations. Children can acquire anxiety or fear responses from what they see or what they think has happened to others. Being told stories, or reading about actual or fictional events, may be sufficient to initiate phobic behaviour.

Following on from the recognition that a child's behaviour is greatly influenced by environmental factors, behaviour therapists have sought techniques to bring about changes in the ways parents interact with their children. At a basic level, some parents need education in the principles of child care. Some of the initial parent training programmes attempted to help parents cope with the special needs of children with moderate or severe learning difficulties. Others attempted to correct abusive situations. More generally, however, it became clear that training parents in the administration of reinforcers, both material and social, could influence the emotional and behavioural development of their children.

Soon interest in applying learning theory principles to parent training extended to attempts to help parents deal with specific behavioural difficulties such as disobedience. Here, there is a powerful change of metaphor towards a systemic perspective. Parents who become more proficient in parenting skills receive direct reinforcement themselves from the improvement in the interactions with their children. The behaviour problems are seen as capable of modification through changes in social relationships and patterns of interactions. To achieve this, the behavioural analysis needs to be extended to the ways in which parents administer rewards and punishments. Parents are helped to become aware of the importance of consistency, and of the timing of such social reinforcers as praise and expressions of interest in what the child has been doing. Parent training programmes for individual couples and for groups have been devised for a wide range of behavioural and medical conditions in children (Callias 1994).

Cognitive behaviour therapy

Behaviour therapy, in common with much of psychology, has undergone a cognitive revolution. Social learning theory had stimulated an interest in intervening variables between stimuli and responses, and also in the importance of mediational processes to explain thinking and language

(Osgood 1953). Evidence was cited that for almost all children the setting of rules is greatly enhanced when combined with verbal explanations. The early techniques of cognitive therapy were directed towards helping adults suffering from depression and anxiety disorders (Beck 1967, 1976; Ellis 1962). The impetus for the development of cognitive methods was partly dissatisfaction with the time taken by psychoanalytical attempts to alleviate distress. The cognitive therapist helps the client identify and systematically challenge irrational thoughts and feelings related to poor self-esteem and subsequent disturbed behaviour. Cognitive therapy with children has extended behaviour modification to focus on the importance of self-esteem and self-worth. There is a degree of overlap here with recent approaches to psychotherapy in adolescents based on applications of attachment theory. From the perspective of the child, self-worth is closely linked to what he or she believes important others think. 'Am I a person worth loving?' This point will be taken up again in the discussion of developments in narrative therapy.

Applications of cognitive behaviour therapy have been developed in the areas of social skills training, assertiveness training, anger management and self-control. Many of the techniques are extensions of traditional behaviour modification. However, in cognitive behaviour therapy there is greater reliance on language, self-instruction and internal representation of difficulties.

Beginning with training in an awareness of self at the level of feelings and mood, it is possible to direct attention to an awareness of some of the effects that the child's behaviour is having on other people. In common with much of behaviour modification, it is training in the timing of the awareness that is of the essence. For example, with oppositional behaviour, the training strategy shifts gradually from increasing the child's awareness of what has been done in past situations, to awareness of behaviour as it occurs, and finally to awareness of situations which might result in conflict and which can be avoided before they escalate.

On becoming more systemic

Independently of cognitive behavioural therapy, family therapy moved the unit of analysis from the problem child to the family. The family systems view helps reduce the pathologising of the child who is exhibiting troublesome behaviour. In this interpretation, in many cases the child has become a symptom carrier for family problems, and the therapist will try to help the family bring about change itself (Hoffman 1981).

The conceptual shift is not from a problem child to a problem family, but rather from a child with problems to a family with problems. In terms of linear causality, interpretation of difficulties is replaced by the recognition of circular causality and a search for new meanings for family problems. Behavioural difficulties in children are seen in the context of the complex interactions of the family construed as a multi-generational social system. Almost all child mental health services now include some form of family therapy in the range of available interventions.

More recently, variations of the systemic metaphor have been adopted by therapists working within the cognitive and behavioural models of therapy (Mahoney 1995; Meichenbaum 1993). One such development in cognitive therapy is the move towards, first, social constructivism, and later social constructionism and the use of narratives.

Social constructivism has its origins in philosophy, cognitive psychology and biology. Philosophical origins can be traced to the British empiricists and to Kant. In cognitive psychology, Piaget's genetic epistemology attributed an active part to the child in constructing representations of the environment and knowledge. Separately, personal construct theory (Kelly 1955) has evolved into an independent approach to psychotherapy, as well as influencing cognitive behaviour therapy more generally and providing examples of how clients can be helped to take an active role in constructing their individual representations of reality. A biological perspective on the active part played by the individual in constructing reality can be found in the work of Maturana and Varela (1980, 1987).

Social constructionism draws attention to ways in which humans make sense of their experiences through narrative. The construction of a concept of self is greatly influenced by each individual's view of the stories which others have about them. These stories are dominant to the extent that they allow insufficient space for the expression of the individual's own preferred story (White and Epston 1990). As in family therapy, social constructionism attempts to rescue the child from the stigma of pathology without blaming the family. Emotionally disturbed children can be helped to construct alternative and less distressing stories to account for their experiences and views of themselves.

Many therapists accept the position that simultaneously adopting different models for intervention constitutes a coherent strategy. It is argued that children can be helped to develop coping strategies using combinations of techniques based on different levels of explanation. The remainder of this chapter will explore applications of these three metaphors for therapy in interventions involving children and adolescents, and examine some of the points of overlap between them.

Behaviour therapy with children

As indicated above, a behavioural analysis will include an assessment of the reinforcement hierarchy of the individual child. This information can be gathered from direct observation and from interviews with the parents and the child. Attempts will be made to identify which rewards matter more than others. There is increasing evidence that for many children social reinforcement and approval or disapproval have a greater influence on behaviour than material gain. If it transpires that the motivation for some of the difficult behaviour is the increased level of attention it gains for the child, then attempts can be made to alter the sequence of events. Becoming the centre of attention for other children, even for just a few minutes, can be a powerful reward for a child who might be finding the attainment of success in schoolwork difficult. The challenge for the teacher is to find ways of reducing the attention given to the disruption without appearing to condone it. The same principles apply to conflict situations in the home. The parent who allows the child to prolong an argument or divert the discussion to irrelevant issues is unwittingly providing social reinforcement for the very behaviours they wish to reduce. Neutral observation or careful history taking can sometimes uncover such behavioural contingencies.

What might be perceived by an adult as a punishment or a negative reaction may not be seen in the same way by the child. For many children, being shouted at has relatively little effect. It has happened so many times before that the response has almost been habituated. The child may even derive some satisfaction from observing the adult appear to lose control or get upset; a different reinforcement from gaining attention. Advising the adult to reduce the amount of attention given to challenging, disruptive or unpleasant behaviour needs to be combined with a warning that the short-term consequence may well be an increase in the intensity of the problem behaviour. On failing to get the usual reaction, the child is likely to intensify attempts to gain attention. In the home situation it is essential that both parents agree to the suggestion to adopt a strategy of reducing attention for it to be successful. Problems arise if the child's bids for attention become dangerous or destructive. The behavioural analysis needs to troubleshoot this far ahead.

Much has been written about the technique of 'time-out' as a means of reducing difficult behaviour. Essentially, it involves removing the child from the situation where the deviant behaviour is being reinforced by social interaction. It is hypothesised that for some children, being alone, or socially isolated, is an unpleasant experience which they will seek to avoid. In the school situation the removal of the child from the class for a short period will only be effective if there is a safe and unstimulating environment available. The child who is able to make faces through a window, or disrupt other children, is unlikely to be changed by the experience.

Spontaneous attempts by parents to enforce their own versions of time-out at home are often unduly harsh and sometimes badly managed. Care is needed to avoid making the parents feel undermined by proposals to adopt a gentler, but more systematic, approach. The child should be sent out of the room or to a bedroom, but it is important that the act of exclusion itself is not allowed to become a new conflict. For both home and school situations, the evidence is that the exclusion, or cooling-off period, does not need to be long to be effective. Unnecessarily long exclusions will be likely to result in boredom and further deviance, and the association between the removal from the room and the original act can become lost. An exclusion of five to ten minutes is often effective. When the child is having a temper tantrum, the timing may need to be contingent on a return to a state of calm behaviour. Parents sometimes make the mistake of ending the exclusion with too much reinforcement in the welcoming back, with the consequence that by a complex process of backward chaining the original difficult behaviour is further rewarded. It is far better to administer praise or provide rewards at an appropriate later time following good behaviour on the part of the child.

The crucial factor in the shaping of pro-social behaviour in difficult and deviant children is the timing and spontaneity of social interaction on the part of parents and teachers. However, some children, particularly those with a short attention span, fail to react to normal patterns of social interaction because they have already switched their attention to some other activity. The adult needs to be made sensitive to these possibilities. Sometimes the administration of more tangible rewards such as tokens or house points may be more effective acknowledgement of acceptable or good behaviour than verbal praise alone. For a reinforcement schedule to be effective, the administration of tokens should not be one which could develop into a source of challenge, and it should be easy to administer.

Perhaps the best known of all behaviour therapy applications is the technique of systematic desensitisation. Based on physiological evidence that anxiety and relaxation cannot coexist, children with phobias, or a tendency to experience excessive anxiety in specific situations such as examinations, are given training in muscle relaxation (Wolpe 1958). About four to six brief training sessions, with some practice between sessions, is usually sufficient for the child to begin to experience pleasure from feeling relaxed. In the meantime, exploratory work will have established a hierarchy of stimulus situations associated with feelings of anxiety. Once in a relaxed state the child can be invited to think about situations associated with relatively low levels of anxiety, and when this can be tolerated it is possible to progress along the hierarchy.

Effective desensitisation is best achieved by moving on to a gradual exposure to real-life situations perceived by the child as threatening. This latter stage may be usefully combined with modelling by the therapist, or even by another child, of coping behaviour. Desensitisation can be effective in some cases of school phobia, when combined with cognitive therapy. It is effective with single phobias, such as fear of lifts or dogs, which might be seriously impairing the child's ability to establish independent behaviour outside the home.

Desensitisation techniques have also been used effectively with children suffering from a range of medical conditions where fear reactions and phobias are resulting in non-compliance with treatment. Needle phobia and fear of injections make it very difficult for many children to cooperate in investigations. A combination of relaxation exercises, desensitisation and training in distraction is usually effective. In some cases it is important to address the level of the parents' anxieties about the illness and procedures in addition to attempting to bring about change in the children. Issues of treatment compliance and feelings of anger are not uncommon in children with long-standing conditions such as diabetes. Interventions in these cases would typically include a combination of behavioural and cognitive methods.

Training in relaxation is in itself a very important therapeutic tool and can be used beneficially with children and adolescents displaying a range of difficult behaviours including aggression. Relaxation not only promotes a sense of well-being, but also serves as a good starting point for training in self-awareness in cognitive therapy.

Some examples of cognitive therapy

Cognitive therapy combined with behavioural techniques has been widely used in attempts to reduce aggressive behaviour in children and to provide training in anger management. Aggressive and challenging behaviour is such a common feature of normal development that it is important to conduct a careful evaluation before attributing labels such as 'deviance' to a child. It needs to be determined whether the disruptive behaviour occurs at home and at school or only in one environment. Recently onset behavioural difficulties, largely associated with the classroom environment, may reflect undetected learning difficulties and psychometric assessment should be considered. Clearly, with recent behaviour change an assessment of recent events and stresses in the family is important.

With or without the identification of background factors, a behavioural analysis will move on to the identification of possible immediate trigger events. Does the child show any worry or remorse afterwards, especially if someone has been hurt or property has been damaged? Is there evidence of stealing or lying in addition to aggressive behaviour?

Research on aggressive children has found that they have a tendency to perceive a high level of hostile cues in their social environment and to perceive threatening intentions in the behaviours of others. Cognitive therapy with these children is aimed at modifying some of the distortions in their attributions of social situations. It also provides training in self-monitoring, including the ability to label feelings and affects. The next stage in the intervention is training in problem-solving skills. Considerable importance will be attached to helping the child to judge when to move away from situations before conflict develops. With increased cognitive awareness, the child eventually becomes better able to calculate the potential consequences of losing control.

Several cognitive behavioural methods have been combined into a programme referred to as 'training in interpersonal cognitive problem solving' (Pellegrini 1994; Spivack, Platt and Shure 1976). The first stage is training in alternative thinking. This involves the child developing the ability to generate a range of possible solutions to an interpersonal problem or to conflict situations. In the original programmes, training took place in group discussions and scripted games. For example, a simple situation described to the children might be that someone has pushed you, and alternatives might be whether to hit him or to tell him that you are angry and do not like what he has done. Similar exercises can be adapted for use in individual therapy sessions. The second stage is training in the ability to judge the immediate and longer-term consequences of alternative actions, labelled 'consequential thinking'. Discussion at this level might examine the consequences of hitting versus telling about anger. Essentially this is training in decision taking. The final stage is training in means–end thinking, or the ability to put together a series of actions to solve a problem.

Problem-solving training can be a useful extension of normal classroom activities. Specific programmes can be designed as group activities for children showing disturbed behaviours. The nature of the tasks will need to vary according to the ages of the children and the types of difficulty involved. With disturbed children the problem-solving activities are likely to need to be preceded by training self-awareness and awareness of the feelings of others.

Self-instructional training (SIT)

A range of cognitive techniques comes under this general heading. The common goal is to help children to be able to regulate their own behaviour through the use of cognitive strategies (Hughes 1988). One aspect of training is to provide strategies specifically designed to help the child slow down or delay acting inappropriately. In classroom situations the impulsive child might be trained to reflect on whether or not the verbal instructions given by the teacher, or in the written question in a test or exercise, has been understood, before rushing on. Initial training may need to be at the level of talking aloud, for example, 'What am I supposed to do for this one?' Following practice, the self-instruction is then to be given quietly, and finally it is allowed to become a silent thought process. To be effective, appropriate social and verbal reinforcement needs to be provided by the therapist, and eventually by the parent or teacher.

With the impulsive and aggressive child, the emphasis in SIT is on helping the child to try to stop and think before lashing out (Meichenbaum and Goodman 1971). In particularly difficult cases, intervention can begin by getting the child to adopt the 'turtle response' of pulling in the arms and legs and lowering the head when confronted by a conflict situation. Training in relaxing through the use of simple breathing exercises or distraction techniques, when in this withdrawn position, can help to make the situation tolerable. Further training can then be given in the use of self-administered verbal instructions such as 'I am not going to let this annoy me'. Variations in training include practice in simple delaying or distraction activities, such as counting backwards from five to one. The effectiveness of SIT in the control of aggressive behaviour is sometimes disappointing. Some children are unwilling to cooperate. To be effective it does require extensive training, and it becomes more effective when combined with other cognitive techniques (Kendall and Braswell 1985) and sometimes with the narrative approaches described in the following section.

When used in group situations SIT can also be combined with modelling. Children can observe the model resisting taunts and adopting different coping behaviours. Further sessions on an individual or group basis will then be required, first for the child to practise recalling the coping strategies, and then to rehearse them. Other training methods include the practising of non-aggressive responses in taunting games (Goodwin and Mahoney 1975).

Variations of SIT procedures can provide an effective intervention when working with disturbed children and adolescents who are being violent or verbally abusive in the home.

Case study

John was a 12-year-old boy who had been living alone with his mother since they were deserted by his father about eight years previously. Mother and son were very close, but John experienced periods when he resented the intensity of the relationship and felt that he had no personal space. In these situations he would be extremely verbally abusive towards his mother, calling her 'a fat old cow' and blaming her for their relative poverty. Just prior to the referral he had also started to hit his mother, which precipitated her decision to seek help. She was beginning to be frightened of his increasing strength. Therapy addressed the intensity of the relationship, and drew attention to the need for the mother to give John more age-appropriate independence. He in turn was required to accept, in stages, a contract of no violence, and then of no verbal abuse. SIT was used to inhibit the violence. He practised saying aloud in the therapy room, on getting up in the mornings and on coming home from school, the self-instruction, 'I will not hit my mother today'. He was also encouraged to develop alternative strategies when he felt angry. Initially this had to involve leaving the room. There were two incidents of pushing his mother during the first two weeks, but the physical violence had stopped by the end of four weeks. It was possible to address the verbal offensiveness at this stage by inviting both mother and son to keep a record of the number of occasions he used abusive language. After a further two weeks he was still arguing with his mother, but had accepted the need to moderate his language in the home.

Others might well have adopted an approach to this case based more on rational–emotive therapy (Ellis 1973). The emphasis could have been placed more on obtaining descriptions of the thoughts associated with the feelings of anger, and then have been followed by the development of a pattern of self-talk to emphasise that these were irrational reactions to the situation. Alternative solutions to the problem of anger could then have been rehearsed.

Social skills training

The importance of social skills training with aggressive and uncooperative children is substantiated by the observation that these children are often unpopular with their peer group. If the report of parents or teachers suggests that the child has few friends, or indeed if the child complains of feeling lonely or rejected, social skills training should be considered as part of the intervention.

Ideally, social skills training should be conducted as a group exercise. This provides opportunities for modelling of appropriate behaviours, which may be difficult to achieve in individual therapy. Several training programmes are available which may be adapted to meet the needs of the particular group. Often, arranging a suitable time for an adolescent group to meet can be difficult and it is necessary to provide training on an individual basis as a part of therapy.

Once again, training in self-awareness forms an important part of cognitive work to improve social skills. Video recordings of therapy sessions can be played back to demonstrate features of conversational style or non-verbal cues such as posture which could benefit from change. Coaching strategies are then used for specific situations in the expectation that there will be some generalisation to similar real-life interactions with teachers or the peer group. It is worth using probing questions to determine whether the child already has an internal template of a role model, for example, 'Tell me about a boy you would like to have as a friend'.

Depression and self-esteem

Depression and sadness are surprisingly common features of children with emotional and behavioural difficulties. A great deal of the angry and anti-social behaviour can be understood as a signal of underlying despair and confusion on the part of an immature individual who has not acquired an awareness of the consequences of challenging social values. The cognitive behavioural approach of choice is an adaptation of the methods used to combat depression in adults. Irrational thoughts need to be detected and strategies for rejecting them will need to be carefully rehearsed. Witnessing parental discord and violence can be particularly distressing for children, with consequential anger and even violent behaviour incorporating an element of modelling of what has been observed. Cognitive behaviour therapy allows a verbalisation of experiences and an opportunity to challenge irrational thoughts that the child was responsible for the parental conflict. Self-esteem can then be addressed using the techniques of narrative therapy referred to below.

Examples of working systemically with individuals

Narrative therapy

Children attending therapy sessions all have a story to tell about what they think others think about them. The therapist is starting from a position that there is no single reality, but rather that views about the family and the world are social constructions. Particularly when working with adolescents, there needs to be an awareness that the individual is living out stories in which they see the parent or teacher as the dominant narrator. The task, then, for the therapist is to listen and gently question to discover those aspects of the adolescent's life experiences which fall outside the dominant story (White and Epston 1990). These experiences are then used as the basis for helping the individual to construct alternative narratives and a view of self that is separate from the problem-saturated version they started with.

Externalising the problem

Externalising is a powerful technique which is sometimes able to release the child from feelings of self-blame for the problem symptom (White 1989). The importance of listening to the child and accepting her/his label for the problem must be stressed. Failure to engage with the child's use of language and meaning system may seriously limit the power of the intervention. In the case of a child with a short attention span and excessive restlessness, the label 'fidget' might emerge. The question to the child would then be, 'What is it about "fidget" which tricks you into getting into trouble in your French lesson?' The therapist and child together can work out strategies for resisting the difficult behaviour. It may also be possible to get parents and other family members to help in the process of distancing the symptom behaviour from the child by joining in the externalising of the difficulty.

Addressing aggressive behaviour and achieving anger management are sometimes possible using externalisation. The technique can be combined with a social constructionist version of narrative therapy. The child is invited to think of times when the behaviour which others complain about was not a problem. 'Let's try to remember how good it used to be before you used to get into fights all the time.' It is also useful to focus on unique outcomes or occasions when the child is able to do something without getting into trouble. 'How are these times different?'

The narrative can be developed in different ways in conversations with the child to reveal alternative constructions of past experiences and of possible future outcomes. This approach has several similarities to a behavioural intervention: there is a logical structure to the exploration of alternatives, exercises are set and irrational explanations are challenged.

Concluding remarks

Emotional and behavioural difficulties in children are often resistant to intervention for the very reason that children have such little direct control over the stresses in their lives. The range of methods now encompassed by cognitive behavioural therapists allow them to take account of the complexities of individual differences and of systemic factors. The combination of behavioural methods to reduce difficult behaviour and promote a sense of well-being, and the cognitive methods of restructuring and narratives provide a means to alleviate many problems.

CHAPTER 8

Psychoanalytic Psychotherapy with Children with Emotional and Behavioural Difficulties

Biddy Youell

For the purposes of this chapter I shall define children with emotional and behavioural difficulties as those who, for reasons of emotional disturbance, cannot make good use of their educational opportunities and are difficult to manage. These are children whose emotional difficulties interfere with their learning, with their relationships with teachers and with their relationships with peers. Children with EBDs usually have parallel difficulties within their families and communities, but this is not always so. In exceptional cases, the split between family and school is such that it is only in the face of authority which is external to the family that the difficulties arise, or only in the face of the demands of formal learning. For many, school is where the difficulties first surface and teachers are the first to put words to what is worrying, puzzling or challenging behaviour.

Many children experience difficulty in making the transition between home and school. With careful nurturing, clear boundaries and thoughtful liaison with parents, most children can and do make the adjustments necessary to fit into school life. Children who appear to manage well may experience periods of difficulty when they move up each year, around the time of secondary transfer, during exam years, or when traumatic events in their families or neighbourhoods intrude upon what might be thought of as the normal developmental path. Some children are sensitive to all kinds of change and transition, and need particular understanding and support at those times. Schools, like families, are more or less successful in meeting children's needs. Where schools do not observe the children in their care and are not thoughtful about their structures, policies, teaching methods and curriculum, the child who is vulnerable may feel uncontained and may begin to behave in a way which challenges these norms.

This chapter will focus specifically on those children at the extreme end of the difficult behaviour continuum, who cannot be managed in the ordinary way in the ordinary classroom. They might be described as hyper-sensitive to anything which disturbs their equilibrium or does not fit in exactly with their personal version of how things should be. These children and young people are extremely difficult to teach. They are difficult to parent and difficult to treat in psychoanalytic psychotherapy. Often their most crippling characteristic is that they cannot or will not allow people to help them. Even when they are in touch with themselves and know what they need, they cannot easily make use of what is offered to them.

It is not my purpose here to dwell on issues of causation. Clearly, some children have real-life experiences which have an adverse effect on their development and render them more vulnerable and more likely to develop EBDs in relation to school and to learning. Other children appear to develop similar difficulties for no obvious reason; they come from 'ordinary' families and are described as having had 'ordinary' experiences. In some cases, it is clear that a child may be seen as 'extraordinary' and unacceptable in one particular school setting but might be entirely acceptable and able to thrive in another.

The picture in the case of each individual child is a complex one and cannot be reduced to a simple matter of cause and effect. It is a picture which is made up of the results of a complicated, dynamic interplay between innate characteristics and experience. Williams (Henry 1983; Williams 1997) introduces us to a notion of 'double deprivation'. She describes the way in which children who have suffered adverse early circumstances are further hampered by the defences which were, of necessity, developed in response to those early deprivations and which render them unable to make use of what is subsequently offered. The main case illustration in this chapter centres on one such boy.

The EBDs population is made up of children from all kinds of background but neglected, abused and traumatised children are over-represented, as are children who have had multiple carers or who are fostered or adopted. Trauma and post-traumatic phenomena are relatively recent areas of study, but have much to teach us in our attempts to understand children with EBDs. Children who have been sexually abused, who have fled from persecution, who have arrived as refugees, who have been in accidents, who have witnessed terrible disasters, or who have been subject to early medical or surgical interventions, are left with a very particular kind of hyperarousal and over-sensitivity. Traumatised children do not simply find it difficult to settle down or to trust adults; they actually suffer from flashbacks, from sudden, overwhelming memories which they re-live in a very concrete way. They tend to be hyper-sensitive to noise, often reacting fearfully to sounds which the rest of us do not hear. They experience physical approaches as threatening and are often preoccupied with memories or are taken over by sudden fearfulness. When the trauma has occurred before a child is old enough to think symbolically, or to describe the experience in words, the effects may be very severe and may result in behaviour which appears random, destructive or aggressive, unprovoked and inexplicable. I am reminded of a boy who had intrusive hospital treatment at ten days old and whose mode of defence, aged three, was to attack the parts of the body in others which had been the focus of his own treatments. He would kick his brothers in the base of the spine (lumbar puncture) and twist and pinch the skin on his mother's wrists (sites of intubation). Caresses would turn into attacks with no warning. The same boy, aged five, would hear a noise three streets away and would instantly throw a toy at his therapist or out of the window. It was all about expulsion, ways of getting rid of his fear of any repetition of the traumatic experience.

The speed with which things changed in this traumatised boy's world was staggering to behold. I have come to think that many of the children who are given the label EBDs suffer in a similar way, although mostly for much less obvious reasons. Things change internally very quickly, without warning, and have a devastating effect on the way in which they can then manage their external worlds. They live with what might be described as an internal hyperactivity and hyperarousal.

Steven, aged eight, was offered three exploratory, individual sessions to see whether psychotherapy might be something which he would find helpful. He had been assessed as having EBDs, not severe enough to warrant special school, but causing his teachers some considerable concern. There were no obvious external reasons for his behaviour and his parents had been told that psychotherapy might be able to make sense of things for them, and for him. He had spent the first session in tears, convinced that the offer of therapy was simply another punishment. The second session had seen him relaxed and talkative; he had apparently forgotten all his reservations about my motives and was keen to make contact. In the third session, he was rummaging through his box of toys and drawing materials, talking in an expansive way about football and smiling appreciatively when I remembered the models he had made the previous week. He was picking up things he had not examined before, naming them and dropping them into the box. He thought he would draw. 'No, maybe I'll use the animals. I could make more models. What's this ball for?' Suddenly, the talk stopped and everything was bundled back into the box without further comment. He rammed the lid on fast and sat back, arms folded. The remaining 40 minutes of the session were spent with him sitting silent and still and with me struggling to make sense of what had happened. I had no clue as to what had triggered this sudden withdrawal and my speculations did not seem to offer any illumination. Eventually, I asked him if he knew what had changed and he shook his head, looking miserable. I felt that he had actually shown me something very important; the way in which his feeling states change, so suddenly and completely, leaving his capacity to think and manage his own behaviour lagging far behind.

What contribution can psychotherapy make to children and young people who suffer in this way? Steven was a boy whose disturbance and distress at home and at school showed in sudden withdrawal, tearfulness and silent, hostile refusal to comply. Sadly, many EBDs children have shifted beyond this into hugely confrontational and aggressive behaviour.

In these cases, there might be an assumption that the one-to-one relationship which is offered in psychotherapy is just what the child needs and would want. Teachers might feel that the psychotherapist will have an easy time of it, with a child who will lap up the attention and not give any trouble. The reality can be very different. The idea that children with difficulties will always function better with individual teaching or in small groups is, to my mind, based on a false premise. It is certainly true that children find very large groups difficult if there is inadequate adult supervision, but it may be that the optimum number is somewhere between large and very small. The crucial element seems to be the ratio of adults to children. For children with EBDs, groups which resemble families are often acutely painful. Feelings of rivalry with siblings, of competing for parental attention, of oedipal conflict, are stirred up in a most powerful way. The child is incapable of managing what is an explosive cocktail of unconscious memories of past experiences and current emotions.

One-to-one work, whatever the setting, carries with it the potential for real change. However, it can also provoke very intense feelings and be difficult to manage for both child and worker. The one-to-one situation may be experienced as a further distilling of emotions in such a way that the child is brought face to face, in the transference, with issues originating in their relationship to their mother or first carer. The therapy room can very quickly become a setting in which passionate feelings (whether of hope, despair or hostility) are aroused, and the success of the work will depend on the therapist's capacity to contain those feelings and the child's capacity to allow her to do so. Psychotherapy is often, mistakenly, characterised as being to do with going back and excavating the past and then restructuring it. In practice, successful work, particularly with acting-out children, needs to be thought of as helping the child or adolescent to make use of current opportunities (with parents, schools, etc.) with a view to a better future. An experience of containment within a therapeutic relationship can enable a child to see similar opportunities elsewhere and to get in touch with a capacity for thought, hope and creativity within themselves.

I intend to illustrate some of the factors which mitigate for and against containment within psychotherapy with material from the treatment of a 13-year-old boy, named Andrew. When we started work, Andrew was attending a day school for children with EBDs and was always on the verge of exclusion. He lived with adoptive parents who had taken him in, with his elder sister, when he was four years old and his sister was six. Nobody could understand why his sister seemed so much better able to settle into the new home. The argument was that she was older and so would surely have clearer memories of her birth mother and the neglect and abuse they suffered with her and with subsequent carers. Andrew was thought to have been too young to know what was going on and so quickly became seen as 'bad', whilst his sister was described as 'delightful'.

I felt that it was Andrew who was in a terrible predicament in relation to his past. He had been abandoned by his mother at two and so the abuse which he suffered occurred during his infancy, before he had developed speech or become truly mobile. He had no access to conscious memories of his family of origin but he was left with all the unconscious damage. He loathed his sister, who he felt to be in a very privileged position. He believed that his adoptive parents did not like him and he did his very best to make himself unlikeable.

When psychotherapy was suggested for Andrew, everybody felt that he would jump at the chance. He was always at his best with one adult. He would enjoy the friendly attention he would receive. In preliminary discussions I alerted his parents and teachers to the inevitability of his developing mixed feelings about the therapy; they were unconvinced. In the event, nobody was prepared for the speed with which he would become engaged with it, nor the intensity of the feelings it would arouse in him. I shall describe the different stages of the therapy and discuss some of the issues raised, both in terms of a psychoanalytic understanding of Andrew's internal world and in terms of the technical challenges involved in working with such patients.

The first three sessions were set up as an exploration, in much the same way as had occurred with Steven. Andrew was told that we would decide together whether or not psychotherapy seemed to be something he would find helpful. In a preliminary meeting with Andrew and both parents, everybody spoke openly about how difficult Andrew's behaviour had become, both at home and at school. I heard about his fights with other boys, about how he threatened his mother and was relentless in his persecution of his sister.

When he and I met alone the following week, it was as if he had never had any difficulty of any kind. For the three 'trial' (his word) sessions, I felt that I was being shown what a lovely boy he was and how lucky I would be if we decided to continue. I felt almost as if I were a prospective adoptive parent who had to be persuaded to go ahead with the adoption. He was quiet, polite and very careful to check the rules before doing anything. He drew pictures and told me how envious his sister was of his having a psychotherapist. 'She doesn't have anything like this.' He was thrilled with the contents of the toy box and told me the room was 'just right'. He spent most of those sessions drawing and colouring in. His need to draw with a ruler and keep the colours neatly within the lines left me feeling anxious, and this did alert me to how hard he was perhaps having to work to keep himself and his behaviour within bounds.

This idealisation of the therapy came to an abrupt end during the gap between these initial sessions and starting regular weekly work. There was a regrettable but unavoidable six week delay and when I met Andrew again he was far less effusive, although still keen to start. I felt that I had, unwittingly, repeated a pattern of broken contact and delay which is so much a part of the experience of children who are fostered and adopted. I had already fallen from an idealised, elevated position as potential rescuer, into one of a fickle, unreliable waste of time. The room continued to be 'wicked' and his box full of good things, but I was soon described as 'lame' and 'sad'. It is inevitable that this will occur where a relationship begins with such idealisation. Denigration follows fast on the heels of idealisation when the child has no solid experience of managing ambivalent feelings. The split is total.

Once Andrew had begun to insult me, he seemed unable to stop and we slipped quickly into a pattern of abuse and provocation which went on for many sessions and which, at one stage, threatened the work. Colleagues in the building were disturbed by the shouting and crashing and felt concerned for my safety. Andrew went on a rampage of verbal abuse and threat in every session. He would ridicule me on a personal level, laughing at my clothes and haircut. He would try to engage me in play in which I was a poor, brainless, pathetic child and he was an all-knowing, all-controlling teacher. His talk was full of obscene language and sexual innuendo. He challenged my minimal rules by going in and out of the door to shout down the corridors and by hanging out of the window to hurl abuse at passers by. He turned furniture upside down, kicked the bin around the room and threatened to hit me. He would accompany all of this with grandiose claims of having 'beaten up' one or other of his teachers, who were variously described as 'pathetic', 'thick' and 'a joke'. He would laugh in a forced, raucous way as he told me how he had terrorised the class, his taxi driver or his sister. He would insist that I found it funny too. All the doubt, fear, weakness and stupidity was projected out into the important figures in Andrew's world and I had joined the cast.

I spent some time thinking about how these sorts of behaviour were being dealt with elsewhere. Not for the first time, I felt relieved to be the psychotherapist, free to think about Andrew without having to deliver the National Curriculum to him or to manage the routines of family life which he seemed intent on destroying. I knew that his teachers at school did their best to reason with him and that his parents sought to appeal to his better nature by trying to make him feel guilty about the things he did. There is a common misconception about guilt, and that is that it will be mobilised if the punishment is sufficiently severe. For children and young people whose capacity to trust in the motives of adults is so seriously impaired, as was Andrew's, punishments simply serve to reinforce denial or, at best, provoke attempts at manic reparation (which is not rooted in real regret). The guilt he experienced was always persecutory.

Throughout this phase of the therapy, I felt I was walking on a tightrope in every session. I was not going to allow him to hurt me physically, nor to do permanent damage to anything in the room, but I knew that to get into a confrontation with him too quickly would only escalate the aggression and violence. At the same time, I felt that he was becoming worried about how far he was going and needed me to intervene in some way. His anxiety often showed itself in a sudden fear that I would tell his parents, and there would be a pseudo-reparative ending to a session, in which he would tidy up and make all sorts of promises about how good he would be next time. This felt placatory and manipulative. In the face of Andrew's aggression, I had to rely on my counter-transference[1] to make some sort of running assessment as to whether or not we were both safe. I was aware that while I sometimes felt furious about how I was being treated, at no point did I feel frightened; I did not think that he was actually going to attack me. I also felt that whilst his behaviour might appear to be out of control, there was an element of posturing in it. However, I was very aware of the danger of tipping him over into an out-of-control state by challenging him too quickly or by provoking him with my interpretations.

I confined myself to very short comments and was careful not to say things which he might experience as humiliating. Alvarez (1992) has been very helpful in developing ideas about how to share insights with patients. She suggests that children in this sort of predicament need their defences and may hear interpretations about their neediness or dependence as con-firmation of their worst fears. They do not feel relieved at being understood, so much as attacked and effectively told that there is no hope for them. This was certainly borne out in my work with Andrew. If I spoke of his minding about his sessions or about me as being anything other than an object of ridicule, he would be wild with indignation and would simply redouble his efforts to convince me of my worthlessness. It was as if everything I said was heard as being for my own narcissistic satisfaction. 'You think you're so clever. You're really up yourself aren't you?' I had to limit myself to short,

---

1   Within psychoanalytic psychotherapy, the therapist tries to understand the nature of the *transference*, or the way in which characters from the patient's internal world are brought into the interaction in the here-and-now in the consulting room. The *counter-transference* is the means whereby the therapist can make sense of the drama which is being enacted. The projections of patients stir up strong responses in the therapist which the therapist takes to be unconscious communication. She attempts to think about her own responses as the key to understanding the patient's experience.

clear statements about what I would not allow him to do and very brief remarks about what might be behind some of the things he was doing. I suggested he was testing me to see if I would manage him and if I would persevere or throw him out. I did not add that I thought he also desperately wanted to stay and to be acceptable to me. I did not challenge the veracity of what he told me about school, but simply observed that he was wanting to impress me and was wanting me to join in with his ridicule of all adults.

In spite of all the provocation, I felt that he wanted me to help him stop the spiralling acting-out, but any flexing of my mental muscles led him further to flex his physical muscles and put the whole contact at risk. When he began to throw a soft toy at me with all his might every time I spoke, and sometimes from very close range, I took hold of it and said it would not be available in future sessions. He was furious and immediately threatened to throw a small table at me, holding it menacingly above my head. I said that I was going to stop the session and he panicked. His aggression turned to fear and he made all sorts of promises, begging me not to tell his mother. After some time, I said that, even though he was now calm, I was going to have to let his mother know that he was finding it difficult to manage in sessions and I would ask her to stay in the waiting room in case we needed to bring a session to an early end. He was desperate that I should think again, but I stuck to my word and spoke to his mother in front of him so that he knew what had been said.

This was my first move to follow up on what I had been trying to achieve with words alone. I did not want to have to go further. I was very anxious not to get stuck in a sequence of having to remove things from his box or from the room or of having to stop sessions early. I had visions of Andrew and I meeting in a room with no furniture and no equipment. I was very worried when, for completely unconnected reasons, I had to cancel his next session. Thinking that he would interpret this as me giving up on him or deliberately punishing him for his behaviour, I offered an alternative time. He could not believe that I had not just taken the opportunity to miss a session with him. Surely I would be relieved not to see him? He was incredulous. We also talked about what he had heard me say to his mother. He had expected me to tell his mother everything he had been doing and I was able to point out that what she had needed to know was that he was having difficulty and needed her to be there.

A turning point had been reached and the sessions became much calmer for the next few months. Andrew began to play games in which he wanted me to be the policeman, arresting him and sentencing him to severe punishments. He wanted me to restrain him physically, which, of course, I would not do, and I would feel him teetering on the brink of another outbreak of destructive behaviour as I tried to point out that there were other ways to manage without provoking people to restrain him. I talked about there being other ways of people getting on together and other aspects of him apart from the 'criminal' which he was allowing to be so much in control. He let me know just how doubtful he was about his own worth when he came in one day in high dudgeon about a man who he said had been bothering him:

> He was there again today. At the school gates. Bastard. What does he think I am? Bum boy! He waved again. I'm going to kill him. Wanker. Pervert. If he's there tomorrow ... I'll ... beat him up. Why is he always there? Every day. My taxi was late so I went inside again. I should have rung the police. What's he want? I'll get him. He'll look at me once too often!

I said that Andrew really did seem worried about this man and what he might be up to. Andrew launched into a new tirade about it not being natural. He must be a pervert. Watching children. Probably a rapist. He would have to get him. Next time he would fetch the Head. No he wouldn't. He would beat him to a pulp. 'Arsehole!'

I commented that Andrew did not really seem sure whether to be frightened, excited or angry, and he suddenly muttered that he thought it was his real dad. Did I think it could be? I felt stunned and momentarily speechless. Was this really what Andrew carried inside as his version of a real father and, if so, what did it say about his view of himself and his own potential for growth? Andrew lapsed into silence and sat very still. I said very little for fear that I would lose control and cry; tears were very close to the surface in me, and I felt I came to a new understanding of why Andrew might opt for anger in preference to tears of sorrow and shame.

Unfortunately, my work with Andrew was brought to a premature end when he and his family moved away at the end of that year. For the most part, the sessions were peaceable and he seemed to value that. When I offered to return the confiscated toy to his box he said he did not need it. He confined himself to drawing as he had in the early sessions, but instead of colouring between the lines, he wanted me to teach him how to draw in three dimensions, box shapes and buildings with insides. This seemed to represent something about the beginnings of an idea of meaning, of looking beyond the surface of mere words or behaviour. It hinted at the development of some notion of a container, an object with an internal space which could hold his projections and think about them. It also seemed to me to carry with it the possibility of space and perspective developing, so that a moment for thought might begin to exist between action and reaction. If Andrew were to have such a moment available to him, it would afford him some protection against instant and complete invasion by contemptuous, persecuting objects (internal figures such as the damaged father described above).

My brief piece of work with Andrew got us to a point at which we could see what might have been possible. He was capable of allowing his entrenched pattern of behaviour to be challenged and a more benign feedback loop to be put in place. Sadly, we were not able to get beyond this stage. As the work came to an end, and he was having to manage leaving his house and neighbourhood, there was a renewal of his provocative and contemptuous behaviour in sessions. He was at pains to let me know that there was absolutely nothing about therapy which he would miss; he was longing to be free of it. Sessions were again 'boring' and I was dismissed as 'sad'. Any comments from me about actual 'sadness' were met with further ridicule. He told me I would be delighted to be rid of him; how could I not be? He wanted to leave early and actually did not come for the final session. He could not manage his own goodbye and I felt he did not want to be exposed to any sadness or regret in me. He had re-grouped his defences in preparation for the move and encounters with new adults and peers. My hope was that just something of what had passed between us might come back to his unconscious mind in his future dealings with adults who would be responsible for him and who would be attempting to offer him something positive.

Andrew taught me a lot about the psychic world which many children with EBDs inhabit. He was both in desperate need of containment and, for the most part, unable to accept it. He invested great hope in the contact before it became a reality, but then felt that everything I did was for my own sadistic pleasure. I set limits only to glory in my superior position and when I used my mind to offer him some understanding, I did so only to triumph over him. Given that these were the assumptions which governed his relationships with the adult world, it is no surprise that he should work so hard to pre-empt matters and attack before being attacked. Kindness was seen as patronising and he was much more comfortable, minute by minute, if people lived up to his worst expectations. However, Andrew was not out of reach. In spite of the actual disappointments he had experienced in his intimate relationships, there remained some element of hopefulness in him.

What Andrew shared with so many children with EBDs was a refusal to feel dependent. It is easy to see how his early experiences would make it extremely hard for him to allow himself to be dependent on anyone; people in his early life were not dependable. Some children with much less apparent reason find it impossible to come to terms with the fact that they are dependent, first on their parents and subsequently on all sorts of adult figures. To acknowledge one's dependency involves acknowledging that there are things one does not know, has not got. This first such acknowledgement occurs between mother and infant in the feeding relationship, where the infant comes to recognise that he does not create the food by magic and that the mother can both provide and withhold. For very young children, the realisation that their mothers are not entirely in their thrall but have got other relationships, notably an intimate one with a partner, is very hard to bear. Some children never forgive their parents for producing younger siblings and never forgive the younger siblings for being born. Within the mainstream classroom, it is possible to observe the children who struggle with just this sort of issue and preoccupation. They have difficulty sharing, are very competitive, refuse to compete or insist that they do not have to do something because they already know it. They seek attention from the adults in the room but are dismissive or contemptuous when they get it.

Money-Kyrle (1968, 1971)[2] writes about the need for human beings to come to terms with three facts of life, or unpalatable truths. He suggests that there is a life-long struggle in all of us to accept and deny these facts. The first two are described above: knowing about one's own dependency and then recognising one's position outside the parental couple. The third he characterises as the need to come to terms with one's mortality, to realise that time moves on and death is inevitable. I would suggest that many children with EBDs work hard, unconsciously, to deny all three facts. Andrew was stuck in a pattern of relating in which he did not allow for dependency. All the need was projected into others, along with all the stupidity, all the envy

2   I am grateful to Hamish Canham at the Tavistock Clinic, who first drew my attention to Money-Kyrle's helpful ideas in his unpublished talk on 'Internal impediments to learning', given to the teachers on the MA in 'Emotional factors in learning and teaching'.

and all the sense of urgency. Children with EBDs, particularly perhaps those who opt out of school attendance altogether, often live in a kind of 'I'll do it tomorrow' way of being. Part of their omnipotence is that there is no hurry, they can always do it later.

Something of this very kind was evident in Mary, a 14-year-old girl in twice-weekly psychotherapeutic treatment. Mary was intelligent and articulate and was thought by her parents and by others to be unusually knowledgeable, talented and mature. She was disparaging of her peer group, she mixed with adults socially and was sexually active. She caused problems in school because of the elaborate stories she told and the way in which she manipulated people. She enjoyed shocking other girls and would pour her heart out to teachers in order to get them to worry about her and to offer her their time. She insisted that everything would be fine when she reached the age of consent, but was also aware that her precocious sexual behaviour and dramatic stories were the only way she knew to get adults to take notice of her and to look after her in the way she craved.

After a year's work in therapy, Mary became genuinely concerned about her performance at school. She no longer stood out as clever for her age (surviving on native wit) but was being left behind by her more diligent peers. She did not know what to do and there was a painful realisation that she had no idea of learning as being a process. She really thought that she was already an adult, already in possession of all necessary knowledge. She did not know how to work, to sit down and concentrate. She said sadly one day, 'There's nowhere for me to start from.' Later in the same session, she rallied some anger against the teachers who she felt were unfair to press her on her work: 'They should assess me on what I *could* do and not on what I do do.' She could see the absurdity of this suggestion and lapsed into silent despair.

In the subsequent session, we started on the same subject but there was no question of my being allowed to re-visit the thoughts or feelings she had been in touch with before. The teachers were now renounced as idiots and I was told that she could not do the work because it was too easy and too boring. When I tried to remind her of the dilemmas we had talked about, she became very panicky and begged me to get out of her head. 'Stop invading me!' It felt as if she had been brought face to face with Money-Kyrle's realities and was trying to turn away from them.

Making an assessment as to whether or not psychoanalytic work can help children like Stephen, Andrew or Mary does seem to involve making some sort of assessment as to whether or not they can bear to look at these realities. Another way of putting it might be that there needs to be evidence of an element of hopefulness or openness still intact. Traumatic experiences, abuse, absent or unreliable parenting, and negative school experiences all serve to put the survival of this at risk.

CHAPTER 9

Working with Vulnerable Children

Early Intervention

Helen Barrett

Introduction

All young children are vulnerable. None is ever completely safe from danger of one kind or another. Similarly, almost all adult interactions with young children involve some form of intervention. On some level, most adults must be constantly mindful of their role in protecting young children and helping those children to learn how to protect themselves from threats to their development or well-being. In this sense, most adults who are involved with small children practise some form of early intervention. They engage in activities which are designed to maximise the chances that the children in their care will develop well and will fulfil as much of their potential as possible.

Nevertheless, carrying out this role is not always easy and some parents face far greater obstacles than others – difficulties such as ill health, poverty, lack of social support or other social disadvantages. In addition, children vary tremendously in the challenges they present to their carers. Some children are distinctly more difficult to manage than others, some need very specialised attention for particular conditions, and while some children appear to sail through relatively trouble-free lives, others are considerably more vulnerable, both to physical and psychological harm.

On the whole, these wide-ranging differences are assumed to be an inevitable part of the rich tapestry of human experience, and the impossibility of organising social and personal resources so that everyone has equal opportunities is accepted. Yet it is also the case that it is rare for any society to be free of troubled or troubling individuals, victims or perpetrators of behaviour which often requires an urgent response. Guarding against this behaviour is clearly preferable to having to deal with the problems it can present. Prevention is better than cure.

This, it would appear, is the rationale behind much of the work involved in early intervention programmes. Appropriate intervention, if made early enough, will function as a prophylactic measure capable of substantially reducing the incidence and nature of troubling behaviour. Underpinning and reinforcing this rationale are two related notions: first, that behaviour is at its most malleable in the early years of life; and second, that early development consists of critical periods at the end of which no amount of input will be able to bring about the desired changes. In other words, workers involved in later intervention (probation officers as opposed to health visitors or pre-school teachers, for example) can expect to encounter far more resistance, will need to use much more complex and comprehensive methods, and are likely to be far less effective.

The challenges of early intervention

Compelling though these arrangements may sound, they do not go uncontested for a number of reasons. It is true that, in the early stages of development, many of the changes which take place are unique to this period, often overtly visible, rapid and, in general, essential for the maturation of abilities of all kinds. It is also true that, in some species and in a limited number of respects (e.g. certain aspects of perceptual and neural development), early development is dependent upon environmental input and, beyond a certain time, deprivation of this input cannot easily be compensated for (Blakemore 1991; Blakemore and Cooper 1970). However, in many other respects, there appears to be less evidence supporting the notion that development in the early years is a critical determinant of later development. Also, more recently, research on human infants has indicated that behaviour which emerges during early development is considerably more dependent upon innate mechanisms than was previously realised. Therefore, the impact of environmental influences, particular discrete alterations within a social nexus, may be relatively small or short-lived (Bremner 1994; Mehler and Dupoux 1994).

Currently popular models of development emphasise the interactive nature of the relationship between environmental and innate factors (see for example Bronfenbrenner 1979; Sameroff 1991) and the multiplicity of pathways through which any one individual may develop. Optimal development in the early years is considered more likely to emerge under circumstances which facilitate adaptive responding and enable the development of germinal skills rather than through the application of universal formulae. Further, since problem behaviour is generally viewed as socially constructed in models of this type, there has been an increasing tendency for early intervention programmes to consider the need for changes in the wider social context within which the behaviour occurs; that is, to examine ways in which this context may support or demand continuation of the problem behaviour.

Early intervention programmes, particularly those adopting an ecological approach of this sort, often carry with them considerable measurement problems (Simeonsson and Bailey 1990). They may also run the risk of making changes where none are required or of making bigger changes than necessary. Metaphorically speaking, early intervention programmes may aim not simply to correct a cleft palate at a developmentally sensitive early age soon after birth, but to correct the palate before the need for correction is definitely indicated. Such measures can be justified only if the benefits of intervention can be shown noticeably to outweigh the risks and costs both of intervention and of non-intervention. As this is not always either possible or easy, early intervention programmes are often highly prone to controversy.

The function of early intervention programmes is also inherently rather ambivalent. On the one hand, they purport to challenge the social order by facilitating an alteration of the 'natural' state of affairs, often involving an attempt to effect a long-term change in the quality of life of people who are socially disadvantaged. On the other hand, they seek to address the fears of the more socially advantaged about threats to this very same social order which works in their favour. In other words, the principal *raison d'être* of early intervention programmes is rarely straightforwardly philanthropic. Improvement of the quality of life of those who are socially disadvantaged, if it happens at all, has often been a somewhat gratuitous by-product of programmes geared towards the interests of, and governed by the values of, the socially advantaged. In this sense, too, early intervention can be seen as somewhat controversial.

Nevertheless, regardless of its tenuous political status and identity, the potential value of early intervention seems incontrovertible, no less so now than in 1944 when Bowlby confidently argued in favour of the early diagnosis, treatment and prevention of delinquency: 'we may look forward to a time when the diagnosis of delinquent character is regularly made in the child's early years. That we can learn to do this there can be not the slightest doubt' (Bowlby 1944, p.126). This chapter explores how much has been learnt about the diagnosis and treatment of problems in early childhood, and considers how professionals might recognise and respond to the needs of very vulnerable young children.

Early identification of problems

The success of early intervention programmes depends as much upon accurate identification of participants as upon the nature of the intervention itself. Accurate identification requires either the selection of individuals whose difficulties are in the early, emergent stages (individual methods of identification) or of young children living in conditions which are more or less unarguably associated with the incidence of problems (epidemiological methods of identification). Although there are difficulties associated with both of these approaches, each has been utilised by workers in the field of early intervention.

Epidemiological methods of identification

Perhaps due to the difficulties associated with identifying the exact beginnings of problematic behaviour in young children, many early intervention programmes have 'worked backwards'. They have started from the premise that certain types of problem are associated with particular social groups, and these groups have been targeted for intervention.

Many educational enrichment programmes, of which Head Start (Zigler and Valentine 1979) and High/Scope (Schweinhart, Weikart and Larner 1986) are perhaps the best known examples, have focused on low-income or socially disadvantaged populations considered to be at high risk of social problems, particularly those associated with alienation from the cultural values embodied in formal educational systems. Much controversy has surrounded claims regarding the success of these programmes. Some have argued that gains are due to a 'Hawthorne effect' (being paid attention raises morale sufficiently to improve performance regardless of the type of intervention) or may 'wash out' over a matter of years. Others have argued that follow-up into adolescence and young adulthood is necessary for benefits to be apparent. Still others have drawn attention to the role of the type of schooling subsequent to pre-school intervention. The recognition that educational input may need to be accompanied by welfare provisions, including medical, dental, nutritional, psychological and social services, in order for programmes to be taken up or have any effect appears to have provoked less controversy.

Other interventions have targeted the children of parents seen as in need of extra support, for example, teenage parents (readers are referred to Phoenix (1991) for a discussion of this population), depressed mothers (see for example Nicol, Stretch and Fundudis 1993; Seeley, Murray and Cooper 1996), abusing parents, parents of children with disabilities or of very low birth-weight and premature or fragile infants (Gilkerson, Gorski and Panitz 1990; O'Brien and Dale 1994), or those with histories of parenting difficulties. Whether or not mothers have a history of difficulties, and even when only short-term support is offered during pregnancy, it has been argued that social support can improve mothers' physical and psychological well-being and facilitate mother–child relationships (Oakley *et al.* 1996). This has obvious benefits in terms of children's welfare. Recently set-up parent support schemes such as Newpin (Cox *et al.* 1991) aim to counter the trend for the most disadvantaged parents to feel alienated and unable to benefit from welfare provisions. Newpin offers peer counselling and the option of participating in a personal development programme which may include psychotherapy on a group or individual basis. Although these schemes can be difficult to evaluate (Oakley *et al.* 1995) and are not invulnerable to funding problems, they appear to offer a relatively cost-effective and user-friendly safety net which may facilitate the identification of difficulties at an early stage.

Early intervention programmes have also drawn attention to the possibility that instructional content is often more effectively delivered in a social context which nurtures children's emotional needs and facilitates social relationships (Campion 1992). It is not possible to state with any certainty what may be the most appropriate, efficient or effective way to remove or manage emotional impediments to children's educational progress. Many methods used for primary school-age children (discussed elsewhere in this book) may also be valuable in work with pre-school children. For some children, nurture groups can provide a safe, contained space within the school setting for them to learn to trust enough to be able to engage with ideas which may otherwise seem intrusive or alien (Bennathan and Boxall 1996). For other children, additional time with classroom assistants may be beneficial. Some schemes aim to give children additional emotional support along psychotherapeutic lines within a classroom setting.

As yet, insufficient research has been carried out for firm conclusions to be drawn concerning the value of these kinds of intervention.

With respect to segregation of children with special educational needs, the wisdom of this has been much disputed and the current trend is away from the more expensive option of this type of extra provision. Nevertheless, some children clearly do not function well in large-group settings and benefit from the opportunity to interact with only a small number of other children. These children may find it very difficult to concentrate on academic tasks without special small-scale provision and additional possibilities for receiving individual attention. They may also need help in recognising that events are predictable, particularly if they have been accustomed to highly erratic or inconsistent home conditions. Providing this more controllable environment while the child is still young may prevent the development of low self-esteem and its accompanying self-defeating patterns of behaviour. However, for special units to be effective, they need to have appropriately trained workers with clearly recognisable aims and boundaries (Campion 1992). The more discernible special units are, the more likely it is that they will be able to operate as integrated units within the overall education system. The danger here, of course, is that discernibility may also entail discriminability or stigmatisation.

Because children are sensitive to differences and capable of making discriminative judgements from a very early age, patterns of coping with being different are soon established. Though some of these may be self-enhancing and adaptive, many are not and may achieve at best only a limited or spurious sense of control. Children may, for example, avoid engaging in activities which threaten self-esteem, or deliberately sabotage their chances of success, so depriving themselves of much needed practice and increasing their disadvantage. Such avoidance may be accomplished by engagement in activities such as fidgeting, daydreaming, clowning, social withdrawal or a range of diversionary tactics. If interventions are to be effective, they must harness the child's need for a sense of control and so encourage engagement in self-enhancing rather than self-defeating strategies. A weighty emphasis on a limited range of academic achievements and competition is often not helpful in this respect, and the establishment of practices which foster respect for differences is vital.

Within mainstream education, it has become an increasingly popular practice to include reflective discussion periods within the class curriculum. In these, children are encouraged to contribute their own personal experiences to the information pool shared by the group. Each child's unique contribution is respected. Report-writing practices and the formulation of individual education plans also reflect a recognition of the value of giving positive feedback on an individual basis. Practical schedules such as precision teaching techniques, which enable children to self-monitor, and behavioural momentum programmes, which focus on rewarding desired responses rather than punishing non-desired ones (Davis and Brady 1993), all reflect a move away from unconstructive confrontation or repeated experiences of failure. Such practices are designed to increase children's sense of self-efficacy and control, and so encourage self-confidence and positive self-esteem.

Particularly with younger children, strategies such as those outlined above may be more effective when carried out in conjunction with the child's parents. Many workers have emphasised the importance of including parents in the work of early intervention, both in parent training programmes and through home visiting by specially trained health visitors, teachers or other professional, paraprofessional or non-professional workers (see for example Farrington 1995; Seitz and Provence 1990; Sutton 1995). It also has to be recognised that not all parents will feel comfortable in a teaching role. Some children may find it more difficult to receive instruction from parents than from people with whom they have a less intense emotional relationship and of whom they are less fearful of rejection or criticism. The importance of coordinating resources and of supporting and offering consultancy services to workers has also been recognised, though there is still much debate about how this might best be achieved (Garner 1995).

An extensive, if somewhat patchy, body of literature exists describing and evaluating the huge number of variety of projects which have used primarily epidemiological methods of identification. However, no systematic overall programme for delivery, evaluation or monitoring of these programmes has operated either in the UK or in the US. In addition, few programmes have included adequate control group comparisons or have been free of confounding variables. As there is insufficient space in this chapter, the reader must be referred elsewhere for an exposition of the complex issue of evaluation (see for example Anastasiow and Harel 1993; Carey and McDevitt 1994; Cooper 1995; Meisels and Shonkoff 1990; Mitchell and Brown 1991; Vernon 1993). Less has been written about individual methods of identification and the extent to which these can be used in work with young children.

Individual methods of identification

In theory, with adequate health care screening programmes, it may seen reasonable to expect early identification of problems in childhood to be a straightforward process. In practice, this is not quite the case. While some conditions are relatively easy to identify (see for example those with clear physical manifestations), identification of the first signs of psychological difficulties is always more complicated and often more labour intensive.

So variable is the course of life for each individual that it is almost impossible to predict with any great certainty how any one individual may develop. Nor is it possible to state with absolute confidence that traits such as aggression, nervousness and impulsivity in young children will carry through into adulthood, or to be sure that an easy-going and sociable toddler will develop into a well-adjusted adult. Similarly, so complex is the nature of society that it is rarely possible to isolate and demonstrate definitively the effect of any one independent variable (separation from mother in early childhood, for example) on any one dependent variable (see for example the ability to relate meaningfully to others).

It is now well established that in populations of children apparently subject to similar environmental, social and personal stresses, although a number may show signs of poor social adjustment, a substantial proportion develop into well-adjusted and socially highly competent adults (Rende and Plomin 1993; Werner and Smith 1982). A poor start in life, in other words, does not inevitably mean a poor outlook. Nevertheless, there do appear to be some continuities across the lifespan: 'The process of development is concerned with change and it is not unreasonable to suppose that the pattern will be set in early life ... continuities will occur because children carry with them the results of earlier learning and of earlier structural and functional change' (Rutter 1989, p.26). While the degree or type of change may vary, some aspects of behaviour in early life and infancy appear capable of giving a general indication of the direction of later development.

ATTACHMENT STYLE

An increasingly large body of studies has gathered evidence for an association between security of attachment and generally successful social relationships, that is, with qualities in children such as greater maturity, sociability, self-control, ego strength, compliance, empathy, popularity, leadership and problem-solving skills, and in adults greater likelihood of achieving satisfying intimate relationships; associations between language and cognitive development have also been found (Van Ijzendoorn *et al.* 1995). Insecure attachment, by contrast, has been associated with negative qualities such as hostility, immaturity, social isolation, withdrawal, peer rejection, fearfulness, anxiety and depression.

Still the most commonly used measure of infant attachment style is the Strange Situation Procedure (Ainsworth and Wittig 1969). This is a cumulative stress paradigm, during which, in the presence of a carer, infants (12–18 months) are introduced to a novel environment, then to an unfamiliar adult, and are subsequently observed during two separation and reunion episodes. Infants' exploratory and attachment behaviours are classified into approximately nine attachment patterns. Infants classified under one of the four 'secure' patterns are more able to use carers to cope with the stress of separation and unfamiliarity; those classified under one of the two 'avoidant' patterns tend not to seek the caregiver when distressed and appear to deny or repress their attachment needs; and those classified under one of the two 'ambivalent/resistant' patterns appear unwilling or unable to seek or gain reassurance when stressed and may be both fearful of separation but uncomfortable when in proximity. A further 'disorganised' group of infants seem highly stressed by separation but unable to coordinate their efforts either to seek or reject the caregiver's attention. Carers of securely attached infants are thought to be the most responsive to their infants' emotional state. Carers of avoidantly attached infants are thought to have difficulty responding to their infants' demands, at times being quite hostile or rejecting. Carers of ambivalently attached infants tend to be somewhat unpredictable, alternating contingent with non-contingent responses. It has been suggested that the disorganised attachment pattern may be highly associated with experience of abuse (Main and Solomon 1990).

The importance of attachment style as a measure of social competence in early infancy therefore seems indisputable. Even so, despite the excitement generated by the rapid proliferation of research findings over the last three decades, there still remains much that is controversial about attachment theory and much reason for exercising caution in utilising its constructs in the work of early intervention. Space prohibits a substantial critique, but the main concern relates to the cultural significance of the value system inherent with attachment theory. Although all three major attachment categories reflect organised behaviour with an adaptive capability, only one is positively labelled – that which occurs most commonly in the majority of samples. The implication here is that that type of interactive relationship may be confounded with the social setting in which it arises, that is, that the secure–insecure division (sometimes also erroneously referred to as adaptive–non-adaptive or health–unhealthy) may reflect a bias towards a particular ordering of society which does not value its members equally (Burman 1994). Given a culturally biased theoretical framework, it may be expected that children with 'secure', more normative attachment patterns will fit better into society than children whose attachment patterns reflect predominantly the culture of non-dominant sectors of society.

While there does seem to be some equivocal evidence for an association between insecure attachment patterns and later behaviour problems, particularly in boys (Greenberg *et al.* 1991; Shaw and Vondra 1993), at this stage there is even less evidence that this association is underpinned by causal relationships. Further, it appears that associations between attachment style and behaviour are mediated by a range of variables, the influence of which is still unclear (Greenberg, Speltz and Deklyen 1993), such as temperament (Fox and Calkins 1993; Seifer *et al.* 1996), biological vulnerability, environmental risk (Easterbrooks, Davidson and Chazan 1993), patterns of caregiving and family stability (Lamb *et al.* 1985).

Attachment theory has intuitive appeal to practitioners in many fields. On the surface it appears to offer a framework within which identification of non-optimal social interactive patterns can provide prescriptive rules for appropriate intervention, such as increasing maternal sensitivity to infant cues (Van Den Boom 1989) or attempting to 'correct' the child's or the parent's attributional style (Dodge 1991). However, at this point in the history of attachment theory research, when very little is known about the precise ecological function of so-called 'insecure' patterns of attachment, it is clearly advisable to utilise the infant attachment classification as though its reliability and validity as a diagnostic and prescriptive tool were proven. At this stage, it is perhaps more appropriately used in conjunction with measures which are known to be culture fair.

TEMPERAMENT

Few would dispute that differences in temperament play an important role throughout the lifespan, both in the emergence of problem behaviour and in its maintenance. Nevertheless, research on temperament has always been prone to controversy due to the methodological and definitional problems which it entails, as well as the complex relationship between temperament and environmental influences. While some researchers argue for a biological explanation of individual differences in temperament, others stress environmental influences, and the problem is complicated by the inter-dependence of genetic and environmental factors (Rutter 1987).

Some of the better established measures of infant temperament have been variably and somewhat confusingly described as 'reactivity', 'irritability', 'negative emotionality' or 'difficultness', depending on the measurement tool used. As it is not always clear how these concepts inter-relate, and as they tend to be poor predictors of later behaviour (Carey and McDevitt 1989), there is, as Bates (1986) suggests, much to be gained from identification of specific response patterns within these larger global categories. For example, within the dimension of reactivity, infants may differ in speed and intensity of reaction, affective tone, speed of recovery and 'soothability'. Different patterns of reaction also appear in relation to fear-eliciting and frustration-eliciting stimuli (Fox and Calkins 1993). Further, as reactivity interacts with the capacity to self-regulate emotionally and this, in turn, may be influenced by the nature of social interactions available, not all highly reactive infants will be rated as difficult, irritable or generally negative in mood (Rothbart and Derryberry 1981). This suggests that the nature of the interaction between infant attributes and the demands and expectations of the environment needs to be included for a comprehensive account of infant temperament. This has been described by Chess and Thomas (1984) as 'goodness of fit'.

One dispositional concept which appears to capture this relationship between the child and his or her environment is behavioural inhibition. Behaviourally inhibited children are very sensitive to novel stimulation, tend to avoid unfamiliar people and situations, and respond fearfully when confronted by them. Kagan, Snidman and Arcus (1993), in a longitudinal study of a large sample of healthy Caucasian children, identified approximately 15 per cent of one- and two-year-olds as behaviourally inhibited. By age eight, half of these children continued to show a behavioural style characterised by timidity and shyness, and few were as emotionally spontaneous, fearless or consistently sociable as the 30 per cent of children identified earlier as uninhibited. Kagan et al. (1993) argued that behavioural inhibition may be, at least partly, hereditary and that its emergency may be preceded at four months of age by a combination of high motor activity and frequent crying in response to novel stimulation (approximately 10% of their sample showed this pattern). Other researchers have also made connections between negative emotionality in early infancy, specific patterns of physiological responses to novel stimulation and quite severe later difficulties in coping with social interactions. These difficulties include social isolation and withdrawal, hostility and peer rejection (Rubin and Lollis 1988). These findings suggest that about 7 per cent of babies are unlikely to develop into children who are vulnerable in social situations. The fearful behaviour of these children may often be reinforced by one or both of their parents. Further, repeated exposure to fearful situations will serve only to increase the intensity of response, and de-sensitisation, if it happens at all, is only likely to be achieved by a schedule of very gradual exposure, possibly accompanied by other forms of intervention such as encouragement to re-appraise the threat or to develop other coping strategies. It would appear, therefore, that this temperament indicator may well be a candidate for selection in an early intervention programme.

It is highly probable that, for children with this pattern of behavioural organisation, experiences such as day care will be highly aversive and, unless handled very carefully, may have long-term ill-effects. In a study of the social experience of children cared for by childminders (Barrett 1991), 8.8 per cent of a retrospective sample of 90 children were described by childminders as never having settled. A few of these children were disturbingly withdrawn and passive; others constantly sought reassurance and were anxious and easily provoked to tears; and some were tense and socially distant or negative in interactions with peers. It seems possible that the difficulties experienced by at least some of these children may have been attributable to behavioural inhibition. If so, this pattern of responding is likely to have been in evidence for some time before day care began. It seems unlikely that behaviourally inhibited children will have the capacity to cope with the extreme stress under which day care places them. Neither will their experience of day care inoculate them against the stress of starting school; on the contrary, it could initiate a non-adaptive mode of coping which may render them less competent in the school setting. There is a need for further research in this area. It is possible that some form of early intervention may be required in order to protect this group of children in the day care situation, as well as in other situations which may cause them more stress than other children.

BEHAVIOURAL INDICATORS

Behavioural measures are perhaps the most easily elicited indicators of the need for early intervention. For example, it has been suggested that neurological dysfunction, which can be identified in very young infants, may underlie the pattern of cognitive deficit and impulsivity associated with much problem behaviour in early childhood (Greenberg *et al.* 1993). There is also some evidence that a significant number of children (approximately half), identified by their parents as hard to manage at age two and three, continue to be difficult in childhood (Campbell *et al.* 1986) and, further, that children assessed as having behaviour problems and poor language skills at age three are more likely to present with conduct disorders or other behavioural problems in middle childhood (Stevenson, Richman and Graham 1985).

Despite these continuities, even using well-tested measures, it is not yet possible to predict reliably whether a toddler considered by his or her mother as hard to manage will later be considered behaviourally disordered by his or her teacher. Only in respect of a small percentage of children do teachers' and parents' ratings appear to agree (Stevenson *et al.* 1985). Given this rather modest level of agreement, the usefulness of early intervention based on parents' observations may seem questionable. Yet retrospective studies of aggression in adults and of children diagnosed as having conduct disorders, oppositional disorders, Attention Deficit Disorder (ADD) or Attention Deficit/Hyperactivity Disorder (AD/HD) frequently reveal a history of management problems. Further, children manifesting problem behaviours often come from families which are stressed, disrupted or disorganised. Particularly when parents express concern to professionals about difficulties with management of their young children, intervention of some sort therefore seems warranted. The question becomes what the nature of that intervention may be.

Intervention can take many different forms. Its delivery may be effected by professional workers, paraprofessionals or non-professionals, or a mixture of these. It may be focused on the child, one or more caregivers, the family, a wider social network or a mixture of these. The programme may be organised as formal standardised instructions, negotiated between deliverer and client, or even haphazardly organised. The number of possible permutations is enormous.

In practice, the choice of intervention often depends as much upon the availability of resources as upon the way need is assessed or the preparedness of the parent to make use of any help offered. Too often, the only person aware of difficulties may be the hard-pressed health visitor whose other work demands, inexperience and cultural background may all mitigate against effective intervention. Under more favourable circumstances, the role of the health visitor in facilitating information sharing between parents can be very valuable. If, in turn, health visitors are able to consult or bring in specialists, either other health visitors with specialist knowledge of emotional and behavioural disorders or other specialists (paediatricians, social workers, child psychologists, etc.), this primary health care network may facilitate early recognition of problems. Unfortunately, even in parts of the UK where health visitors' case loads do not preclude this kind of preventive work, women of lower socio-economic status tend to be under-represented among service users. It is often therefore necessary to make special provisions to overcome class barriers which can limit the potential effectiveness of informal intervention at these early stages.

In other ways, too, political concerns can interfere with the management and diagnosis of behaviour problems in the early years. This is particularly noticeable in respect of AD/HD and ADD, where competition between the educational and the medical professions has tended to discourage the use of combined therapies and, in some cases, appears to have led to a refusal to contemplate the possibility that there may be even a limited role for some forms of treatment (Cooper and Ideus 1995). During the pre-school years, especially where a child is cared for at home, it may be particularly difficult to ensure the availability of the kind of professional collaboration necessary for a comprehensive assessment which takes into account both child and environment attributes. Even within the school or nursery setting, this is not always easy (Cocker 1995). Further, it may be extremely difficult for professionals working under considerable financial constraints to inform themselves about the full range of possible treatments. Privatisation and increased competition between services may also militate against the open-minded approach required to ensure that treatment plans are flexible, well monitored and accessible.

Where children's fears are reinforced by parental anxiety, intervention is often more effective if it also involves the parent. Where parents or carers are able to carry out and feel comfortable in the role of supplementary therapist, this approach can work quite well, and the parent, in helping their child, may be able to accept help for themselves. However, particularly where negative patterns of interaction are persistent, it may be more useful in some circumstances to work directly with the parent. It is beyond the scope of this chapter to give more than the briefest outline of the numerous possible interventions which may be beneficial, and there is no reason to believe that any one approach will be more effective than another (Luborsky et al. 1993).

Therapies may vary in many ways, such as in length (time limited versus no time limit), content (focusing on specific or general skills or on personal development issues), delivery (group or individual, directive or non-directive, etc.) and structure.

Programmes focused primarily on teaching specific skills may aim to help parents identify and respond to infant cues which may otherwise be overlooked or responded to inappropriately. Other programmes may teach general practical parenting skills, such as those related to child development, discipline issues or time management. Programmes focused primarily on personal development or emotional issues will often aim to help parents recognise ways in which their own emotional needs or inappropriate negative attributions may affect the care they offer to their children. For example, it has been suggested that among some abusing carers, there may be a tendency to attribute inappropriate negative intentions to infants, such as 'he's screaming at me because he hates me', 'he's refusing to eat to wind me up', 'he's just trying to show me up'. Using a cognitive behaviour modification approach, these negative attributions may be systematically examined and replaced with more age-appropriate and less incriminating responses, such as 'he's screaming because he's the sort of baby who needs a lot of reassurance. This is no reflection on my ability to care for him.' Alternatively, a psychodynamically oriented approach may help carers to recognise and address their own emotional needs and, by differentiating more clearly between these and the needs of their children, free them to respond more appropriately. Many programmes (such as Newpin, mentioned earlier) will offer a more eclectic approach designed to meet each carer's needs on a more individual basis.

In this chapter it has only been possible to present a very broad overview of early intervention work with vulnerable children. It is hoped, however, that the reader will have gained some impression of the enormous variety of potential approaches available and of the tremendous range of individual situations and social contexts within which work may take place. It is also hoped that they will have gained some insights into the many controversial and exciting issues which are involved in the work of early intervention and that they will be inspired to continue to explore ways in which the most vulnerable children in any society may be helped to achieve as much as possible of their potential.

CHAPTER 10

Coping with Children with Emotional and Behavioural Difficulties in the Primary Classroom

Diane Montgomery

Introduction

Children who are distressed for whatever reason may 'act out' their distress and perhaps become fidgety, noisy, attention seeking or disruptive; they may lie, steal and bully other children or they may become withdrawn, passive, dreamy and isolated, disappearing into the background, hardly noticed as long as they produce a little work now and again. When such behaviour shows a persistent pattern across a range of subjects and activities, and often with a range of teachers, then it is regarded as an emotional and behavioural difficulty.

The tendency to 'act out' or externalise problems is said to result from believing that the source of reinforcement is beyond control due to some external factor such as chance. If such an external locus of control (Rotter 1954) is held, there is little incentive to invest personal effort to strive for success. A common consequence of an external locus of control is poor social skills and poor adaptive behaviour (Gresham, Elliott and Black 1987; Knight 1992).

Boys tend to act out their problems more than girls (Rutter, Tizard and Whitmore 1970). If they fail to understand or cope with classroom work, they tend more often to regard it as the teacher's fault, not theirs, whereas girls tend to feel the reverse (Good and Brophy 1985). Some pupils may regard their failure as a depressing consequence of their low ability, and their self-esteem and motivation to work are diminished (Cooper 1984). The more difficult and disruptive the behaviour, the lower the sense of self-esteem has been found to be (Wilson and Evans 1980).

The tendency has, in the past, been to regard the child as 'owning the problem', but more recently the strategy has been to redirect attention to the disturbing or challenging behaviour (Galloway and Goodwin 1987) and to consider the problem from an ecological perspective (Mittler 1990). In this model the interaction of a range of factors contributes to, and causes, problems. This means that an ecosystemic approach to intervention (Molnar and Lindquist 1989) is required. According to Cooper and Upton (1991, p.23), the approach combines the following elements:

- a management function – it aims to control and change behaviour

- a developmental function – it emphasises building cooperative relationships

- a reflexive function – it depends upon self-scrutiny by teachers.

Associated with this has been a move towards positive approaches to discipline (Cheeseman and Watts 1985; Chisholm *et al.* 1986; Luton *et al.* 1991; Wheldall and Merritt 1984). The Elton Report (1989), a major survey of discipline in schools, in fact found that 'punitive regimes are associated with worse rather than better standards of behaviour' (S 4.47).

Types of behavioural difficulties which teachers have to manage

The most difficult pupils can be calm and sensible in a tutorial session, separate from the class. In a small group they can become a bit of a nuisance and produce little work, but in a class of 30 they can cause disruption. Coping with difficult or 'challenging' behaviour in class can be a continual problem for teachers. Croll and Moses (1985) found that in any primary classroom there was usually one pupil likely to prove disruptive, another three who would be so if unfavourable conditions arose and seven who might occasionally be disruptive.

There is a continuum of overt misbehaviour, from mild attention seeking at one end to major upheaval and disruption at the other. According to the Department of Education and Science (1979) and the Elton Report (1989), disruptive behaviour is that which interferes with the learning and opportunities of other pupils and places undue stress upon the teacher. However, it is not usually that scale of problem with which the teacher has to deal. It is instead the continuous chattering when pupils should be working which presents them with a challenge and which they find most wearing (Elton Report 1989). A common description of such nuisance or attention-seeking behaviours is:

> They fidget, tap rulers, pencils or feet, whistle or sing ostentatiously, swing on chairs tipped dangerously backwards, roam around the room, crawl about under desks, snatch others' books and pencils, and most irritating of all, talk continuously. Sometimes they just engage in low muttering, at other times they call out answers to the teacher's questions and shout abuse across the room, interrupting their own and others' work. (Section 4.47)

It is little wonder that teachers become tired and irritable with the sheer effort of dealing with this continual harassment. In such a climate, it is difficult to pursue curriculum goals in a steady and uninterrupted way. A teacher who ignores misbehaviour will find that before long it has escalated to major proportions, with most of the class inattentive and several who have become disruptive (Scott MacDonald 1971).

According to Mongon and Hart (1989), challenging behaviour is just the visible tip of a problem of disaffection which is widespread in the school population and becomes even worse in the secondary school. As such, it cannot be effectively tackled in isolation from a systematic programme of school improvement. Although the Elton Report was a response to what was seen as a major increase in behaviour problems in schools as reported by the media, the surveys showed that only two per cent of 3600 teachers reported that they had been the target of physical aggression at some time. Deliberate attacks upon teachers were rare. It is, however, aggressive behaviour which worries teachers most and was according to Gross (1993), the most common reason for suspension and referral for special provision. Other surveys have shown that whilst problems have increased in some schools in some areas, other schools remain the same with few difficulties and in yet others difficulties have decreased (Farringdon 1994).

It is perhaps not so surprising that pupils will occasionally tend to make a nuisance of themselves when we consider their circumstances. It is a most unnatural thing to expect a group of 30 or more lively youngsters to be confined in a classroom for a whole day together for weeks on end and also to expect them to remain seated and quietly attentive. Any novelty effect will soon wear off. If the tasks they are asked to do are boring and mundane, presented in a vague or unstimulating manner, exact little mental challenge and do not seem relevant, it is clear that the children will protest in the only way they can by chattering and being a nuisance as they try to entertain themselves in other ways. It is, however, very distressing to a well-prepared teacher with a keen interest in the subject to find a noisy and inattentive class after ten minutes of best effort.

Even more serious in the long term are those who are withdrawn, passive and perhaps depressed (Cashdan 1976). Their problems, often deep seated and emotional, may never be addressed in school, only to emerge later in a more serious form (Kraupl-Taylor 1966).

Some possible origins of behavioural difficulties

Perhaps a helpful way of thinking about this is to consider the continuum of behavioural difficulties as being beset along its length by a range of 'at risk' factors which will interact to make some pupils become less attentive and gradually switch off or become negative. Several strategies may thus be needed to recover this situation. Even two teachers looking at the same behaviour may regard it quite differently. If a child shouts out answers in class, one teacher may see this as misbehaviour, which, if repeated after a warning, must be punished. However, another may treat it as high spirits which need to be calmed. The consequences of punishment can have a negative effect on the child, leading to protestations, negativism and resentment, whereas calming acts as a positive recognition of the child's energy and enthusiasm, and gives a second chance to produce a considered response. Behaviour problems are very much a matter of social perception and this affects how we deal with them.

Reframing

> To change the conceptual/emotional setting or viewpoint in relation to which situation is experienced and to place it in another frame which fits the 'facts' of the same concrete situation equally as well or even better, and thereby changes its entire meaning. (Watzlawick, Weakland and Fisch 1974, p.75)

Reframing has recently come back into prominence and been given a wider applicability. Its purpose is to help teachers to look at a behaviour in a new light. Reframing can enable them to view behaviour problems in a more positive manner and can open up a wider range of coping strategies. Similarly, reframing by pupils in a bullying situation may help the bully see his or her actions from the victim's point of view and engender empathy, enabling it to stop (Knox 1992).

Social 'at risk' factors which may predispose towards problems

'At risk' factors may reside within the social background of an individual child so that, for example, home discipline is too severe or inconsistent, creating a resistance to normal control techniques which have at their core a respect for persons and a willingness to listen to others (Robins 1966). The child may have adopted models which are deviant and anti-school or belong to a subculture which is disaffected from school and society, seeking comfort and esteem only from its own peers and through the promotion of its own anti-authority goals (Jenkins 1966). Another social setting may be over-indulgent and pander to the child's every whim, making it difficult for him or her to treat other children as equals. Family relationships themselves might be disturbed and stressful, with marital discord and violent quarrelling creating great distress amongst the children (Rutter 1975). Some children might feel that others in the family are more preferred and respected than they are, or there may be a new baby which is demanding the parents' time, contributing to the feeling of rejection in the older siblings. All these may predispose an individual to become attention seeking or a nuisance in class. If this is coupled with an awkward temperament or a mild difficulty, even temporary, in learning, then that child can be set on a career in misbehaviour and disruption as the factors multiply, interact and intensify some otherwise trivial incident.

Learning difficulties as 'at risk' factors

Learning difficulties of a mild to moderate nature which prevent the child 'catching on' when others do, or from working quite as quickly and learning as fast as other children, can lead to feelings of failure and fear of the learning situation. There may be a progressive withdrawal from any learning experience with a challenge to it and sometimes a refusal to participate in learning at all (Holt 1984; Stott 1981). This can also be seen in children with learning disabilities such as dyslexia (specific learning difficulties in reading and spelling). Such children may use a range of strategies to conceal their difficulties and so defend their self-esteem. These include:

- withdrawal
- avoidance

- evasion

- distraction

- digression

- disruption

- clowning

- daydreaming

- negativism

- absenteeism

- cheating.

Similar behaviour may be observed in children with handwriting coordination difficulties, where no matter how hard they try they cannot produce a neat print. Continual pressure to copy and write neatly will cause increasing distress and frustration, leading to disaffection from school as a hostile learning environment (Cotterell 1985; Myklebust 1973). Much distress of this sort can be alleviated by teaching a fully joined hand from the very first and linking it to spelling (Montgomery 1990; Morse 1991). Reading and spelling problems themselves can be identified in the first few months in school (Bradley and Bryant 1985; Montgomery 1990, 1997a), and can be addressed by using phonological, linguistic and cognitive strategies built into any literacy programme (Goswami 1994; Hickey 1977; Montgomery 1997a, b).

Schooling as an 'at risk' factor

Schools and the schooling process itself seem to be able to create powerful 'at risk' factors. Kellmer Pringle (1973) linked violent and disruptive behaviour with a curriculum which placed too little emphasis on individual non-academic achievement and too much on competition. According to Rutter *et al.* (1979) and Hargreaves (1984), such schools gave an over-emphasis to academic goals and neglected childrens' personal needs, thus disposing more children to fail and become a 'problem' in the school's eyes. These differences, however, could not be attributed to the catchment areas which the schools served (Galloway and Goodwin 1987); it depended more upon the school they happened to be attending rather than the pupils themselves or their families. Mongon and Hart (1989) found that many pupils lived in a state of fear, despite the good and kindly intentions of their teachers, and that too many schools exerted a coercive rather than a therapeutic educational influence. This is why it is so important for the ethos of the school and the classroom climate to be positive, constructive and supportive. In this way the most vulnerable children will be protected and classroom work can proceed in a regular and orderly way.

Negative disciplining techniques can be a major contribution to disruption (Scott MacDonald 1971). Negative sanctions which teachers use are:

- withholding praise and support
- using desists
- stopping the flow of nuisance behaviour by reprimand
- nagging and crossly stopping the behaviour
- watching and intervening on every occasion possible
- withholding stars or 'treats'
- writing pupil's name on board
- sending to another part of the room on own
- sending to another room
- sending to the head or deputy
- keeping in to complete work
- giving additional or repeat work
- putting on report
- reporting to parents
- putting in detention
- confiscations on a temporary basis.

These are negative responses to the pupil's behaviour. Other children and the attention seeker can soon grow used to them, so that the more the sanctions are used the less effective they become. Keeping children in after school or in detention and sending them out of the room may have dangerous or legal consequences and should be avoided.

Some emotional difficulties creating 'at risk' factors
Whilst it can be seen that difficult social, school and learning circumstances can induce anxiety and distress and lead to behaviour problems, it is also

possible that some children are particularly vulnerable. They are likely to react more strongly and suffer greater distress than siblings and peers, and thus they can become ill. Others may already have inherited a vulnerability to emotional illness and it takes only a trigger experience to plunge them into a phobic, depressive or psychosomatic response, or into obsessional compulsive rituals which prevent them functioning in school or society. Child abuse frequently leads to depressive symptoms even in the youngest of children, making them sad and weepy, often prone to tantrums, overt inappropriate sexuality and aggression (Kempe and Kempe 1984). Children who have been violently rejected in hostility by their parents are particularly sad cases and deeply troubled, acting out their suffering in violence and aggression on peers, school and society at large (Jenkins 1966). Their problems are deep seated and they need specialist psychiatric help (Herbert 1985; Rutter 1975). If they do not act out their problems but become withdrawn, then their suffering may be missed and only in later life might they develop severe psychiatric problems which may by then be more difficult to treat (Oppe 1979).

If children do show signs of emotional distress and illness then specialist help and support should be summoned immediately. The teacher can support the therapeutic programme by ensuring that the educational ethos is calm, secure and safe, positive and supportive. When the distress manifests itself, it is important that the behaviour is understood, the emotions accepted and the pupil affirmed (Bowers and Wells 1988). This *in extremis* may even involve permitting the pupil to sit under the teacher's desk in the smallest, safest place to be found whilst he or she grapples with the phobia. In one case, encouraging two such pupils, one phobic and one depressed and almost continually crying, to work together and giving access to a small office where they could withdraw to work and play when needed, helped them to help each other and kept them both in school.

Observing and targeting problem behaviours

It is extremely important to identify precisely which behaviour needs to be changed and what has precipitated it. This is often identified as the ABC of intervention that is, antecedents – behaviours – consequences. It is also important to describe the behaviour seen rather than one's inferences about it. For example, 'Sue hit Jamie' is a factual statement, whereas 'Sue is aggressive' is an inference, not necessarily true and certainly not a fact. When a pupil is being particularly problematic, it is helpful to write down several observations of the problem behaviour as follows:

> James stood up, looked around the room, saw me watching him, sat down, picked up a piece of paper, turned round in his chair and then stood up and walked slowly to the sand tray. He dribbled sand through his fingers on to the floor, watched Emma filling pots and making pies. Moved over to the large boxes, saw empty trike, climbed on to it. Pedalled it round room and outside.

This small segment shows nothing unusual on its own but when it is repeated day in and day out, and is precipitated each time by any activity which requires James to sit down and try to write his name and his news or read, then it has a significance. James's wandering behaviour is of concern. It enables him to avoid sitting down at a desk and preparing to read or write. As he wanders, so he can disturb and annoy other children working. However, the wandering behaviour of itself is clearly not the problem: James most likely has a handwriting coordination problem and difficulties with reading and spelling which need to be addressed directly through an assessment through teaching strategy (Montgomery 1997a). We might also decide to change his behaviour by giving him praise and support every time he sits at his desk and looks at a piece of paper or a book, trying to extend his on-seat time each day rather than catching him out of his seat and remonstrating with him. Systematic classroom observation is a powerful tool for teachers in the improvement of classroom performance (Bailey 1991; Montgomery 1985).

Ecosystemic management functions: controlling and changing behaviour

Changing the learning climate and changing the behaviour using CBG

CBG stands for 'catch them being good'. There is a considerable amount of research which shows that teachers spend most of their time attending to pupils when they are 'off target', not working and being disruptive (Kounin 1970; Scott MacDonald 1971; Wheldall and Merritt 1986). When they are working and being constructive they receive little positive support and encouragement, the teacher accepting their good behaviour without question.

Pupils who receive little attention, support and approval at home will tend to seek it at school from teachers or, failing that, from peers. If they cannot gain this attention and recognition through their work, they will find other means to satisfy their needs.

The strategy of CBG is one which every teacher thinks they use. However, when they are recorded, the number of desist and negative unsupportive behaviours and comments outweigh the positive and supportive ones. The less successful the teacher, the fewer the positive responses; failing teachers give none (Scott MacDonald 1971).

The CBG strategy requires that:

- The teacher positively reinforces any pupil's correct responses with nods and smiles, paraphrasing their correct responses and statements, with 'Yes, good', 'Well done'. Incorrect responses should not be negated but the pupil should be encouraged to have another try.

- The response should be, 'Yes, nearly' and 'Yes, and what else …?', 'Good so far, can anyone help [him or her] out?' and so on.

- It is very important to remember to CBG behaviour as well as answers to questions. This needs to be done more discreetly. It consists of going to children when they are on task and working, and making quiet supportive statements and comments, not expecting them automatically to settle down to work.

- When pupils are working and it is not a good idea to interrupt them at that moment, simply standing near them and looking at their work and smiling is very supportive. Detailed looking at work as they are doing it and moving on shows them you are interested in it and them. They know or feel that you will intervene if there is a problem, even if you yourself are just looking.

- CBG makes pupils feel that you are actively involved with them and the work they are doing and that you consider it important to give it and them your attention. If a teacher sits at the front and marks the books of another class it demonstrates an 'us versus them' attitude, with tasks handed down to the lower orders without them having any intrinsic worth. Even if the teacher is marking that class's work and is calling individuals up, it is far better to be out and around the room doing the marking.

At its simplest, CBG is one form of behaviour modification technique in which the teacher positively reinforces desirable behaviours emitted by the child, gradually shaping them towards desirable ends determined by the teacher without the child being aware of the process or the goal (Blackham and Silberman 1971).

In the original researches, the teachers were told to ignore any undesirable behaviour and to support only those directed towards the targets. This of course has deleterious effects on the other children who see the target child getting away with misbehaviour, and so the behaviour of the whole class can deteriorate. To avoid this situation, it may be necessary to tell the child to stop talking, sit down, open their book and start reading, but then *immediately* the child does this, give attention, support and encouragement for the on-task behaviour. Children learn vicariously how to behave in classrooms as much from what happens to other children as from what happens to them, and thus it is important to stop unwanted behaviours at the outset. Where a child is very disturbed it may be possible within these parameters to ignore a significant proportion of the unwanted behaviour, if the other children identify him or her as a special case. In some circumstances, it may be necessary to seek the support of the rest of the children in helping an individual to gain mastery over unwanted behaviour.

General classroom management strategies: the three Ms

The three Ms represents a series of tactics which effective teachers can use to gain and maintain pupils' attention whatever teaching method or style they subsequently use. When teachers with classroom management disciplining problems were taught to use these strategies in observation and feedback sessions, they became more effective teachers (Montgomery 1984, 1989).

PHASE 1: MANAGEMENT

The teacher makes an *attention-gaining noise* such as 'Right!', 'OK class 3', 'Good morning, everybody', 'Uhummm!' or bangs the door or desk, claps hands. Some teachers simply wait quietly until the noise subsides as the pupils notice he or she is present. Next, the teacher gives a *short verbal instruction* such as 'Everybody sit down', 'Get out your English folders', 'Come and sit on the mat' or 'Sit down and listen carefully'. At this point 20 of the pupils will do as requested and 10 will not. The effective teacher pauses, looks round, spots those who are not doing as requested and quietly *names* these pupils and individually instructs them to stop what they are doing and to listen. This is usually quite sufficient if a *check back* look is given to bring the whole class to attention. The mistake that the ineffective teacher makes is to begin to shout 'Be quiet' and 'Sit down', as a general instruction to all pupils. The raising of the teacher's voice and the general command to those who are already behaving as requested begins to engender hostility in them. Some who were attending now begin to chat, causing the instruction to be repeated louder and thus contributing to the general level of classroom noise. This transmits the information that the teacher is not quite in control and can surreptitiously be disobeyed by an even larger group. Thus in a short period of time, the class has become out of control. The teacher at this point usually becomes very exasperated and red in the face and shouts the class into submission. These 'shock tactics' become less and less effective the more they are used, and it takes a considerable amount of time and effort to reconstruct this teacher's behaviour to make it effective, allowing the opportunity actually to teach something (Montgomery and Hadfield 1989, 1990). Many give up the struggle and 'teach' over the noise, so that the level of attention and achievement of all pupils are lowered.

The effective teacher, having gained the pupils' attention and silence, will immediately launch into the introduction to the session or begin to read the story. During the teacher's talk or story it is necessary for a range of attention gaining and maintaining tactics to be employed. For example:

- pausing in exposition to look at a pupil who is talking until she or he stops
- walking to a pupil and gently removing a tapping pencil or note
- asking the talking or inattentive pupil a question
- placing a calming hand on head or shoulder
- repeating the phrase just given
- inserting 'and Goldilocks said to the three bears!' in the middle of the story, looking hard at the miscreant
- using hand signal or finger on lips cue to quieten
- using 'stink look'.

The main point about this phase of the lesson is that the material and mode of delivery should be reconsidered if a lot of controlling techniques need to be used.

PHASE 2: MONITORING

As soon as there is a change of activity, from pupils listening to getting out books and writing, or going back to places to work, disruption can and does arise. The monitoring strategy needs to be brief, perhaps lasting no more than 30 seconds. As soon as the pupils are at their places, the teacher should move quickly round the room to each group or table and quietly settle them down to work. It is essential not to linger to give detailed explanations at this point, but to say that you will come back shortly to help. Go to the noisiest group first but make sure all are visited. If there is not a lot of space to move around, then a vantage point should be selected and monitoring directed from there by calming gestures and quiet naming.

In addition to activity change, monitoring should be used when pupils are engaged with tasks and the noise level and attention seem to be slipping. This can be noted at any time by the well-attuned ear, and usually only requires that the teacher look up and round the room to the talker. A pointed look or very quiet naming may well be all that is required. The important thing is not to nag and be noisy about criticism. Having told a pupil to be quiet, look up and check back on him or her within three to five seconds.

PHASE 3: MAINTENANCE

Once the pupils have been settled to the task by the monitoring techniques, it is advisable for the teacher to move around the class to each individual to find out how the work is progressing. In the maintenance period, all the requests and queries of individuals can be dealt with. During a lesson period or period of study within a curriculum area, each pupil should expect to receive some form of individual constructive and developmental comment on the work. This has been called *positive cognitive intervention* (Montgomery 1984, 1994, 1996). In this steady move around the room, the teacher should look at the pupil's work with them and offer developmental advice which makes a positive statement about progress. They should then offer ideas and suggestions for extension, or through constructive questioning help the pupils see how to make the work better or achieve the goals they have set themselves. When the work has been completed, there should again be written or spoken comments as appropriate and further ideas and suggestions: 'Jason, I enjoyed your story very much. The beginning section was very good, it set the murky scene very well. I think you should look at some of Roald Dahl's characters to help in writing about your people. If you look up one or two I will show you what I mean'. Or, 'Chrissy, the colours in your picture are beautiful. Next time I want you to explore the effect when you only use three'.

During the maintenance period the noise will fluctuate. As soon as the level goes above 'interested work' or an individual's voice is clearly audible and does not stop after a few moments, a quick monitoring session should ensue. This may only need to be the raising of the teacher's head to look in the direction of the noise to cue the pupil to silence, or it may again involve a 'stink look' and quiet naming. If this does not suffice then it may be necessary to go over and settle the problem. A noisy pupil who continually causes the teacher to go and attend to him or her needs further consideration, for this is an attentional problem which is gaining illegitimate satisfaction, which will in itself maintain the unwanted behaviour. At this point it may become necessary to institute some behavioural modification procedures to cause the pupil to spend more time on their task in their seat. There may well be a learning difficulty underlying this behaviour which needs direct and individual teaching to be overcome. In addition, the lesson/session plan and pedagogy need to be reviewed to assess whether these can contribute to restoring general good classroom behaviour.

Some individual behaviour management strategies

Behaviour modification strategies are most frequently advised upon by the School Psychological Services, which may also offer training courses to help the management of particularly difficult, often disruptive, pupils. BATPACK courses (Wheldall and Merritt 1984, 1985) and their books on positive approaches to teaching are all based on the principles of reinforcement established by Skinner (1954) in his studies of operant conditioning, and most books on classroom management and managing difficult behaviour include this (Cheeseman and Watts 1985; Chisholm *et al.* 1986; Luton *et al.* 1991). The pupil emits unwanted responses which the teacher learns to ignore, instead reinforcing the closest opposite and desirable response. By a process of continuous positive reinforcement, the behaviour is gradually shaped towards more desirable ends. Elements of all of this have been described in the foregoing, as well as some of the problems which can result if it is not used well. The difference in the case of a disruptive pupil is that close observation and identification of the target behaviour are needed, together with the drawing up of a reinforcement schedule and school behaviour management plan. Even so, it is impossible to reinforce each occurrence of the desirable behaviour, and it may be better to put the pupil in a much smaller class – a group of 8–12 – with a specially trained teacher whilst the main part of the programme is being implemented. Rogers (1994a) suggests withdrawing disruptives for regular 20 minute sessions of social skills and behaviour management training from trained teachers.

Other colleagues, including playground and canteen helpers, need to be made aware of the main elements of the 'therapy' if all the work in the classroom is not to be undone. Many of the studies in the USA used positive reinforcements which not only included giving merit points for good behaviour, but also enabled them to be saved up to spend time on hobbies, games or to buy sweets, paints and even make-up. As a rule, it was found that when the novelty had worn off the pupil decided not to work for more credits. This was supported by the work of Deci and Ryan (1983) and Ryan, Connell and Deci (1985), who found that extrinsic rewards such as these actually caused a decline in motivation over time, whereas intrinsic motivation was raised by a positive, supportive learning environment. It is thus the teacher who is the real source of motivation, and it is the teacher's smile and genuine support and praise which is the all-pervading and prime motivator. Young children love to earn stars and merit points, but it is mainly because they are the tangible expression of the teacher's appreciation that they are so effective.

Another strategy the teacher may use is *modelling* (Blackham and Silberman 1971). At its simplest level, this involves the teacher saying such things as 'Very well done, the Green table is ready', 'Show me who is ready', 'Michael was really listening, so he is doing it well', 'Sharon has a good idea, watch how she does it', 'I like the way Gary helped him', and so on. Other children learn vicariously by watching the reinforced model (Bandura and Walters 1966). In a more sophisticated version, the model is reinforced and then the pupil watching is reinforced for any approximation towards the good behaviour of the model. It is important to select a range of different models so that one child does not become a 'star' for the others to dislike and even bully.

Time out (Blackham and Silberman 1971) is another recommended strategy. Where pupils have become overexcited or distressed, are upset or having a tantrum, a 'time out' corner, cushion or seat can be very useful. Pupils can take themselves there to have 30 seconds' peace and quiet to recover, or they can be sent there knowing no other pupil must look at them or speak to them until they come out, or it is agreed that they can come out now they are calm. It is not advisable to send them out of the classroom, for they may run away and be involved in an incident outside. If a pupil is unmanageable, it is wisest to send another responsible child to the head or deputy to summon help.

Disruption on this scale is serious and, of course, the parents would need to be consulted about underlying difficulties and joint efforts to help the child. For a period of time it may be essential to draw up a *behaviour contract* with the pupil and parents, stating attainable goals (Rogers 1994a) and the ways in which the pupil will behave; this will be signed by all the parties. The class teacher and any specialist teachers will sign a record at the end of each session or write a comment on the pupil's conduct. At the end of the day, the record is inspected by the head or deputy and commented upon. This should only need to be kept up for two or three weeks and then the pupil should be officially signed off for good behaviour and the record filed. Such periods can give an opportunity for attitude change and a detailed review of the child's needs, and may be enough to deal with the problem. The contract may have to be redrawn at a later stage as some new factor arises. It is very often found that the counselling relationship which is established between the pupil and the person to whom the daily report is made develops strongly enough to make the pupil want to work for the good opinion of that person. They may seriously try to iron out what before may have seemed to be insuperable difficulties.

Coping with confrontations and disruption

These are most often explosive episodes involving an individual pupil and teacher or pairs of pupils in a fight. There may have been little provocation for the outburst or it may be the end of an episode of noisy disruption culminating in verbal abuse which the teacher in desperation seeks to stem. The teacher may already have tried calming strategies and may have asked the pupil to stop the tirade or to sit still and get on with his or her work. The pupil has thrown down the gauntlet and challenged the teacher verbally or physically. The teacher has a range of options to select from: summon help if necessary; offer choices (Rogers 1994a,b); or recover the situation (Montgomery 1989). This can be done by *deflecting* the confrontation, putting it on *hold* (giving time for things to cool down and for brains to be engaged), *normalising* (continuing with the lesson as though nothing has happened and supporting the work effort) and keeping the pupil behind at the end of the lesson for *counselling.*

The ecosystemic developmental function

The Behavioural Support Teacher (BHT)

In some schools a BHT or a coordinator may be responsible for developing team approaches to disruption within an education authority. It may be more economical to appoint BHTs than to establish units for children with emotional and behavioural difficulties even though these may be attached to schools. The evidence is not yet available. The most important activities of the BHT, as recorded by Rennie (1993, p.9) are:

- withdrawing 'problem' children
- counselling them
- supporting other staff in their classes
- devising behaviour modification programmes
- supporting individual children
- advising other staff on class management.

It can be seen once again that some training in counselling is an important requirement, and in particular the Rogerian approach is favoured (Hall and Hall 1988; Knox 1992; Rogers 1980) and offers opportunities for reframing and personal insight.

Assertive discipline

Assertive discipline was developed by Lee and Marlene Cantor in the USA in 1976. It is a method of disciplining based on behaviour modification. It consists of a highly structured and administered system of rewards and punishments. Rewards may be stars, merit marks, play time, and even tangible rewards such as prizes and gifts earned by the collection of tokens or merit points. Gifts are less popular in this country than in the USA. The punishments or consequences are at five levels of increasing severity: having one's name put on the board; being kept in for five minutes at playtime; isolation for a short period; reporting to the head; informing parents. At the first infringement a warning is given. Having one's name put on the board five times leads inevitably to the next stage of punishment, and the penalties are non-negotiable. This method can ensure a quiet, calming discipline. Cantor and Cantor (1991) insists that no child's name should be put on the board or the list until two others have been praised. The system is graded according to individual schools' policies and the staff team must agree to implement it systematically. Teachers learn to establish no more than five clear rules; for example: follow instructions the first time they are given; put your hands up to answer questions; keep the noise level low; keep your hands, feet and objects to yourself; do not talk whilst the teacher or other pupils are talking.

Behaviour Management Products Ltd was set up in the UK in 1991 to carry out assertive discipline training. It claims that over 2000 schools are now using the system. Makins (1991) reported that schools adopting the system were able to see a difference within a day. However, all staff need to commit themselves to the system and it breaks down when they do not. Older pupils are less responsive to it and often find peer esteem in gaining the maximum 'score', thereby defeating the objective.

Developing social and communication skills

It has already been noted that pupils with emotional and behavioural difficulties often lack these skills, so that programmes of learning which incorporate skills development, mediation and confrontation management can be particularly helpful (Bowers and Wells 1988; Curry and Bromfield 1994). Not all cooperative learning, however, is truly cooperative (Galton, Simon and Croll 1980; Bennett 1986), and so the materials and methods need to be carefully researched. Some useful examples may be found in Rawlings's (1996) *Ways and Means Today*. This includes work on 'circle time', conflict management, collaboration and mediation, all useful techniques in coping with emotional and behavioural difficulties and developing social and communication skills.

Developing personal controls and keeping the team informed and involved

A not infrequent experience is of emotionally disturbed children such as Lisa, who at five years of age would scream and scream and bang the chairs and tables and throw things about whenever the teacher tried to call the class together on the mat for a story or teaching input. She made such a noise that the other children were frightened and could not hear what the teacher said. We agreed that the teacher would tell Lisa that she would not be given the teacher's attention in these episodes, but she would get it when she came and sat down and listened. The teacher explained to the other children what would happen and that they would all work together in this way to help Lisa regain her place in the class and that it would be difficult for a little while.

The strategy was also explained to colleagues and agreed with the head. There would be no intervention except to stop the child harming herself or others. The story session began. Lisa sat at a distance quietly, then opened the music cupboard, got out the drum and chime bars, and banged and screamed for a full 15 minutes. She was given no response, the teacher quietly keeping the others on the mat. Suddenly Lisa put down the instruments and said 'Oh you!', and then went and sat on the mat with the others. The story was continued and she was welcomed with a smile and a cuddle.

Parents as partners and team members

Parents should wherever possible be regarded as part of the discipline management team. Most will agree to support the school's strategy at home, although some may need help to change their own disciplining techniques or extend the quality time they spend with their child. The BHT may be able to offer this counselling and support as a form of family therapy (de Shazer 1985; Hoffman 1981).

Ecosystemics and reflexive teaching

These depend upon self-scrutiny by teachers and once again reframing can be a powerful strategy.

There are a range of ways in which this can be promoted. These include through the processes of reflection on professional issues which arise from peer discussion, attendance at in-service courses, reading about and viewing practice issues, and appraisal and review.

Observation and recording of professional activities

Looking again at the organisation of a room, considering the space for movement around it and changing the positions from which to teach can all contribute to easier classroom management (Montgomery 1989). Seating in rows instead of groups fits some learning activities better (Hastings 1995).

Tactical lesson planning

This involves focusing directly upon what the pupils are doing at any point and is a major support to learning and teaching. A tactical plan simply means that each phase of the lesson has been constructed and timed to create an activity change for the pupils, from listening, to writing, to reading, to speaking, to practical activity, to writing (recording), to speaking (reporting) and so on. Changing the tactics can cause marked changes in pupils' responses, which can feed into the reflective process.

Critical thinking about teaching and learning

It will be found that a move from more didactic methods towards cognitive process pedagogies or teaching methods which facilitate a greater amount of learning will also reduce the amount of time available for misbehaviour and inattention. These methods in themselves induce intrinsic motivation, so that the pupils want to work rather than have to be made to. A brief outline of these methods will be found in Chapter 11. Where these methods have been used, teachers found that they themselves began to rethink their practices (Fisher 1990; Montgomery 1994).

Summary

The problems which arise when coping with children with emotional and behavioural difficulties in classrooms face all teachers at some time. The methods required are not punitive and harsh, but are calming, firm, fair, supportive and constructive. Too often pupils with such difficulties have been exposed to an excess of poor and inconsistent disciplining techniques and to inappropriate models for behaviour in environments in which their sense of self-worth has been diminished.

An ecological model of the difficulties has been used as the context for the discussion and an ecosystemic approach to intervention has been outlined.

The role of learning difficulties and disaffection from schooling has been stressed. Classroom management practices which gain and maintain control have been described, followed by individual and team behaviour management procedures which can help teachers to cope.

CHAPTER II

Supporting 'Able Misfits' in the Primary Classroom

Diane Montgomery

Introduction

It is more than 25 years since Mia Kellmer-Pringle, former Director of the National Children's Bureau, first wrote about children she called 'able misfits'. She put the problems of quite a large group of individuals on the agenda of concerned professionals for the first time. She indicated that these concerns about the able were legitimate and that they might be suffering, discriminated against and failing in the school system, a system which at that time was more flexible than the current one. It was generally thought then, and even now, that ability was a gift which would enable 'bright' children to succeed against all odds, whatever their circumstances. How wrong this view was.

Kellmer-Pringle's researches showed that able under-achievers as a group showed a characteristic profile:

- a sense of inadequacy and limited ambition
- a dislike of schoolwork and book learning
- poor work habits
- unsatisfactory relationships with peers
- a high incidence of emotional difficulties.

Many people working with schools will have met a number of such children whose early promise remains unfulfilled; those who will not work and those whose emotional difficulties come between them and success. It is often difficult to determine whether their emotional problems lead to their failure and poor relationships or arise directly because of them. Distressing family circumstances can, of course, give rise to anxiety in most children which they may 'act out' in the classroom. Such children are regarded as pupils with 'challenging' behaviour. They may become alienated from school, or they may become passive and withdrawn and so of concern.

There are also children who are highly intelligent but who fail to learn to read and spell, an extremely handicapping condition. To some extent this defies common understanding, for people will wonder how a child can be termed 'clever' if he or she cannot do what even slower learners learn to do and some bright children can do at the age of three, self-taught. These children also fit into the group of 'able misfits', and of course there are others. The purpose of this chapter is to help the identification of these different patterns of under-functioning and lower attainment, and to suggest what might be done to recover the situation.

As a first step it must be firmly established that when we speak of the able, the talented and the gifted, clever or bright children, there are far more of them than most people think. In any classroom of mixed-ability pupils, there will be at least five who are able; one may be gifted and several will be talented. Fifty per cent of them or more might have untapped gifts and talents. Identifying under-functioning cannot, of course, be achieved in a classroom where a teacher insists that in ten years of experience he or she has never met a gifted child. What is happening here is that the teacher is looking for a child prodigy, not realising that these are also made rather than born (Radford 1990). It also reflects a narrow concept of ability more typical of the nineteenth century than the present. What, then, is currently considered to be high ability and talent?

Early concepts of giftedness and talent

In the nineteenth century, concepts of high ability were reinforced by studies of the eminent (mainly men), notably by Galton (1869), and then by biographical studies (Cox 1926). It was Terman who undertook the first longitudinal study identifying 1450 highly able children with intelligence quotients (IQs) of 140 plus. These children were followed up into adulthood by Terman and his co-workers (Terman 1925, 1937; Terman and Oden 1945). His group had a mean IQ of 155, and over a 30 year span he was able to investigate the relationships between ability and attainment. By the end of the study he was convinced that the IQ test was not a reliable indicator of high ability, although it was more so in the average and lower ranges.

Only one of his subjects was regarded as having achieved eminence; six had attained national reputations, but probably in a hundred years no one would have heard of them. In a sense, then, all of his subjects were under-achieving and under-functioning on a massive scale. When he compared the relative successes of his higher achievers with that of the lowest there was no difference in the IQ scores but patterns of personal and social characteristics were different. Persistence, emotional stability, independence of thought and a positive, supportive social and cultural background, plus opportunity, enabled individuals to achieve. The highest levels of measured IQs (such as 180) did not even lead to success. In fact, it has since been indicated that a base level of about 120 is quite sufficient for high achievement in any sphere (Getzels and Jackson 1962; Torrance 1966). Given that IQ tests have inbuilt standard errors, the baseline may actually be anywhere between 115 and 125.

During the middle decades of the twentieth century, these findings led to an expanded and multidimensional view of high ability, then called 'giftedness'. Creativity, much more difficult to measure, was seen to play a more significant role in giftedness. Cropley (1994) has suggested that there is no 'true giftedness' without creativity. Intelligence tests are thus limited in their assessments because they test only the convergent aspects of intellectual functioning.

Modern concepts of giftedness and talent

Giftedness is now generally defined as 'high ability' and the capacity for performance in any potentially valuable area of human endeavour. This expanded notion was first crystallised by Renzulli (1977, 1995) in his three-ring concept, shown in Figure 11.1.

This much broader definition of giftedness encompasses Terman's and Torrance's findings, and shows that there is a much larger group of people who can be considered to be potentially gifted and of whom we can have high expectations. More emphasis in the last ten years has been placed upon the influence for good or bad of the social and cultural environment (Monks 1992). Freeman (1991) concluded in her longitudinal study of nearly 200 highly able children that disadvantaged environments could constrain achievements and the realisation of abilities. High-quality schooling then becomes crucial. However, according to Passow (1990), in his review of 25 years of research and practice in gifted education, high-quality schooling

Figure 11.1 The three-ring concept of giftedness

which will stimulate the highly able and improve the achievements of the disadvantaged has escaped the wit of educators, legislators and researchers alike.

Talent

Talent is usually defined as a domain or specific gift or ability such as seen in art, music, science, ballet, chess or mathematics. The characteristic form is that the individual appears to have a high ability or precocious talent in the presence quite often of seemingly modest abilities in other areas. For example, Peggy Somerville was a talented painter with a mature style at three years. Mozart at seven composed and played well. It does not mean, however, that talent development is automatic; it requires the complex interaction of opportunity, diligence, interest and motivation, belief in oneself, and models and mentors who facilitate the vision and crystallise the experience (Elshout 1990). Of course, some people are multi-talented and have very high measured IQs as well. Many children will never be exposed to such facilitating experiences and environments, and their talents will never be uncovered. In teaching it is best to assume that every child does have some special talent or ability which can be uncovered with perseverance and an appropriate learning environment. This has been borne out even with slower learners (Montgomery 1990).

Creativity

Creativity refers to an innovative, ingenious and productive response to ordinary problems. This is often characterised by a flexible approach to thinking, the capacity for induction, and the use of analogies and models in new and productive ways. According to Simonton (1988), the creative person is particularly good at producing associations and then recognising the significance of the new configuration which has occurred. There is hence a need for inclusion of flexibility and creativity training and experience in education (Feldhusen 1990) if the country is to maintain its economic position or even improve upon it.

Incorporating creativity opportunities into the National Curriculum in the UK has been particularly problematic, despite Dearing's (1994) attempt to cut down its content. Opportunities to play with materials and ideas are associated with creative thinkers and producers but have little place in our current system of education.

Multi-dimensional concepts of ability as opposed to multiple intelligences

The multi-dimensional nature of ability and talent was first proposed by De Haan and Havighurst in 1957. The talents they identified were:

- intellectual ability, evidenced in aptitude for school subjects
- creative thinking
- scientific ability
- social leadership
- mechanical skill or ingenuity
- talent in a fine arts area.

It is a short step from this position to the current theory of Gardner (1983, 1993) of 'multiple intelligences' in the following areas: linguistic, musical, logico-mechanical, and personal intellectual about self and about others. His data are, however, somewhat limited and anecdotal, and it is Sternberg's (1986) triarchic model which has gained wider acceptance and upon which proposed curriculum provision is based.

Sternberg proposed three sub-theories in his model of ability. Sub-theory One he termed *componential*, and this also has three parts:

- *metacomponents* – executive processes needed for planning, monitoring and decision making in a problem-solving situation
- *performance components* – processes needed for executing the task
- *knowledge acquisition components* – used in the selective encoding, combination and comparison operations.

Sub-theory Two is termed *experiential*: the ability to deal with novelty and to automise or habituate information processing.

Sub-theory Three is *contextual*: selecting, shaping and adapting to real-world environments.

As can be seen, this theory is very much about the control and executive processes which we can identify as higher-order thinking processes. It is these with which education for all students should be involved (Paul 1990; Resnick 1989) and it is greatly to the disadvantage of the able when it is not. The more creative the able pupil, the more frustrating and mundane a didactic curriculum can become, with the consequences to be described.

Identifying under-functioning able pupils

Identifying the able is not always simple and straightforward, but identifying the under-functioning able can be even more problematic. In a family, one child may be of average ability and attainment, another may be of high ability and doing very well in school, and the third may be of even higher ability but functioning in school at a level lower than the average. Parents very often know that such a child is under-functioning but the school sees only the poor attainment. It can conclude the pupil is of low ability or lazy and may refuse to investigate further. It can be difficult for parents to secure an assessment through the school, as there are often many other children whose special needs seem more severe. Even if an independent psychological assessment is obtained there is no guarantee that it will show high ability – or that special provision will be made if it does. Parents are on hand to observe the challenging questions raised by their child and the ingenious ways he or she may solve problems and how quickly they 'catch on' when being given an explanation or demonstration. They can note the different profiles of development. Teachers with large classes do not always have time to observe these nuances. Teacher judgement can, however, be facilitated where there has been in-service training in identification strategies (Denton and Postlethwaite 1985). Such teachers will often have developed and tested checklists which can assist in the identification and so make their judgements more stable. Primary school teachers who see the pupil across a range of curriculum areas tend to make more reliable judgements than a single-subject tutor.

In test conditions some highly able children work very slowly; others see uniquely different answers to items and problems, and so their scores may appear artificially low until their performance and rationales are explored. A few children will deliberately exploit the tests and give wrong answers so as to remain with their friends or not appear to be noticeably different. If schools obtain high test scores and then pupils fail to shine in school subjects, there is a tendency to perceive this as laziness and failure to pursue school goals. Pupils' reports read 'could do better', 'has good ability but ...', 'must work harder', and so on. This negative stance adopted by the school can be very frustrating for the pupil, who may not know why nothing ever seems to satisfy them – a scene set up to create an alienated able misfit. Sometimes the promise seen in the early years of education is not fulfilled and once again a range of reasons is cast – misassessment, favouritism, burn out, laziness, the challenge of the more advanced curriculum – when quite often the reverse is the case. There may be insufficient challenge and a mundane curriculum with days of boredom stretching into infinity. Trapped in this 'psychic prison' (De Mink 1995), the pupil switches off and daydreams the time away. Others may seek the cognitive stimulation in that favourite past-time of all pupils – tormenting the teacher. Able pupils, however, are so much cleverer at this and think of many different ways to disturb others. They may clown and fool about, enjoying the excitement and thrill of making their peers laugh and driving teachers to the brink of distraction without necessarily pushing them quite over the edge. This activity is interpreted by teachers as 'challenging', and all too easily a pupil may become set on a career in disruption as people fail to recognise the signs and over-react in their disciplining techniques. Problem pupils such as this are said not to fit into the school regime and are excluded as soon as is feasible. Nevertheless, it must be said that there are many schools which go to great lengths to try to counsel and keep such pupils on track. However, it is very difficult to break these habits once they are well established, and especially when they are driven by some inner emotional need or tension arising from personal or family conflicts and fears.

What we do know is that boredom and lack of cognitive challenge in the daily curriculum play a significant role in causing pupils across the ability range to behave in this way. Where there is a pressure for so-called academic standards to the exclusion of a concern for individuals and their needs

(Galloway and Goodwin 1987; Hargreaves 1984), then this will predispose many children to feel alienated from schoolwork. In the minds of many legislators there is a confusion between what is regarded as 'academic' and 'standards in education' and the reality. Their 'standards' are too often concerned with a didactic mode of teaching (lecture style) and an overfilled curriculum. These are unsuitable for the able and slower learner alike (Montgomery 1990, 1996a). They do not engage the brain in a challenging and interesting way; they require the memorisation of large quantities of inert information to be reproduced for later tests, and never to be used in real-world problem solving (Freeman 1992). We can suggest that the more imaginative and creative the pupils, the more likely they are to be switched off by this form of curriculum and pedagogy. Even the most able and least creative, after mopping up all the knowledge and skills of the primary and early secondary years, may perceive increasing redundancy in the knowledge input or feel the 'brakes' are permanently on. The disparity in ability and knowledge can become so wide that didactics can no longer reach them. Thus differentiation has become an important consideration in curriculum provision for the able, a policy endorsed by HMI (1992).

The able and learning disabled

Whilst there is a wide range of learning disabilities (specific learning difficulties), the most common and the most detrimental to school success is dyslexia.

It has been a hard struggle for parents and dyslexia tutors to gain recognition for this severely disabling condition in which, often in the presence of high ability, there is a serious and unexplained decrement in reading and spelling skills. When pupils have high ability, the fact that they can hardly read and write only seems to confirm the idea that they are really not very able at all. Imagine the frustration of a six- or seven-year-old with an IQ of 146 on the WISC – R and an inability to read and write. It is not surprising that he or she may become disruptive every time the class is settled down to these activities. This is the reason why many parents have chosen to have their child tested rather than accept the school's view that he or she is disturbed and of low ability, potentially a candidate for the unit for children with emotional and behavioural difficulties.

It is important for professionals to identify these disparities as such (Montgomery 1990, 1997), and to know the patterns of specific difficulty which children may suffer.

These patterns are:

- *Reading and spelling difficulties.* The spelling is the more intransigent problem and remedial strategies applied to spelling improve both reading and spelling; however, the reverse is not the case. A structured multisensory specialist, APSL (Alphabetic – Phonic – Syllabic – Linguistic) programme is needed, and this must be carefully followed: a 'pick and mix' approach does not work (Ridehalgh 1996). The terms used are 'developmental dyslexia' or 'specific learning difficulties in reading and spelling'.

- *Spelling difficulties in the presence of average or even very good reading skills* (Frith 1980). An APSL programme is needed for remediation for the early stages, and a cognitive strategies programme (Montgomery 1997) for the later stages. This is known as 'developmental dysorthographia'.

- *Handwriting difficulties.* A motor coordination problem which needs to be addressed through a multisensory training in cursive (joined up) writing. This also enhances spelling skills (Cripps 1989). Cursive should be taught to all pupils from the first day in school (Montgomery 1990, 1997; Morse 1991). The condition is known as 'developmental dysgraphia'.

- *Complex specific learning difficulties.* A condition in which all of the above are found, together with a range of other specific difficulties. These include language difficulties, general coordination difficulties typified as clumsiness (Gubbay 1976), and attention deficit disorders which prevent attentional set so that it is difficult for the child to sit still long enough to learn. These pupils need more than a remedial withdrawal programme – they need a fully integrated teaching and learning programme which can only be provided in a specialist unit. Despite the need for specialist teaching, referrals are few and still only taking place after five years of little progress in the ordinary classroom.

- *Language difficulties.* Although in the majority of cases these are usually mild, such as word-finding difficulties, delayed language development and mild articulation problems, they can lead to damaging responses. Adults may regard such children as babyish as their language or impatiently ignore them; peers will most often bully them and make them frightened to contribute in schoolwork or even to come to school at all. There will, of course, be a few who, despite more severe language difficulties, demonstrate a specific talent or ability which does not demand linguistic skills. AFASIC (Association For All Speech-Impaired Children) offers good advice on teaching needs and provision. Language difficulties are more commonly associated with children of low ability and thus areas of high ability, can be overlooked. Giftedness and learning disability have been regarded until recently as mutually exclusive terms and conditions, and many academics and employers still seem unable to regard as intelligent anyone who cannot spell perfectly.

The career gifted

This group of able and under-functioning pupils was first identified by Freeman (1991). In her longitudinal study, she found the 'career gifted' had been nominated by parents or identification procedures as gifted at an early age. These children had enjoyed the aura that the title could bring but feared failure and also suspected that they might not really be worthy of it and would be found wanting. They would thus say that they could not be bothered to try with schoolwork, that the work was too uninteresting and boring, or that it was beneath them. By failing to involve themselves in schoolwork, they fell further behind, so that eventually the only sign of high ability was on tests which required very little prior knowledge.

As can be imagined, one of these individuals in the classroom could be a sore trial to the teacher. Because he or she is avoiding work, there is much time which can be spent on other, sometimes disruptive, activities. It is also upsetting to be told that everything you provide is 'boring', and it can also be catching, so that other children may decide to tell the teacher this and so obtain some more attention or freedom to choose something different.

The gifted handicapped

This term first appeared in the literature in the 1970s. It includes individuals with visual, hearing, physical, emotional and learning disabilities. Often provision has been made for them in special education, and this has led to the neglect of the high ability and talent which some possess. In the case of hearing-impaired pupils their disability is not highly visible, and there is a tendency to regard them as heedless and less able if they are unable to understand exactly what is said to them.

Where there is a stereotype that the highly able must 'look bright' (Karnes and Johnson 1991), then those who look different in some way may be considered to be less able than they really are. The UK stereotype is of a white male, weedy, bespectacled, given to solitary reading, referred to as the 'little professor' by peers and often by teachers, sounding and looking old fashioned (Freeman 1991, p.22).

According to Yewchuk and Bibby (1989), the characteristics of high ability which teachers perceived in the gifted handicapped were found to be similar to those in the non-handicapped. Thus we can use the same criteria for identifying them and be very much aware that failure to find them is much to do with misleading stereotypes and to structurally or system-induced 'blindness'.

Cultural differences and disadvantage

Being 'culturally different' refers to differences in racial/ethnic status, language, religious beliefs, values and the way in which children are socialised in families. Disadvantage is taken to mean being brought up in homes or environments where financial resources are limited and educational traditions are not strong. These groups were found by Gallagher (1985) and Gallagher and Gallagher (1994) to be under-represented in gifted programmes in the USA. Cultural differences and disadvantage are commonly observed in minority groups in this country, and thus pupils from them can be doubly disadvantaged. Both groups are under-represented, even in the current expanded university system in the UK (Ashworth 1996). Creative curiosity, critical remarks and questions, physical activity and sociability may all be seen as a challenge and affront to teacher authority. It may seem particularly unacceptable when couched in the language of a subculture. In a disadvantaged area, the school and environment may hold low expectations of its children and parents, and teachers can become blind to high ability.

Gender and under-functioning

Freeman's stereotype of the gifted child did not include images of girls and women in the national psyche. If the highly able girl does not achieve the highest grades in the curriculum, then there will be little recognition of her ability. Often, even when she does achieve them it is regarded as the result of very hard work and persistence but seldom of flair or real ability. It is very easy for girls to under-function because their patterns of behaviour tend to be quieter and they are left to their own devices. Those who do 'act out' their frustrations will become regarded as problem pupils (Good and Brophy 1985), to be persuaded to leave as soon as possible. Being a girl can thus be a double handicap; being a girl from a disadvantaged background or ethnic minority can be a triple handicap. Add dyslexia to this and the prognosis is very poor.

Girls are not significantly different from boys in their patterns of ability, creativity and talent, but they may be more likely to be taught to under-function in home and in school (Butler-Por 1987). Spender (1983) observed that boys gained two-thirds of all the attention in class and regarded it as their rightful share. They complained of favouritism towards the girls when Spender and her co-workers tried to even out their attention giving. In Good and Brophy's (1985) research, it was found that teachers would give boys more information when they asked questions, whereas girls who asked similar questions were quietened, ignored or regarded as domineering. Although overt sexism is now less apparent, structural sexism is still in operation (Fawcett Society 1995), so that the sexes are not treated as equal citizens.

Deeply rooted attitudes are difficult to change and lead to many forms of covert discrimination. In all arenas where attention should be equally shared between members in groups, committees or assemblies, the contributions of females can be seen to be passed over. Both men and women discriminate against girls unfairly, causing them to under-function on a major scale and creating a progressive weakening in their psychological make-up and, frequently, a learned helplessness in all their decision making.

'Able misfits': what the teacher can do

Differentiation

In 1989 it became a statutory requirement that state schools in England and Wales should provide a differentiated curriculum. Primary classes are most often mixed-ability groups and good mixed-ability teaching requires skilled differentiation. Structural methods involve accelerating the learner through the curriculum contents by streaming, setting, vertical grouping, grade 'skipping', compacting, and so on. Even some so-called 'enrichment materials' merely teach what the learner could expect to learn in another phase of education. A more sophisticated form is needed which is integral to the normal curriculum (Montgomery 1996b). Because it is integral, or built into the whole curriculum, all children can have an opportunity to profit from the enrichment, and tests of ability are not required to determine who shall and shall not have it. Most structural approaches tend to be product or content based, using didactic methods, whereas integral approaches are concerned with processes, in particular cognitive processes such as those described by Sternberg (1986), as well as contents. A particular form of differentiation is recommended:

DEVELOPMENTAL DIFFERENTIATION

This is the setting of common tasks to which all children can contribute their own inputs. They can thus progress from surface to deep learning and be enabled to achieve more advanced learning outcomes.

Developmental differentiation can take account of the range of individual differences and assumes that even in so-called homogeneous groups the range of differences in thinking abilities, knowledge, language and literacy skills, social, emotional and perceptual development will vary considerably, as does the experience and learning history which each individual brings to the curriculum task.

The key features of developmental differentiation are:

- an identification through provision strategy
- the National Curriculum as the subject content
- the use of cognitive process teaching and learning methods
- assessments which are both formative and diagnostic.

These can be converted into objectives and fulfilled, not by bolt-on enrichment, but by incorporating teaching and learning methods into class teaching which will promote cognitive functioning and metacognition as defined by Sternberg (1986).

Cognitive process teaching methods

These are the core of developmental differentiation and enable it to be achieved. They are based in critical thinking theory (Paul 1990; Resnick 1989) and are the means by which higher-order thinking and metacognitive skills can be developed through the ordinary curriculum (Montgomery 1995, 1996 a and b; Renzulli 1994, 1995).

The Taxonomy of Educational Objectives constructed by Bloom (1956) can be used to help assess the levels of operation which the materials are able to help the pupils achieve. Success is counted as operations at the higher levels of analysis, synthesis and evaluation, but also including all of recall, comprehension and applications. Examples of cognitive process pedagogies are:

- games and simulations
- cognitive process study skills
- real problem solving and investigative learning
- experiential learning
- collaborative learning
- language experience methods.

GAMES AND SIMULATIONS

Simulation games contain the elements of real situations, and groups interact with and can become part of the reality. Role playing is often an important part of the game; for example, in working with a class of children on the problems of bullying or stealing, it is often useful to organise small-group role play so that individuals can practise expressing their own and other's feelings as well as analyse the issues and suggest solutions or resolutions to the problems. Characteristic of all games is that they must be followed by a discussion – a debriefing session about what transpired so that educational and metacognitive objectives can be achieved. In this case, it can also have therapeutic outcomes.

'Place the castle' is a curriculum game which can be used to introduce the subject of medieval castles in historical and geographical studies. Groups are given a ground plan of an area marked off with six potential sites. Each group has to study its area and prepare a marketing brief to persuade the noble lord and lady to decide to build the castle on their site. Each group gives a brief presentation of the attributes of the site for castle location and building. In the concluding section the teacher can use the experience to help the class reflect upon which features make the best site, and then they can look at real sites and apply their knowledge. The method brings them to a deeper realisation of the needs and purposes of castle builders than a question and answer introduction might have done. At the same time, the children can contribute their own knowledge, develop discussion, negotiation, communication and presentation skills, and have fun.

COGNITIVE PROCESS STUDY SKILLS

Study skills are a form of self-directed learning and frequently involve active work on verbal, pictorial or textual material. Although reading skills are taught in primary school, it is not usual to teach higher-order and cognitive skills such as these in secondary school, although they are considered to be essential to the educated person and a requirement for success in higher education.

The following can be applied across the curriculum:

- locating the main and subordinate points
- flow charting
- completion and prediction activities
- sequencing
- comparing and contrasting
- drafting and editing
- marking and assessing work using external and internal criteria
- organising – tabulating, classifying, ordering, diagramming, categorising
- drawing inferences, abstractions and analogies
- recognising intent, bias and propaganda
- planning and monitoring one's own learning
- micro teaching
- managing one's own learning and keeping it on schedule.

These sorts of study skill (Montgomery 1983) are different from those which involve lower-order activities such as using a dictionary or an index, finding one's way about a book and what its main contents are, or recovering factual information from text and making notes.

REAL PROBLEM SOLVING AND INVESTIGATIVE LEARNING

Human nature is such that if you present a person with an open-ended situation in which the answer is not given, the mind automatically tries to solve and make closure. This notion of the human as scientific problem solver and investigator from birth was put forward by Kelly (1955). Although not everything can be converted into a problem, there is considerable scope for doing so across the curriculum. For example, in didactics a study of homes usually consists of showing the children pictures and videos of different types of building in which people live, including one type which they might describe as 'home on stilts'. The cognitive process method is to show them pictures of the terrain, probably a video clip of a monsoon, and describe the flora and fauna and the tools available to the people. The pupils in groups are then set to design the most appropriate form of home for those conditions. Their designs – treehouses, boats, homes on stilts – can then be presented, discussed and compared with the reality. This form of learning is not only more memorable and meaningful to the pupils, but also encourages argument, teamwork, organising, planning, researching and presentation skills.

Characteristic of the approach is that there needs to be plenty of content material for their research, to help develop ideas and strategies or verify solutions. Because the activities start from the children's own ideas and knowledge, each is building up their own cognitive structures and knowledge hierarchies and can thus interrogate the various sources. The teacher in this setting is only one of the resources, and is also the manager and facilitator of learning.

EXPERIENTIAL LEARNING

In 1984 Kolb defined the experiential learning cycle in which it was important that practical experience was reflected upon in order to achieve higher-order learning. However, a learning spiral might be a more accurate interpretation of the process (Montgomery 1993), for at each turn the talking about the experience and then the reflecting upon the learning process add to the sum of knowledge and skills, changing the process and the understanding in an additive way. At each point, mediation – judicious questioning – by the teacher (Feuerstein 1993) can facilitate the process. Experiential learning is essentially *action learning*, and it is surprising to what degree children can remain passive in classroom learning.

Although learners may learn without direct experience by observing and modelling others, and able learners are particularly adept at this, this does not mean that direct experience is not useful. The experience does, however, have to be cognitively challenging.

COLLABORATIVE LEARNING

Collaboration means that children work with each other towards the framing and design of problems, as well as in their resolution or solution. Frequently, what is meant to be cooperative group work is no more than pupils sitting together in groups doing individual work. Studies have shown that interactions within the groups are mainly between children of the same sex and not related to the task in hand (Bennett 1986; Galton, Simon and Croll 1985). Pupils in groups on average spent two-thirds of their time on individual work, interacting with no one. The five per cent of time actually spent talking about the task was most likely to consist of requests for information. It was the exception rather than the rule to find a group working as one.

Bennett (1986), using a computer program to provide decision-making tasks, observed triads in homogeneous and heterogeneous groups, and found that the high-ability children understood the decisions and attained 95 per cent success whichever type of group they worked in. Thus working with average and low attainers did not damage their capacity for achievement, a concern which has frequently been raised.

One of the most useful sources on practical collaborative learning activities is Bowers and Wells (1988), updated by Rawlings (1996). Circle time, conflict management and many other creative and problem-solving activities are described and can be applied to real-world problems. The strategies can also be incorporated into content areas, as well as the resolution process: definition – expressing feelings – creating options – goal setting – actioning one 'best fit' option – and verifying, evaluating and modifying a solution.

Brainstorming, role plays and a wide range of action learning strategies are illustrated, and have been well tried and tested in schools and colleges. The pedagogies already described all profit from having pupils working together in cooperative pairs and groups.

LANGUAGE EXPERIENCE METHODS

These were first described in relation to the teaching of language and literacy in children with reading difficulties. Where these pupils were having difficulties acquiring basic literacy skills, their own words and stories were used as the texts for them to learn to read. Frequently now, the word processor is used instead of a scribe to assist pairs in story writing (Peters and Smith 1986). The edit, spell check and print facilities are particularly encouraging to the young writer. The material can be made into story books with pictures, and can have a motivating effect, encouraging much more redrafting and rewriting than would otherwise be the case.

One very powerful motivation is for the writers to prepare their books to read to much younger children, and class books may also be compiled. Gardner (1990) showed how able children's creative abilities could be developed and extended by a mixture of study skills and language experience approaches.

Summary and conclusions

The term 'able misfit' has now been replaced with the concept of 'under-functioning able' to refer to those who have high ability but are not demonstrating this in school subjects. They may have profound knowledge and interest in a subject outside the school curriculum or they may not. Their failure and frustration at school may lead many of them to become alienated and a problem to themselves and others, so that the school may feel it can no longer contain the pupil safely and constructively; this can lead to exclusion. Others under-function and pass quietly through the system.

It has been suggested that lack of cognitive challenge in the curriculum can cause under-functioning, as well as a range of learning disabilities and difficulties which conceal learning potential. Stereotypic views of the 'good' pupil and the 'able child' can also cause pupils' abilities to be overlooked and lead to under-functioning as expectations are lowered.

There are a wide range of structural strategies which can be employed to help motivate pupils who can easily be identified as able, such as acceleration, setting, mentoring, distance learning and compacting. In this chapter the focus has, however, been on developmental differentiation and what the mainstream class teacher can do within the National Curriculum to improve the quality of cognitive challenge across the subjects for mixed-ability groups. The methods suggested are cognitive process pedagogies. These methods also offer an identification through provision strategy (Birenbaum 1994) which enables so many more to find their abilities and reveal them to their teachers, often with the most surprising results.

CHAPTER 12

Teaching Children Who Have Profound and Multiple Learning Difficulties

Rob Ashdown

Introduction

It is a sad and disturbing fact that there are many children with profound learning difficulties who behave in ways which cause deep distress to their parents, siblings, carers, teachers and others. Their behaviour may be just bizarre, but frequently it can be seriously destructive or dangerous to themselves or others. By its very nature, this behaviour isolates them from people, prevents their participation in appropriate educational activities, reduces the opportunities for their involvement in family social and leisure activities, disrupts the education of other children and restricts the options available for continuing education when they finally leave school.

The focus of this chapter is on a group of children who are usually described as having 'profound and multiple learning difficulties' (PMLDs) and who constitute an increasing proportion (probably between 25 and 50%) of the pupil population in special schools for pupils with 'severe learning difficulties' (see Ouvry and Saunders 1996). Not all children with PMLDs will present seriously challenging behaviours, and many pupils with less severe learning difficulties will also challenge staff and parents greatly.

The development of the communication and language skills of pupils with PMLDs is very severely delayed. Many have additional moderate to severe physical disabilities, resulting in high dependency on adults (Ouvry 1987). Many have severe visual impairments and/or hearing impairments too, and for them the world must often seem to be a confusing place with unexpected sounds, touches and other sensations. Many pupils are able to walk and may be very active and highly mobile. A significant proportion of these pupils may be regarded as having autism, which is a life-long condition with many implications for families and schools (Jordan and Powell 1995).

It is usually assumed that some kind of organic damage occurring before, during or after birth and/or a biochemical dysfunction is the most likely root cause of the problems of most of these pupils (Clements 1987; Ouvry 1987). However, the challenging behaviours shown by these children are not an inevitable consequence of the biological damage they have suffered. Instead, they are more likely to be the result of a complex interaction of their disabilities and their life experiences. Nevertheless, it is still common to encounter people who, perhaps subconsciously, belittle these children's capacity for learning and deny that they have the same needs, sensibilities and emotions as other children. People with learning difficulties have been perceived and labelled variously in ways which suggested that they are subhuman, more like animals than humans, even vegetable-like, and a potential menace to society (Ryan and Thomas 1987). However, modern educational practice has shown that much more can be achieved in terms of the education of pupils with PMLDs than was considered to be the case for many years (see for example Ouvry 1987; Ware 1995a).

The nature of their learning difficulties

If we are to be successful in meeting the highly individual needs of these children, it is necessary to be aware of the implications of their learning difficulties, albeit in general terms. Our problem is that we have difficulty in understanding what the world must seem like to them, precisely because their language and cognitive problems mean that they are not good subjects for the usual psychological studies. The research literature relates mainly to children and adults with severe learning difficulties rather than to children with PMLDs, but it can still give us some insights into the psychological reality of their learning difficulties. Readers seeking introductory reviews may refer to Clements (1987), Coupe and Porter (1986) and Ouvry (1987). Also, a growing number of publications have provided useful suggestions for appropriate curricula (see for example Coupe and Goldbart 1988; Hewett and Nind 1996; Kiernan, Jordan and Saunders 1978; Nind and Hewett 1994; Ouvry 1987; Ouvry and Saunders 1996; Ware 1995a, 1996; Wyman 1986).

Even though the organs of the senses may be intact, some children with PMLDs can show inconsistent reactions to stimuli, and this holds true of all senses and includes reactions to pain. When stimuli are presented at normal levels, such children may show very little or no reaction or they may over-react and show signs of distress and panic. Jordan and Powell (1995) describe how this is particularly true of some children with autism, who often also seem to be unable to cope with irregularities in their environment (see for example changes from the normal classroom routines, new people in the room). Therefore, it is essential that teachers plan to create areas in classrooms with minimal distractions and avoid a lot of free activity and high levels of noise or types of noise which provoke anxiety.

Memory and attention deficits are often implicated; to a certain extent, these problems may relate to inability to perceive the aim of a teaching activity and may be minimised by slowing down the rate of presentation of stimuli, allowing sufficient time for a response or using prompts and cues to draw attention to the relevant stimuli. Failure to use spontaneously learned skills and knowledge outside the original teaching setting is frequently observed. Modern educational theory therefore emphasises the value of overlearning and explicit planning to teach the use of learned skills in naturalistic settings beyond the original teaching situation.

The teacher has to structure the learning environment so that it is largely predictable and non-threatening, but a certain degree of challenge must be introduced in a carefully controlled fashion. Failure must be accompanied with clear cues and demonstrations of alternative and more appropriate responses.

The communication and language development of these children is very seriously delayed. When they communicate, it tends to be in terms of learned rote responses to gain satisfaction of basic needs only; they are much less likely to try to communicate ideas or initiate social interactions or make comments, for instance. Actually, although they have feelings like other children, many of these children may be unaware of their needs; for instance, they may experience hunger pains but not recognise that they need to eat and they may suffer from cramps but not know that a person could massage them to provide relief. Although they may cry when in distress or laugh when elated, they may fail to recognise the communicative effect of their vocalisations and body language. Even though some children may learn to use a few spoken words, they do not use these for a greater range of functions. In practice, they show equal difficulty in using non-vocal means of communication (see for example sign language, gesture, pictorial symbols or even communication systems using photos and objects), reinforcing the impression that they simply do not understand what communication is about.

It falls to their teachers, parents and carers to put all the effort into developing communication exchanges by responding as though these children are communicating with intent and, thus, show them that their behaviour can have an influence on people around them. Reciprocal interaction is encouraged when adults are responsive, behave in interesting and enjoyable ways, and when they allow time for pupils to respond and prompt this if no response is forthcoming (Coupe-O'Kane and Goldbart 1998; Goldbart 1995; Hewett and Nind 1996; Nind and Hewett 1994; Ware 1995b, 1996).

'Total communication' is advocated rather than a reliance on speech alone, and therefore signs, symbols, gestures, photos and objects all have their place as part of a non-vocal augmentative system for communication (Kiernan, Reid and Goldbart 1987; Ockelford 1994). Systematic use might be made of touch cues so that visually impaired pupils come to learn that a touch cue to a particular part of the body has a specific meaning (see for example time for a drink or time to be toileted). Teachers must ensure that there are reasons for pupils to communicate and, therefore, it is vitally important that adults should not anticipate and provide for all their wants. Indeed, teachers may use 'sabotage' to engineer situations where children have to communicate their need, say, for something that has been hidden or put out of reach.

These children have considerable difficulties in understanding that others may have thoughts and feelings or even that they do themselves. They do not have the language and cognitive skills to understand social contexts and recognise the social signals that are given out in the course of normal human interactions. They probably find social contexts and the behaviour of people within them utterly confusing and, in the case of some children with autism, even stressful or frightening (Jordan and Powell 1995).

Other possible consequences of their problems with social understanding are that they may lack empathy; they may be poor at expressing emotions; they have no understanding of what others can be expected to know; they have no idea that their behaviour might affect how others think or feel and, therefore, have no conscience and no motivation to please; and they may have limited or no interest in social interactions with others. Children may often appear to be withdrawn into a self-stimulatory world and resist intrusions, and those children who do seek out other people may approach them in primitive and bizarre ways, often using basic exploratory behaviours of smelling, biting, mouthing or stroking. Of course, they simply do not realise that their bizarre behaviour offends social convention and, to compound problems, will have difficulty in recognising models for more appropriate behaviours. Obviously, aspects of social and moral behaviour may be taught, but it is never possible to teach the whole range of behaviours that most children easily learn.

Inevitably, emotional disturbance often follows from such extreme developmental difficulties. The normal bonding processes can be seriously disrupted or fail to develop at all; attachment to others may not be motivated by the emotional bonds as we usually understand them, but because of the way in which people behave, for instance, as agents for satisfying needs or providers of interesting things. These children may also have considerable difficulty in recognising emotional expression in others (see for example facial expressions, body language, gesture, tone of voice, etc.) and they may even not notice or appreciate the reactions of others to their behaviour (Clements 1987; Jordan and Powell 1995). If people are seen as confusing or aversive, this could lead to withdrawal and a failure to engage with people. In fact, even gestures of comfort or affection may not be understood or may be rejected along with other forms of normal intimate contact. It may therefore be necessary to break down any barriers to normal physical contact, perhaps through a desensitisation programme aimed at developing tolerance of the presence of others. In the face of quite difficult behaviours, teachers, parents and carers need to remain responsive and show these children explicitly that they value interactions with them and that these can be enjoyable for them also. Adults must make themselves predictable and behave consistently so that the children are more likely to turn to them for help in coping with the events of daily life and so that they come to view them as a source of security.

What behaviour is challenging?

There have been a number of surveys which have identified a wide range of behaviours which staff in special schools considered to be seriously challenging (see for example Harris, Cook and Upton 1995).

Self-injury can be particularly upsetting for staff and parents. This may take the form of skin picking and scratching, self-biting, head punching or slapping, head-to-object banging and body-to-object banging. Less commonly reported forms of self-mutilation are body punching/slapping, hair removal, eye poking, skin pinching, anal poking, lip chewing, teeth banging, nail removal, and cutting or banging with tools (Oliver, Murphy and Corbett 1987).

Much stress is created by physical aggression and violence, destructiveness and non-compliance. General disruptiveness, spitting, verbal abuse, tantrums, deliberate soiling or wetting and smearing of faeces, masturbation and other inappropriate sexual behaviour all cause problems for school and home.

Often behaviour is not actually offensive but constitutes a formidable block to development, such as repetitive ritualistic or stereotypic behaviour and lack of interest in normal social interactions. Unpredictable anxieties and lack of awareness of common hazards are also cited as problematic.

On the whole, children who are mobile may show several challenging behaviours, with physical attacks on others and temper tantrums being particularly common. Pupils with physical disabilities, due to their immobility, largely present just one or two extreme behaviours, with self-injurious behaviour and destructive behaviour being quite commonly shown. It must be stressed that extreme forms of avoidance of social interactions or failure to participate in these also occur, and these must be regarded as seriously challenging too, even though they cause no management problems.

Reasons for challenging behaviour

There are a number of pupil characteristics which may be associated with challenging behaviours (Clements 1987; Fraser and Rao 1991; Harris *et al.* 1995; Murphy and Oliver 1987). First, there is compelling evidence that many (but not all) challenging behaviours have communicative functions (see for example as a protest, an expression of rejection or a way of gaining attention). It is not that children deliberately set out to challenge but that they have learned that such behaviour achieves the desired results. Second, these children are socially inept and lack understanding of social situations to the extent that they may become confused or anxious about what is happening. Third, their behavioural repertoires may be so impoverished that they may become exclusively preoccupied with repetitive, stereotyped behaviours, such as spinning objects, flapping fingers, and so on. Fourth, challenging behaviours are sometimes the result of an extreme reaction to aspects of their environment which they find particularly aversive (see for example lights, noise or the presence of people in close proximity). Finally, children may behave badly because they are in pain or discomfort for some medical reason

(see for example ear ache, menstrual pain, unpleasant effects of ep.
effects of medication, muscle spasms and cramps) but they ₁.
understand what is happening to them.

In addition, there is a possibility in the case of a very few children t₁
certain behaviours may not be under voluntary control and that they are due
to neural disturbance. For instance, a study in Canada by Gedye (1989)
suggests that sudden rages may be due to 'frontal lobe seizures'. Prader-Willi
syndrome has been linked with excessive eating and Lesch-Nyan with
self-injurious behaviour (Murphy and Oliver 1987). However, there is no
hard evidence to suggest that a direct link between organic damage and
challenging behaviour is likely other than in some very rare syndromes
(Clements 1987; Fraser and Rao 1991).

There is some evidence that people with sensory disabilities will seek
different means of self-stimulation in the absence of normal stimulation.
Murphy and Oliver (1987) discuss the possibility that behaviours such as eye
poking, twirling, hand flapping and rocking are done because of their
sensory consequences. However, they cite studies which have demonstrated
dramatic reductions in the occurrence of these behaviours when alternative
sensory stimulation is made available. Such findings remind us that boredom
or lack of access to appropriate activities are important factors.

The challenge to teachers, parents and carers is to develop appropriate
styles of interaction with these children. Many people are just uncertain
about how to behave towards these children. However, all too often
challenging behaviours can be the result of people failing to see things from
the child's point of view: for instance, they may make requests or give
instructions which the child finds difficult to understand; they may favour
rigid routines; they may suddenly change activities or established routines; or
they may insist that children should do things which they find boring or
incomprehensible.

Behaviour modification

The STAR approach

It must be recognised that challenging behaviours are often an unacceptable
means of achieving acceptable ends. Therefore, the focus of intervention
should be on teaching children more appropriate and desirable ways of
achieving these legitimate targets. This section describes the STAR approach
(Zarkowska and Clements 1994), which is representative of the very

sophisticated and benign approaches to the management of challenging behaviours which are available today. There are many other useful books which give similar guidelines, although they may not use precisely the same terminology (see for example Donellan *et al.* 1988; Harris *et al.* 1995; Murphy and Oliver 1987).

The STAR approach requires an analysis of the function of challenging behaviours and intervention at four different levels: settings, triggers, actions and results:

- *Settings* are the context in which behaviour occurs and determine the individual's motivation to achieve and work for results which might be available. Settings can be internal or external to the individual. The major external or environmental setting conditions are the physical climate (see for example noise level, temperature, crowding), the social climate (see for example quality and style of relationships, levels of conflict) and the occupational climate (see for example level and type of stimulation, access to appropriate, high-quality activities). The major internal or personal setting conditions are the physical state of the individual (see for example pain, tiredness and poor physical health), his or her psychological state (see for example anxiety states, sadness and depression following trauma) and levels of cognitive development (see for example communication problems, disordered thinking, lack of social understanding).

- *Triggers* are the particular signals or stimuli in a situation which 'set off' specific actions. They are those things which occur just before the behaviour: they may signal the availability of a thing a person may want; they may suggest the imminent threat of something occurring which the person may not want; they may trigger habitual behaviour which has always followed that particular stimulus; they may directly elicit an automatic reaction; or they may cause a sharp and rapid increase in arousal or emotion.

- *Actions* are the actual behaviour which causes concern and any new behaviours which need to be taught.

- *Results* are the consequences which immediately follow an action: they may be reinforcers which increase the likelihood that an action will be performed again under similar circumstances (see for example removal of threats, acquisition of material rewards); they may be punishers which decrease the likelihood that an action will be performed again under similar circumstances (see for example scolding); and they may be neutral results which, if they consistently follow a behaviour, will result in a decrease in the likelihood that that action will be performed again under similar circumstances.

The components of the STAR package are:

- a comprehensive assessment of the individual and the behaviour of concern
- modifying settings
- modifying triggers
- teaching appropriate alternative skills
- removing or altering results achieved by challenging behaviours.

Implementing interventions requires careful planning, deliberate use of prompts, cues and special reinforcers, and a graded approach to change. Programmes may be introduced gradually: for instance, the initial focus may be on one setting and gradually the intervention will be extended across other settings; or intervention may target only one behaviour at first and is subsequently extended to other challenging behaviours one at a time. Above all, teachers, parents and carers must work to achieve a consensus view about the nature and goals of the intervention. Achieving this is dependent upon a number of factors: making a precise definition of the behaviours which are the focus of the intervention; agreeing the aims of the intervention; producing written plans which describe the methods to be used; and devising an objective system for monitoring progress.

An essential preliminary is assessment. Zarkowska and Clements (1994) describe a variety of interview and observation procedures which may be used to determine the results that a challenging behaviour appears to achieve, as well as apparent triggers, relevant setting conditions, relevant skills deficits and a general statement of needs. The statement of needs is used to prioritise teaching objectives and establish management plans. It is therefore important that the individual's needs are stated in terms of positive behavioural outcomes rather than as a catalogue of all the negative things about the individual. Finally, it is necessary to break the long-term objectives into achievable steps and organise the steps into a sequence for teaching.

The STAR approach involves developing appropriate strategies at various levels. One thrust involves preventing the challenging behaviour from achieving positive results and finding ways of communicating to the child that this behaviour is unacceptable. Another thrust is to teach more appropriate alternatives to the challenging behaviour, either by reinforcing behaviours the child already has in his or her repertoire or by teaching specific, relevant skills. As a third tactic, 'risk factors' are reduced by altering the settings and triggers which are associated with challenging behaviour and establishing conditions under which the child seems to learn best and the challenging behaviour is rarely seen. It is necessary to consider most carefully whether the child's environment (social and physical) may be contributing unnecessarily in some way to the problems. If this is the case, consideration should be given to making changes wherever this is reasonable and practicable. For instance, it might be appropriate to increase the range of activities which are meaningful, interesting and pleasurable for the child and reduce the amount of time spent in unstructured activities. There may be a need to alter the relationship which currently exists between adults and children by, for example, giving more opportunities to choose activities or giving unconditional positive attention.

As noted above, the STAR approach aims to establish an acceptable alternative behaviour when seeking to suppress a challenging behaviour. Appropriate skills may not be much in evidence because they do not achieve the results which the challenging behaviours do. Therefore, it should be an aim to increase the value of the results for the appropriate behaviour as well as to prevent the undesirable behaviours from achieving results. For instance, a child may have learned that when he wants a toy, screaming is followed by an adult giving it to him. Therefore, a possible strategy might be to ignore the screaming, prompt the child to point to the toy, and straight away give it as immediate and positive reinforcement. A number of such episodes should have the effect of demonstrating to the child that the challenging behaviour achieves no useful result but that pointing to the desired item does.

'Extinction' is the name given to the systematic prevention or with-holding of reinforcement which is thought to be maintaining a behaviour. This is a well-documented procedure and certain findings are frequently replicated in research studies (Murphy and Oliver 1987; Zarkowska and Clements 1994). First, the child may work harder to get the results he or she is accustomed to receiving: there may be an increase in intensity and/or frequency of the challenging behaviour and the child may even resort to a range of other challenging behaviours to achieve results. Second, if the behaviour is reinforced intermittently rather than continuously, extinction takes longer. This means that it is important that positive results are withheld every time that challenging behaviour occurs because, if they are occasionally given, the challenging behaviour is likely to become even more persistent. Hence the need for a consistent approach among all people dealing with the child.

Many behaviour modification studies have reported the use of punishers as consequences for challenging behaviour (Clements 1987; Murphy and Oliver 1987), although Zarkowska and Clements (1994) stress that the use of punishers should be a last resort for all kinds of ethical and practical reasons. A punishment procedure is only likely to be effective when combined with strategies for teaching and encouraging appropriate alternatives and will tend only temporarily to suppress challenging behaviours. If appropriate alternative skills are not taught, there can be concurrent increases in other types of challenging behaviour as the target behaviours decrease. It is also important to make no assumptions about what is reinforcing and what is punishing: for instance, it is not unusual for children to actually find it rewarding to be excluded from a classroom activity because they find a quiet corridor soothing in comparison with a noisy classroom. Finally, the use of punishment may harm any relationships between staff and pupil which may be developing and may cause much psychological harm. It is for such reasons that professionals working with people who present challenging behaviour have increasingly sought to develop educational methods which do not involve the use of punishment at all (see for example Donellan *et al.* 1988).

Intensive interaction

A radically different approach, called 'Intensive Interaction', has been developed by Nind and Hewett (1994; see also Hewett and Nind 1996). Their concern was that there was too much emphasis upon punishment in orthodox approaches to the management of challenging behaviours and that these resulted in interactions that were so formalised and controlling that they seemed to deny the humanity of the individuals involved. Intensive Interaction explicitly values the individual with learning difficulties as a social and communicative person whose behaviours have meaning. The approach does not set out to suppress behaviour which is uncomfortable or inappropriate. In fact, Intensive Interaction was not developed as a method for managing challenging behaviours but as an approach to teaching communication and other skills to people who had profound learning difficulties. Challenging behaviours may diminish because avenues of communication are opened and new opportunities for learning new skills are offered, but this is regarded as a spin-off rather than the main motivation for the use of Intensive Interaction. Nind and Hewett state that Intensive Interaction is relevant for those children who are not at a stage where they use or understand verbal or symbolic communication, and they claim that it can reach learners who remain untouched by traditional approaches.

Intensive Interaction lacks the formal structure seen in orthodox teaching techniques with pupils with PMLDs. Although a great deal of consideration is given to the learning environment and providing appropriate stimulation, what happens during Intensive Interaction is profoundly influenced by the fact that the teacher follows the lead given by the child's interests and behaviour. Behavioural outcomes are seen as less important than the actual process of interaction, and the teacher's work is interpretative rather than directive. The aims are to develop sociability, communication, cognitive abilities, emotional well-being and constructive interactions with the people and things in the child's environment.

Important basic principles are that the process must be mutually enjoyable and, potentially, any behaviour or interests of the child can form the basis for the development of interactive games. These games are evolved by the teacher painstakingly imitating the actions and noises made by the child, and physical contact features a great deal. As the child attends more to the behaviour of the teacher and comes to enjoy the games, the teacher can begin to introduce new stimuli and new actions gently to guide the development of new skills.

Nind and Hewett (1994; see also Hewett and Nind 1996) and Watson (1995) furnish anecdotal evidence of the success of Intensive Interaction. At the outset, the child may be wholly unresponsive and withdrawn or may behave in ways which are provocative, repugnant or even frightening. Therefore, the teachers will bear the entire responsibility for making rewarding interactions happen. However, after a while, the child should begin to participate momentarily and begin to show reciprocal behaviours, such as smiling, contact seeking, touching and looking. Increasingly, it should become easier to engage the child in interactions and the child will initiate them too. Eventually, a stage should be reached where there is give and take on both sides and the child should show a readiness to learn new skills and participate in a wider range of activities.

Intensive Interaction is marked by avoidance of punishment and coercion, which are clearly incompatible with its underlying philosophy. The main strategies for dealing with challenging behaviours seem to involve giving them as little value as possible: thus eye contact might be avoided and physical contact kept to the barest possible minimum. Indeed, any behaviour which could be taken to imply rejection of the teacher's attempts to initiate interactions would be respected and the teacher would withdraw, to return at a later time. Attempts at self-injury or physical violence to others would be interrupted to ensure safety but in a minimally intrusive manner.

Intensive Interaction was originally developed in a hospital special school which eventually became fully geared to the use of this approach as the main way of meeting the needs of the difficult young adults with profound learning difficulties who were on roll. In terms of specialised activities, staffing and staff support systems, this school must have been rather different from the typical community special schools of today. Therefore, there are resource, staffing and curriculum implications for schools interested in developing Intensive Interaction. Another problem is that the proponents of Intensive Interaction cannot point to any methodologically rigorous studies to support their claims. Nevertheless, Intensive Interaction may well succeed where more orthodox methods have failed and merits further research to determine its potential uses in special schools.

Medical interventions

A variety of medical treatments for different forms of challenging behaviour have been tried over many years. Treatment through drugs has its proponents and its critics. One view is that medication is an immoral way of reducing people to a controllable state and should be avoided at all costs. However, at the other extreme there is still a strongly held view that benign, sophisticated drugs are available and should be tried. In practice, there is some suggestive evidence that medical treatments or 'pharmacotherapy' may have a positive role, especially when used in conjunction with educational regimes. However, systematic research has not been extensive or of very good quality for various reasons (Aman 1987; Fraser and Rao 1991).

Aman (1987) is adamant that very little can actually be concluded about the precise nature of drug effects and the theoretical basis for such treatments remains largely speculative. There is no clear evidence for their effectiveness in controlling challenging behaviour, especially in the long term. Nevertheless, teachers may well encounter children for whom drugs are prescribed to complement an educational package aimed at managing challenging behaviour.

Developing a whole-school approach

Teaching these children is not easy. Teaching demands good classroom organisation and specific strategies to create an effective learning environment (Lacey 1991; Ware 1995c, 1996). In addition, staff dealing with children who present challenging behaviours may have to learn a whole new philosophy and a new set of teaching practices. Mere commonsense and intuition are no longer sufficient. There are major issues here which the senior staff of schools have to address. They must:

- ensure adequate staffing levels
- lay down clear procedures for devising individual education plans, keeping records and reviewing these
- provide adequate in-service training and induction training
- provide moral support for staff who have to deal with the challenging behaviour on a daily basis
- provide clear guidelines about acceptable control and restraint methods.

All the advice points to the need for regular reviews and rigorous documentation, both to guide and protect staff and to evaluate the effectiveness and appropriateness of interventions. Identified senior teachers (see for example head teacher, Child Protection Coordinator) will need to scrutinise teachers' records and be closely involved in the development of interventions.

The emphasis in this chapter has been upon teaching pupils with PMLDs in a school context, but these interventions should occur in other living environments too. They will have limited effectiveness if they do not continue at home and if they do not have the support and active participation of the pupil's families and carers. Parents have the right to be involved fully in decisions about the education of their child. Often, they are frustrated or depressed about the challenging behaviours that their child presents at home and are looking for advice about what to do. After all, most pupils spend only a small proportion of their waking hours away from their parents and family.

Schools must be seen to listen to parents' views and concerns, respond to them, and engage them effectively in the development and maintenance of any interventions with their child.

Fortunately, there are effective models for developing agreed policies and procedures (see for example Harris *et al.* 1995; Zarkowska and Clements 1994). The National Autistic Society (1991) has produced guidelines about acceptable practice in the management of feeding difficulties and extreme food fads. The legal commentary by Lyon (1994), DfE Circular 9/94 (DfE 1994) and DfE Circular 10/98 (DfE 1998), clearly show the requirements for good practice in the use of rewards, sanctions, devising individual education plans, the use of control and restraint, and the recording of incidents. The National Autistic Society and the British Institute of Learning Disabilities have produced a guide to the legal framework and models for good policies and practice (British Institute of Learning Disabilities 1996).

Inevitably, there are many differences between schools in terms of the numbers and range of ability of pupils, the available resources and the particular strengths of the staff. Therefore, each school has to develop its own particular ethos. All staff must have the opportunity to be involved in a process of developing a policy which expresses the school's own set of values and beliefs. This should include statements of intended positive outcomes, agreed approaches to the management of challenging behaviours, and methods of liaison with parents and other significant people in the lives of the pupils. Staff face severe tests of their skills and character, often without sufficient resources and support from external experts. However, the process of formulating a policy can show individuals that they do not have to face these pressures alone and will identify how the collective skills of staff may be harnessed to create quality support systems that will sustain good practice.

CHAPTER 13

Parenting and Children with Emotional and Behavioural Difficulties

Peter Lloyd Bennett

Introduction

Children with emotional and behavioural difficulties may have witnessed or been part of domestic situations which most professionals have never experienced, such as a situation during a family quarrel in which a child was encouraged by his father to kick and spit on his mother. The lack of a nurturing environment can result in children growing up with special educational needs and EBDs. These children often develop very powerful weapons which they have few inhibitions about using – choosing scapegoats, showing physical and verbal aggression. However, these techniques do not enhance their ability to live in peace and comfort with everyone else. This chapter focuses on the nature of the home environment in which emotionally and behaviorally disturbed children develop (referred to throughout in the male gender) and in particular the principal figures in this environment – the parents/carers.

Terminology

A complex network of terminology has been developed to describe and clarify this area of personality disorder. Cleckly (1941) identified the cardinal features of a 'psychopath' (this term is rarely used now in reference to children), among them an absent sense of responsibility, refusal to accept blame for wrongdoing and lack of goal directedness in a chaotic lifestyle. Bowlby (1944) identified 'affectionless character', where children's early histories are marked by prolonged separation from their mothers and foster mothers, which was linked to child conduct problems. In line with the trend of employing new terms to avoid social censure through negative labelling, the term 'emotionally and behaviourally disturbed or disordered' found favour over the term 'maladjusted', which focused on norms and a child's inability to function within the norm. More recently, the emotional component has been dropped from many of the terms in current usage – oppositional-defiant disorder, psychopathic personality, delinquent, anti-social personality disorder, to name only a few. A useful distinction has been drawn between children with socialised and unsocialised aggression. DSM III (American Psychiatric Association 1980) identifies 'socialised' as having one or more friends, avoiding blaming others and sharing concerns for the welfare of others. Children with socialised aggression employ the undesirable currency of violence as a means of achieving social goals such as wealth and social status. EBDs children who display unsocialised aggression have few friends and are not verbally articulate; they are both victim and perpetrator. DSM IIIR (American Psychiatric Association 1987) identified the more general term 'conduct disorder', which refers to truanting, lying, stealing, running away, starting fires, burglary, robbery, initiating fights, using weapons, forcing sex, and being cruel to animals and people. The term 'conduct disorder' has been further refined into pervasive aggression and situational aggression. However, exactly how these labels fit on to individual children is not always clear. Professionals, particularly in the education system, are often wary of employing labels, and even a brief glance at our schools shows that children do not generally fit into neat categories. In particular, a prolonged period of teaching designated 'EBDs' children indicated to me that the majority of these children did not substantially differ from others in kind, but they did have a high preponderance of negative symptoms and a tendency to escalate situations of conflict. Further discussion of alternative terms and their meanings is beyond the remit of this chapter, and has been described elsewhere (American Psychiatric Association 1994; World Health Organisation 1992).

Factors in the development of EBDs

Serious juvenile crime is sometimes seen as an inevitable fact of life in an increasingly violent society. In America, arrests of those under 18 years of age for murder and non-negligent manslaughter rose by 60.1 per cent between 1981 and 1990 (Federal Bureau of Investigation 1991). The development of EBDs is multiply determined by a wide variety of factors operating through interactional processes at a number of different levels. These factors include parenting style, maternal and paternal roles, divorce, and parental abuse and neglect, as well as the wider social trends (e.g. bonding to deviant peer groups, availability of drugs and guns) and economic influences (e.g. poverty). Rutter (1979) identified six family variables significantly associated with childhood psychiatric disorder: marital discord, low socio-economic status, large family size, paternal criminality, maternal psychiatric disorder and child welfare intervention. Children with just one of these risk factors were no more at risk of disorder than those with none. Yet as the number of risk factors increased, children were very much more likely to develop psychiatric disorder.

Parental abuse

Parental abuse and neglect of children are risk factors which have a wide variety of causal agents, including historical, cultural and situational. The experience of childhood maltreatment undoubtedly puts individuals at risk of becoming abusive themselves, but the path between these points is far from direct or inevitable. Mueller and Silverman (1989) proposed that an abused child internalises both sides of the abusive relationship, learning the roles of both abuser and abused. Crittenden (1985) observed different types of parents interacting with their children and concluded that abusing parents behaved as though they perceived the world from an adverserial perspective which demanded that they gain control to satisfy wants that must be imposed on others in spite of their resistance. This tendency may be the result of the parents' own childhood experiences but researchers are now cautious of assuming that parents necessarily pass on to their children what they themselves experienced as children. Parents with histories of maltreatment who did not perpetuate the inter-generational transmission of maltreatment had more extensive social supports, had experienced a non-abusive and supportive relationship with one parent while growing up, or were more openly angry and better able to give a detailed account of earlier abuse than parents who themselves became abusers (Belsky 1993). Abusive parents may not have developed a coherent practice of graduated rewards and punishments and they are more likely to rely on physical punishment and negative acts – hitting, grabbing and pushing. What may start as a justified attempt to discipline their child may result in major acts of violence.

Physical abuse, which is generally defined as the presence of a non-accidental injury resulting from an adult's use of overt physical violence or excessive punishment, has been linked with adolescent aggression

(Malinosky-Rummell and Hansen 1993). Children who had been physically abused and were receiving mental health treatment exhibited more aggressive behaviour than their non-abused peers. A general pattern emerging from research suggests that physical abuse on its own may not lead to children's behavioural problems, but that in the presence of other factors emotional and behavioural problems may emerge. Physical abuse as part of a package of behaviours which include lack of supervision, parental conflict and aggression have been found to account for a significant amount of variance in violent crimes. Hunter and Kilstrom (1979) interviewed prospective mothers who had not yet had the opportunity to abuse their children. They concluded that although a high percentage of their sample may have been physically abused, the experience of abuse does not necessarily result in perpetrating abuse. On the other hand, Bernard and Bernard (1983) found that 75 per cent of abusive subjects used the same form of violence on their dating partners as they had experienced or observed in childhood. However, gender differences are important in this area, as childhood abuse among women was found to predict received violence rather than inflicted violence (Marshall and Rose 1988). Abused mothers who do not abuse their children tend to have higher intelligence scores than abusive mothers who continue the cycle of abuse on their own children; abusive mothers also show more emotional instability as well as anxiety and depression. Emotional stability, intelligence, the presence of a supportive spouse and the ability to articulate clearly the parent's own experience of abuse all contribute to reducing the risk of perpetuating the cycle of abuse. Exposure to family violence and distress is associated with internalising and externalising negative behaviours and social incompetence. The consequences of physical abuse in childhood are varied and complex, but strong links have been found between the presence of male aggression and the childhood experience of physical abuse.

Evidence for the occurrence of physical abuse rests on the identification of inadequately explained injuries and awareness of parental neglect relies on the observation of inadequate standards of care, whereas the recognition of sexual abuse depends on listening to what a child has to say, which is more likely to be a process than a single event. One of the difficulties in the identification of sexual abuse is the possible traumatising effect of the abuse on the child's recall of what happened to him. Reported prevalence rates are thought to underestimate cases of child sexual abuse; Finkelhor et al. (1990) found that 27 per cent of adult females and 16 per cent of adult males reported childhood experience of sexual abuse. Short- and long-term negative consequences of sexual abuse include depression, anxiety, guilt and anger, as well as problems in interpersonal relationships. Treatment interventions involving groups of sexually abused girls appear to be helpful in reducing some of the negative effects of sexual abuse in terms of self-esteem and behaviour problems (De Luca *et al.* 1995). Dysfunctional family relations constitute one of the risk factors for childhood sexual abuse (Peters 1988).

Divorce

Children of divorced families tend to exhibit higher levels of externalising problems, such as aggression and conduct disorder, than children from intact families (Grych and Fincham 1992). Conduct problems in boys tend to be more prevalent and persistent than for girls, whose difficulties in peer interactions were apparent only shortly after their parents' divorce (Hetherington, Cox and Cox 1979). The effects of divorce are thought to be dependent on a variety of factors, including the quality of the parent–child relationship, the gender of the custodial parent and whether he or she has re-married, and the parenting style. However, studies of children of divorced parents rarely examine the quality of family relationships prior to divorce, and its effects are likely to be due to factors such as the previous consistency of parenting and degree of marital conflict rather than physical separation of the parents. There is a complex interaction of parental factors, such as emotional and physical insecurity, disruption of parenting, and inconsistent management both within and between parents, and child factors such as non-compliance, reduced concentration, and being angry and demanding. Custodial parents may experience increased responsibilities as stressful and over-zealous financial pursuit of non-custodial parents by government agencies has ended in a number of suicides. Financial resources are sometimes reduced in one-parent families, and the number of children in families on income support rose, in the United Kingdom, from 7 per cent in 1979 to 26 per cent in 1994 (*The Guardian,* 27 September 1995).

Paternal role

Very little research has been carried out on the paternal role in childrens' psychological disturbance. Caplan and Hall-McCorquodale (1985) reviewed publications in nine clinical journals, and found that 72 different kinds of child psychopathology were attributed to mothers whereas none were attributed to fathers. Mothers were never described in solely positive terms whereas fathers were often mentioned as the solely positive influence on a child. Researchers may assume that many children do not have contact with fathers because of parental divorce. In the United States only 67 per cent of children under the age of 18 years live with both parents. However, a review by Woollett, White and Lyon (1982) found that fathers were no more difficult to research than mothers; subject refusal was more related to number of data collections and time involvement than to gender of the parent. Reeves *et al.* (1987) compared fathers of conduct-disordered children with a control group of fathers of normal children, and found that fathers of children with conduct disorder (89% of whom also had a diagnosis of Attention Deficit/Hyperactivity Disorder) were more likely to be alcoholic and have anti-social personality disorder than fathers in the control group. Fathers of the conduct-disordered children were also more likely to have a history of aggression, arrest and imprisonment than fathers of other clinically referred children. Overall, a strong link has been found between children's (mostly boys') conduct disorder and paternal psychiatric disorder and to a lesser extent maternal psychiatric disorder (Phares and Compas 1992). In the past, physical aggression has primarily been attributed to the male gender; however, press reports in the United Kingdom suggest that a gradual shift may be taking place with regard to a small but noticeable number of women acting in a physically violent manner (e.g. 'Masked Woman Goes on Armed Robbery Spree', *Telegraph,* 1 September 1995).

Parenting style

Parenting style refers to a constellation of attitudes towards children that are communicated to them and create an emotional climate in which parents' behaviours are expressed. Darling and Steinberg (1993) focused on two main aspects of parents' behaviour: specific goal-directed behaviours through which parents perform their duties (e.g. 'come and have your tea') and non-goal-directed behaviours such as gestures, changes in tone of voice or spontaneous expression of emotion. Though attitudes are thought to be more influential than behaviours, it is difficult to study the former without the latter. Children described as instrumentally competent were thought to be products of parenting which was warm, established clear rational guidelines while allowing autonomy within those boundaries, and where parents clearly communicated their expectations and the reasoning behind them (Baumrind 1970). Baumrind suggested that one of the primary aims of parenting is to socialise children to conform to the necessary demands of others while maintaining a sense of personal integrity. The battle to achieve this balance is particularly difficult for emotionally and behaviourally disturbed children, and indeed continues to be a source of reflection for many of us throughout adulthood.

Socially maladjusted children who withdraw from peers have relatively negative views of social interaction, expecting to be disliked and excluded from peer activities (Crick and Dodge 1994). Children approach social situations with a set of biologically limited capabilities and a database of past experiences. Earls (1995) proposed that the most profound problem with conduct disorder is children's inability to view social encounters as events that require thinking about the feelings and rights of others. Social information processing is likely to be automatic, rapid and irrational. Most developmental theories emphasise the role of early experiences in shaping neural paths which become increasingly efficient and complex but also rigid and resistant to change. Maladjusted children may perceive many social situations as threatening and the concomitant emotional arousal has a disabling effect on their ability to interpret situations accurately. For example, verbal and physical aggression become common channels of communication and the child's lack of sensitivity to other family members, which could partially be the result of parenting style, can enhance the parents' sense of powerlessness and justify their withdrawal of support and care for the child.

Children of depressed mothers often show disturbance in emotions, behaviour and development. Parent–child relationships are marked by high maternal criticism and coercion; the child may seek attention from his mother by increasingly negative behaviour. Parent–child relationships are affected by a maze of inter-correlated factors, including adversity in housing conditions as well as negative relationships with spouse and neighbours, which may contribute to the start of difficulties in mother–child interaction and these difficulties may gather their own momentum, persisting even when external circumstances improve (Cox *et al.* 1987). When parent–child interaction is inconsistent, resulting from a number of factors including the parents' strong punitive action over one in a series of otherwise ignored misdemeanors, a child may exhibit negative behaviour as a matter of course, seeking predictability and attention. Parents who lack sensitivity to their children's needs may seek to gratify their own emotional needs without recognising their child's individuality and development. Children's EBDs may develop when emotional abuse has become an intrinsic part of the parenting style.

Factors within the child

Before proceeding to a discussion of parent training programmes, consideration needs to be given to child-centred risk factors in the development of emotional and behavioural disorder. McGhee, Silva and Willaims (1984) identified perinatal risks such as prematurity, low birth weight and anoxia as being associated with persistent parent- and teacher-rated behaviour problems. Components of temperament, such as adaptability to change, mood intensity and sociability, may affect the development of anti-social behaviour. The child's cognitive ability and skill in expressing himself through language may also be linked to EBDs.

Parent training

The central aim of parent training is to teach parents appropriate principles and strategies so that they can alter their parenting style and the nature of parent–child interaction, with a consequent improvement in their children's behaviour. Parent training has become an increasingly popular approach to helping parents with their children's emotional and behavioural problems.

Parent training programmes

Psychologists and other professionals who are responsive to media reports of children's extreme anti-social behaviour and have an awareness of clients' needs within their own professional practices, have developed a variety of parent training programmes which have been developed from social learning theory, cognitive psychology and psychodynamic principles. Becker (1971) drew up a programme encouraging the use of positive rewards, outlining ten group sessions aimed at helping parents use specific reinforcement and avoid using general statements such as 'show me more respect' as well as increasing their awareness of giving praise and criticism.

Appleton and Minchom (1991) identified four predominant approaches to partnerships between professionals and parents. The first of these is the expert model, in which only the professionals own the knowledge and skills necessary to identify and define the problems as well as prescribe and evaluate the solutions. The second is the transplant model, in which parents are expected to carry out programmes or treatments according to detailed information and instruction. The third model is the consumer rights model, highlighting individual choice and the principle that the parents know best. The fourth approach is the social network/systems model, encouraging fluidity, flexibility and facilitative rather than directive professional input.

Parent training programmes represent a major shift in approach from therapeutic intervention, where the therapist works directly with the child, to the therapist working with the parent in order to effect therapeutic or behavioural change in the child. This shift in approach has brought with it an increasing awareness that children's behaviour is largely contingent upon influences within the family. Parent training provides education in parenting skills generally, as well as preparation for parenthood and guidance for parents who are failing in their role of bringing up their children. Early intervention programmes, such as Portage, involve parents in a well-organised structured system for enhancing children's development. Other approaches using self-help and support groups include the use of telephone lines (e.g. Helpline), volunteer home visiting (e.g. Homestart) and group meetings where peers provide the main source of assistance. Useful information in the form of simple leaflets is widely distributed to parents aiming to reduce child maltreatment by agencies such as social services.

Patterson (1982) developed a programme for parents of conduct-disordered children starting with the teaching of social learning principles followed by tests and the description of skills for observing and recording problems. Effective disciplinary methods, monitoring of children's out-of-home activities, problem solving and negotiating strategies were also included in the programme.

Programmes may involve the therapist sitting behind a one-way screen observing the parent interacting with the child during a game-playing session. The therapist instructs the parent on appropriate strategies for directed and non-directed tasks using a bug-in-ear device (see for example Forehand and MacMahon 1981). Many programmes have been informed by cognitive behaviour approaches and problem-solving ideas in which parents are invited to prioritise undesired behaviour and consider its anticedents, as well as developing enjoyable interactions with their children.

Effectiveness of parent training

Individual training enhances opportunities for programmes to be designed specifically for individual needs, whereas group training maximises the use of limited resources and encourages the development of peer support systems. In general, methods involving active participation are more effective than didactic methods alone. Different approaches used – such as group training sessions, telephone communication and home visits – yield equally positive results (Callias 1995; Sutton 1995). Teaching the principles as well as practical skills does not improve the acquisition of such skills, but it does enhance the long-term effectiveness of training. Cohn and Daro (1987) evaluated a large number of treatment programmes and reported some improvement, but success rates were not high and they concluded that a comprehensive package of services addressing concrete and interpersonal needs of all family members is needed. Long-term effectiveness of parent programmes is likely to be highly dependent on the establishment of social and emotional bonds between at-risk parents. The very old joke – 'How many psychologists does it take to change a light bulb?' Answer: 'One, although the light bulb has to really want to change' – highlights the key role of parents' attitudes and willingness to implement ideas to enable treatment programmes to be effective. Parent views of what behaviour is acceptable or unacceptable may vary both between and within cultures, and many parents choose not to take part or drop out before programme completion. Sensitive canvassing, adequate child care arrangements and convenient locations all facilitate family involvement. Also, therapist characteristics are influential – Wilding (1982) reported that some professional experts involved in programmes rendered people less able to cope with the ordinary problems of day-to-day living.

Parent training programmes have partially developed from a surge of social concern over individual incidents which have shocked and challenged public views of acceptable behaviour, not least because of the apparent impotence of local communities. However, authoritarian approaches in parent programmes have been accused of operating as a means of social control and uniformity. Feminist views question the core belief that womanhood and motherhood are inter-meshed. More fundamental social change may be needed to address issues that are primarily seen in terms of individualistic sites of conflict within families. Allan (1994) proposes that parent programmes should provide opportunities for parents to explore the influence of socially constructed dominant ideologies, though more immediate gains are likely to be made through cognitive behaviour therapy and problem-solving approaches. Delinquency has been found to exhibit characteristics that are particularly amenable to primary intervention, such as early age of onset and high stability (Yoshikawa 1994). Family support and education on child-rearing practices over an extended period, high-quality day care and pre-school provision, and emotional and financial support are likely to help reduce emotional and behavioural disturbance in children.

A parent's account

In conclusion, a parent's own account of the development of her child with EBDs is presented. Many of the factors in the research literature can be noted in this account, which provides an insight into family circumstances and the mother's view of the difficulties. The parent's own words have been recorded and no changes have been made, except to names and places in order to maintain confidentiality.

The parent's own parenting

My mum had her own children on her own on social security and she went with different men, she was married three times and she was a drinker. I had a rough life, I had very few clothes and I did not have the things I wanted. I want to give these things to my kids so I compensated for what I did not have as well and when I had the three of them on social, that is what finally cracked me, I could not put shoes on them and I knew that a foster parent would.

Circumstances around Roger's birth

My husband went into prison; obviously we separated and I went into a battered wives' home because he beat me when he was drunk. He came out of prison, we had a flat and my daughter was living with my mother at the time because I could not cope, and I thought 'well we will give it another try' and so I went back to him on a trial basis. I got pregnant in that month and at the end of the month I did not really want to stay with him. I was pregnant and I had to make a decision – I could get rid of the baby and stay in the home or go back to him and try yet again to make a go of it. I did not really want to have an abortion so I decided to go back and I got my daughter back from my mum as well. So I started again but he had not really changed in any way and when I gave birth I did not really want the baby and I did not want my husband. The minute I gave birth to him, the nurse said 'have a look at your baby' and I said 'get that rat away from me'. It was so big, it was nine pounds and four ounces, it was like a three-month-old baby and I looked at it and said 'good grief', but after a few days I sort of took to him and started to feel towards the baby and so it went all right from then on.

We stayed together but my husband kept hitting me, and my little girl who was then about two or three years old used to scream 'daddy, daddy don't hit mummy' and all this stuff. Roger was still in the pram at this stage and sitting up. I thought 'I've got to get away now because if Roger sees all this stuff it will affect him and he will be hitting other children', so I made the decision to leave and I went into bed and breakfast. That was very difficult – a cot and a bed and everything in one room, they are dirty dodgy places, my health visitor visited and there was a little bit of contact from his dad but it was a long way to travel. Basically at that stage I had become a heavy drinker, I started to drink every day if I could and not eat, so I lost a lot of weight but still I would say I was a good mother – they always had what they wanted even though I did drink. As the years progressed so much happened to me, it was incredible to think who went where. I had four children, Christine was the eldest, followed by Bill and Roger, then Trevor who is my youngest child.

Early development

I got a flat in east London and I was drinking a lot and I could not cope, the kids were running riot, they were getting hit on the street and I could not cope with that. So I took Christine and Bill, who were about six and eight years old, to social services and told them I wanted them put into care. Roger was very difficult as well – he climbed everywhere, up curtains, into everything, he was just literally everywhere. I had to watch him constantly, I probably swore at that stage and he told me to f*** off at two years old and things like that. He used to be a very naughty child, very demanding and forceful. At four years old he was very big and he suffered from clumsiness and a lot of his naughtiness I put down to being clumsy, always knocking things over and falling over stuff. In supermarkets he went knocking things off shelves and aggravating people.

When he was naughty I just smacked him, he got harder and harder, as the years went on he just got harder and in the end it got to the point when I smacked him quite hard and he was laughing. On a few occasions when he was about six or seven years old, I hit him with a dog lead out of frustration, I just did not know what else to do. It just made him more angry and determined to battle against me. Social services became involved and they said they would give me a break and take him for respite care on Saturdays. By the time I got him there and got back home it was time to go and get him again. One weekend I just did not want to bring him home at all so I just left him there altogether. In the meantime they kept phoning me up and they told me he was hitting people and breaking windows as well as hitting teachers at school. Social workers came to persuade me to take him back and I did not want to but eventually I agreed.

Family relationships

When the two older children went into care, I had Roger on his own and I spoiled him, bought him clothes and spent a lot of time with him. This was just before I got re-married and it was just him and me for about a year and a half. Anywhere I went, he went with me. He was spoiled, he had everything he wanted because I was able to give and I think that is a lot where I went wrong. When my new husband Tom came along, Roger resented me and my husband resented Roger as well, so there was a battle between them right from the start and I did not know what to do. If Roger played up I kept it from Tom as I did not want Tom to take it out on Roger. I never involved my husband in my child being disciplined because he was not his dad. Tom wanted to discipline him but I thought he was too strict and I was too careful because I knew that step-dads do not feel the same way about children as their real dads. I was frightened that he might physically abuse him by hitting him too hard so I could not find a way of involving him. I was stuck in the middle with lots of people doing lots of different things without letting everyone know what was going on. Even up to a year ago it was happening, just imagine I am dealing with a situation in the bedroom and trying to keep quiet as well so that the person in the front room did not know. Everything that was going on was covered up, my husband never knew that Roger was aggressive towards me, not till recently. He knew that Roger was abusive towards me but he never knew that it was physical or that Roger was hitting his younger brother, ever. So I drank to relieve the pressure, the trouble is that I found I drank on a daily basis because I just could not handle life. The more I drank the more the kids got away with because I did not want to control them. When I had a drink I just wanted to be by myself and do what I wanted to do and they just got on with it. If Roger asked me for money I would say 'take it, go on, out you go', they got everything they wanted, especially him. I did not control, I just let him get away with everything.

CHAPTER 14

The Further Evolution of Emotional and Behavioural Difficulties

Bringing the Biopsychosocial Approach into Education

Paul Cooper

Introduction

As the opening chapter suggested, a prominent theme in educational and psychological approaches to emotional and behavioural difficulties has been a debate about the relative contributions of nature and nurture in human development. Other chapters in this book have shown awareness of the ways in which nature and nurture factors might interact. However, when we consider the dominance of the technologies of behavioural psychology (see for example Wheldall 1992) and the preference shown among psychologists of education for psycho-social explanations and interventions, including those based on systems theory (Burden 1985; Campion 1985; Cooper and Upton 1990) and socio-cultural theories of learning (see for example Bruner and Haste 1987), this reveals the emphasis on 'nurture' which educationists and psychologists have, by and large, chosen to make in this debate. This emphasis has formed the backbone of educational psychology for much of the era of state education in the UK, at least in part because of a second (laudable) preoccupation of educational psychologists and psychologists of education, namely the desire to make psychology useful in the service of education (see for example Lindsay 1998).

Recently, however, there has been some disturbance to the theoretical status quo, in relation to the relative importance of nature and nurture in EBDs, that has been fuelled by the phenomenon of Attention Deficit/

Hyperactivity Disorder (AD/HD) (the diagnosis of the American Psychiatric Association which describes severe problems of inattentiveness, impulsivity and hyperactivity that are regarded as having a biological basis see for example Barkley 1990, 1997). In response to both an increase in the numbers of children diagnosed with AD/HD and a large-scale demand for the diagnosis among parents of children with attentional and activity problems; the British Psychological Society (BPS) launched an inquiry under the aegis of its Professional Affairs Board. The final report of this inquiry (BPS 1996) took the form of an appraisal of some of the available research evidence concerning the nature, aetiology and management of the condition. The report concludes with a cautious acceptance of the diagnosis and recommends that professional educational psychologists familiarise themselves with the condition. The report emphasises, however, that AD/HD is a concept which is still in the process of evolution and repeatedly stresses the need for it to be dealt with cautiously by practitioners.

In many respects the BPS's AD/HD report is a sensible and academically useful document, which ultimately presents a generally well-balanced and even-handed appraisal of the scientific underpinnings of the concept of AD/HD. It is, in fact, a succinct 'primer' that could be commended to anyone seeking a brief critical overview of the research base of the condition. What the document fails to address, however, is anything of the social and political impact of the AD/HD concept on the profession of educational psychology and its traditions. This is surprising when we consider that the report was produced not by a BPS scientific affairs committee but by a professional affairs committee.

The document fails to acknowledge the historical origins of the profession of educational psychology in relation to the medical model. It fails to acknowledge the possibility that some professional psychologists, for essentially professional, cultural and historical reasons, may be ideologically predisposed to reject a concept which suggests that up to five per cent of the childhood population may suffer from a severely debilitating behavioural condition that often has a biological basis, and that is often treated, in part, with stimulant medication.

The problem of AD/HD for UK educational professionals

AD/HD, coming as it does from a medical background, is seen by some psychologists and educationists as a threat to the progress that has been made in securing educational and social rights for previously disenfranchised groups (Cooper and Ideus, 1995c). Slee (1995, p.74) expresses this view forcefully:

> The monism of locating the nature of disruption in the neurological infrastructure of the child is myopic and convenient. As complex sites of interaction on a range of levels, classrooms provide opportunity for dysfunction across a number of fronts ... The search for institutional dysfunction is ignored by the diagnosticians' probes. ADDS [*sic*] simply refines and extends the individualising and depoliticizing of disruption in schools.

Slee's perspective seems to resonate with Boreham *et al.*'s (1995) research study into parents' and educational psychologists' ways of construing EBDs in which the educational psychologists are portrayed as 'system fixers', demonstrating 'a ready capacity to perceive hidden motives' (p.20), especially in relation to the information they are given by parents and teachers about a child's EBDs. Their common reaction to individualised explanations of EBDs is to 'see through' them, and to identify social-systemic patterns of influence on the problem in hand. The clear implication here is that the educational psychologists in Boreham (*et al.*'s) study, like those of Slee, are not prepared to entertain the possibility that there may be individual, within-child factors at work in given cases of EBDs. Such a view, it is suggested, were it to be widely held, would have the effect of hindering the development of effective responses to AD/HD by attributing to AD/HD the identity of a 'Trojan Horse' under the cover of which the medical profession would regain territory currently occupied by educational psychologists and other educationists (Cooper and Ideus 1995c).

In these circumstances, the BPS report might be seen as a subtle and effective means of neutralising the AD/HD phenomenon, by 'damning with faint praise' the concept of AD/HD. Unfortunately, this has been the preferred interpretation of some informed commentators (see for example Kewley 1997), who have dismissed the report on these grounds and portrayed its purpose as being subtly to undermine the AD/HD concept so as to keep medical professionals from trespassing on the turf of the educational psychologist.

The rise of client power

The central point being made here is that the impact of the emotive, professional and political elements of debates such as that surrounding

AD/HD are often left unexamined (Usher and Edwards 1994). This makes full and open dialogue about the issues difficult. It also makes for misunderstandings and sometimes unnecessary conflict between those who relate the same science (e.g. research on the biological correlates of cognitive and behavioural characteristics) with different value positions (e.g. on the one hand eugenics, and on the other hand the human rights of disabled people). The problem here is that the lay person, whose interests are meant to be served by the deliberations of applied scientists and other warring professionals, is left at best bewildered and at worst utterly unconvinced about the value of science in relation to the problems of everyday life.

There is no simple solution to this problem. What is necessary, however, is for a greater awareness to be shown of such value bases, along with a willingness to engage in frank and open dialogue which encourages the explication and exploration of different value positions. This dialogue should involve academics from different disciplines, professionals from different professions and those 'clients' and 'subjects' with whom professionals and academics work and for whom they often claim to speak.

An interesting parallel to the AD/HD debate is provided by the philosopher Jonathan Glover (1998), who has argued for the need to avoid the tendency of some commentators to reject the science of genetic engineering because of its associations with the Nazi eugenics programmes. His argument is that modern applications of these biotechnologies are often directed at the relief of suffering and the extension of human rights (e.g. to the infertile). The biologist Steven Rose (1997) has identified similar connections between the over-zealousness of contemporary genetic researchers and the Nazi eugenicists, and in doing so has made explicit reference to AD/HD. If such arguments were to remain in the province of dusty academics, they might not have such important ethical consequences. As it is, however, it is increasingly the case that non-scientists tune into these discussions. 'Clients' are increasingly eschewing the passive role assigned to them by the labelling theorists and demanding the application of certain labels as means of gaining access to scarce resources and services (Susman 1994). If they are to be helped towards making the best choices, then they must be served with information that cannot be dismissed as simply serving professional and political interests.

Furthermore, those, such as Steven Rose and Roger Slee, who express concerns about the possible misuse of ideas such as AD/HD, have an important and valid point. AD/HD could be, and in some cases perhaps is, used for negative purposes. It can be used as a simple and convenient excuse for more complex problems. Medication can be used as a cheap and cynical 'chemical cosh' to control troublesome students. On the other hand, almost any concept can be misused and any intervention used for negative purposes. The concept of AD/HD is compatible with many of the approaches to EBDs that are traditionally accepted by UK educational psychologists. There are psychologists and teachers in the UK who are working constructively and effectively with AD/HD (Cooper, in press). Effective approaches to AD/HD in children almost always involve the use of educational interventions and never rely on medication alone (Barkley 1990; Hinshaw 1994). The further development of successful interventions that preclude the need for medication is likely to depend on educationists and psychologists developing an understanding of the nature of AD/HD, rather than attempting to ignore or deride it. In fact, it might well be the case that the strategy of ignoring and deriding AD/HD will be counterproductive, creating a conflict between the medical and educational professions in which the parents of many children suspected of having AD/HD will take the medical side.

The value of a biopsychosocial perspective

One of the problems of being locked into a particular mindset is that it encourages the dismissal of certain items and forms of knowledge. Roger Slee's reaction to AD/HD is to dismiss it out of hand, simply because it derives from a medical origin and implies some degree of individual impairment. For Slee, it would seem, notions of individual pathology and the idea that deviant behaviour in school is socially constructed are mutually exclusive. Similarly, the educational psychologists in Boreham's *et al.*'s study seem to imply that one must choose between individual and systemic explanations. Such positions, it is suggested, are untenable for the following reasons.

Biology is not destiny

The fact is that certain people are placed at greater risk of developing certain forms of EBDs by virtue of their personal make-up, whether it be their socio-economic status, their gender, their ethnicity or aspects of their biological predisposition. The path to deviance is influenced by a combination of these individual characteristics and the social and political environment that children encounter in school and the wider community. There is clear evidence that our schools and other social institutions are often discriminatory towards ethnic minorities and females (see for example Arnot 1985). Similarly, there is a tendency for our schools to reward the kinds of pupil knowledge and styles of learning that are most readily acquired in middle-class families (see for example Willis 1978). By the same token, the biological aspect of AD/HD places children who possess it at risk of behaving in ways that are misconstrued by parents and teachers as wilful misconduct, and thus is likely to lead the child to be subject to unfair criticism and blame for not exercising sufficient control over their impulses. Children with AD/HD, therefore, just like children from ethnic minorities and low SES (socio-economic status) backgrounds, are placed at risk because schools are often intolerant of behaviours and social styles that fall outside a fairly narrow band of preferred behaviours, and social and learning styles. In other words, children with AD/HD are often exposed to inappropriate expectations and educational experiences.

Bio-medical and psycho-social understandings can combine powerfully

When teachers and other educational professionals bring their existing knowledge together with that of medical scientists, the result is what Gregory Bateson (1972) would call a 'bonus'. The bonus is provided by the bringing together of two different ideas, which when combined produce a new idea or set of ideas that amounts to more than the sum of the two original ideas. In the case of AD/HD, a predominantly medical perspective on the condition may emphasise the neurological aspects of aetiology and medication therapy as the most suitable response. A purely educational perspective on AD/HD is more likely to emphasise the contribution that different teaching strategies and patterns of educational organisation and management make to the child's educational performance. A combined educational-medical approach to AD/HD is likely to look at ways in which medical and educational approaches may complement one another. Central to such an approach would be the need to ask questions about the kinds of expectation that are being made of the child in the educational setting and the ways in which these relate to the difficulties expressed by the child. Are the demands being made by the educational setting educationally necessary or desirable, or are they placing undue strain on a child's areas of specific weakness (e.g. their attentional capacities, level of impulse control or distractibility)? In each case, what is the precise blend of medical, educational and psychological input necessary to enable the child to participate fully and effectively in the social and educational experiences of schooling? Recent research, for example, indicates that children with attentional deficits and problems of overactivity, including in some cases children diagnosed as having AD/HD, can be helped to demonstrate improvements in self-controlling behaviours and on-task behaviour through the manipulation of recess (i.e. breaktime) timing (Pellegrini, Davis-Huberty and Jones 1996; Pellegrini and Horvat 1995). It would be a gross over-simplification to generalise from this research that all children with AD/HD would benefit in this way from this type of intervention. The role of the interdisciplinary team is to develop ways of working that are informed by the insights of other professionals as well as the client(s). In the case of AD/HD, the use of medication as an intervention in the educational context will only be justifiable when more directly educational measures have been tried and found to be unsuccessful. And even then medication is almost never seen as a sufficient intervention on its own, always requiring the accompaniment of psycho-social interventions, including educational adaptations (Barkley 1990; Goldstein and Goldstein 1990; Hinshaw 1994). The appropriateness of specific educational interventions will, again, be partly judged on the basis of an informed understanding of the nature of AD/HD. Thus, for example, an awareness of a specific child's difficulties of auditory discrimination and difficulties of focusing on specific stimuli (which are common aspects of AD/HD) may suggest to a teacher that this child's concentration and behavioural difficulties will be exacerbated by placement in groups for particular learning activities. In this case, pairwork may be a preferred option.

Multi-dimensional problems require multi-professional cooperation

Medical professionals often have little training in, or knowledge of, the workings of schools. As a result, they may develop distorted ideas about what goes on in schools and what can be done in schools to help children with AD/HD. The idea, however, that medical practitioners are necessarily wedded to a disease model whereby individuals are automatically pathologised is outdated and inaccurate. This book, for one, illustrates the way in which some medical practitioners embrace systemic thinking, with the emphasis being on the ways in which apparently individual behavioural difficulties are very often the product of an interaction between individual and external factors (Barker 1990; Dare 1990; Higgins 1990). The emphasis in the clinical literature on AD/HD on the use of family therapy underpins this point (see for example Barkley 1990).

One of the ways in which doctors will come to learn more about the possibilities for change inherent in educational settings is by interacting in a cooperative way with teachers and other educational professionals in multi-disciplinary teams, where each member is assertive of their professional expertise as well as respectful of, and receptive to, the expertise of other professionals.

The AD/HD diagnosis can provide a useful basis for professional–client cooperation

The final point here relates to issues of what might be termed the 'civil rights of AD/HD'. Notions of the stigmatising nature of disability labels and their use as instruments of social control and suppression are increasingly anachronistic, particularly in relation to the issue of AD/HD (a precursor of this is, perhaps, dyslexia). The fact is that AD/HD sufferers are to some degree a self-defined group characterised by the desire to find a non-stigmatising explanation and treatment for EBDs that have been previously ignored and/or misconstrued by professionals. In these circumstances, the AD/HD diagnosis is seen as a definition of a problem which brings with it clear lines to follow towards a potential solution. In this way it can be contrasted with the vague and ill-defined, yet utterly stigmatising, label of EBDs. Parent and adult sufferer movements, such as Children and Adults with Attention Deficit Disorder in the US and the many recently formed groups in the UK, are testimony to the way in which the AD/HD diagnosis is being seen as a route towards finding solutions to problems rather than a problem in itself, in that it provides individuals with a basis for securing access to appropriate help and professional support.

This aspect of the disability rights movement (Susman 1994) carries with it, of course, dangers of the disorder becoming a band wagon that will be sought by persons seeking more than their fair share of limited educational and other resources. The way to tackle this problem is for professionals, such as teachers and educational psychologists, to become sufficiently informed about AD/HD to know the difference between genuine AD/HD and 'pseudo-AD/HD' (Hallowell and Ratey 1994), and to be aware of the necessary components of a comprehensive and rigorous assessment process (see for example Detweiler, Hicks and Hicks 1995).

On the positive side, this enthusiasm for the AD/HD concept can be seen as helpful to professionals working with children with EBDs. It is too often the case that issues surrounding EBDs and indiscipline in schools are clouded by feelings of guilt and the apportioning of blame. Sometimes the blame is placed on teachers; at other times it is placed on parents, and at other times on children. The most rudimentary acquaintance with humanistic psychology tells us about the destructive effects of blame and guilt. It is not surprising, therefore, that well-meaning attempts to help teachers in schools and parents in their homes to improve their behaviour management skills often meet with resistance. AD/HD, by removing the issue of culpability from certain children's behavioural problems, opens the door for teachers, pupils and parents to attempt new ways of thinking and behaving that may lead to solutions to difficulties without the attempt being seen as an admission of guilt.

The need for multiple perspectives

If services for children with EBDs are to develop effectively and efficiently, they must draw on the best available knowledge from as wide a range of sources as possible. In the case of AD/HD, there is a massive body of peer-reviewed research literature which supports the existence of a condition defined by activity, impulse control and attention problems, in which cognitive processes are implicated, and which is often associated with neurological abnormalities and patterns of genetic inheritance (Tannock 1998). AD/HD research which sheds light on the cognitive mechanisms which underlie self-regulation and impulse control (Barkley 1997; Tannock 1998) is likely to be of particular value to educators. Furthermore, strong evidence exists to suggest that the particular manifestation of these problems, for example in relation to childhood aggression, can be influenced by experiential factors, in particular the personality characteristics (Nigg and Hinshaw 1998) and child management practices of parents (Woodward, Taylor and Dowdney 1998). Patterns of influence would seem to be bi-directional and recursive rather than uni-directional (Barkley 1990). That is, the biology may create initial difficulties for the child, in terms of attentional and activity problems, which place stress on parents, which leads to negative treatment of the child, which leads to the child behaving worse, which leads to parental stress, and so on. Thus the explanation being offered here is not that the problems are caused by bad parenting or bad teaching, but rather that the parent and teacher strategies are rendered inappropriate by the AD/HD condition.

The possibility that such a condition may affect as many as 5 per cent of all children makes this a serious problem that all professionals who are concerned with childhood EBDs should know about and understand. This is not to say that everything is known about AD/HD that needs to be known. A great deal is still unknown about this condition. More than anything, research is needed into the ways in which the biological and experiential/ environmental influences interact with one another. This can only be achieved through multi-disciplinary research which moves beyond the psycho-social domain and begins to incorporate bio-medical under-standings.

Conclusion: EBDs – past, present and future

This and the opening chapter have explored the development of dominant perspectives on what we now call EBDs over the past 100 years. This is a complex topic with many facets. A key issue throughout these chapters has been that many of the developments described have had their origins in a liberal and humanist educational and psychological tradition. As such, they have many positive implications for children with EBDs.

The final major development to have occurred since 1981 that is dealt with here is the return to centre stage of the debate about the role of individual pathology in the development of EBDs. The main focus of this area of concern is the recent widespread interest that has been shown in AD/HD. The arguments about AD/HD highlight some of the limitations of dominant ways of construing EBDs that have developed among UK professionals since the 1960s and 1970s. It is suggested that the rejection of the AD/HD concept on the grounds that it represents a simple return to the discredited 'medical model' of the 1945 health regulations is founded on a mistaken view of the nature and significance of AD/HD. It is argued that there are social, political, educational and empirical reasons why AD/HD should be taken seriously by educational and other professionals dealing with children with EBDs. If this happens, then the late 1990s will see the burgeoning of the inclusive biopsychosocial approach to EBDs, which will draw on and synthesise the best of existing conceptualisations.

Challenges to the validity of the diagnosis based on a blanket rejection of the 'medical model' will serve only to create a barrier between educational and medical professionals, leaving vulnerable clients (i.e. children and their parents) in an invidious 'piggy in the middle' position. Furthermore, such is the force and seductive power of many current developments in the field of genetics (Cook-Deegan 1994), that we may be on the edge of a new era of biological determinism, in which it will be a popular belief that such outcomes as low cognitive ability (Herrnstein and Murray 1994) and adult criminality (Moir and Jessel 1995) are genetically determined and, therefore, controllable through selective breeding and other measures designed to 'cleanse' the gene pool. If educationists and others concerned with the welfare of children with EBDs wish to contribute to the prevention of a new age of eugenics, we must face up to the role that biology plays in influencing human make-up. An understanding of the biological dimension will enable those opposed to the dangerous excesses of biological determinism to argue from an informed position. The substance of this argument should be that, whilst biology may create propensities for certain social and behavioural outcomes, biology is always mediated by environment and culture. Also, such a comprehensive understanding of the different kinds of influence (biological, psychological and social) which affect behaviour will surely strengthen our ability to meet the needs of children and others with EBDs.

References

Abrams, D., Simpson, A. and Hogg, M.A. (1987) 'Different views: the impact of sex, area of residence, and victimisation on teenagers' explanations for delinquency'. *Journal of Youth and Adolescence 16*, 401–413.

Achenbach, T.M. and Edelbrock, C.S. (1983) *Manual for Child Behaviour: Checklist and Revised Child Behaviour Profile*. Burlington: University of Vermont, Department of Psychiatry.

Ainscow, M. (1994) *Special Needs in the Classroom: A Teacher Education Guide*. London: Jessica Kingsley Publishers.

Ainsworth, M.D.S. and Wittig, B. (1969) Attachment and exploratory behavior of one-year-olds in a strange situation. In B. Foss (ed) *Determinants of Infant Behavior, Vol. IV*. London: Tavistock, pp.113–136.

Allan, J. (1994) 'Parenting education in Australia'. *Children and Society 8*, 4, 344–359.

Alvarez, A. (1992) *Live Company*. London and New York: Tavistock/Routledge.

Aman, M.G. (1987) 'Overview of pharmacotherapy: current status and future directions'. *Journal of Mental Deficiency Research 31*, 121–130.

American Psychiatric Association (1980) *Diagnostic and Statistical Manual of Mental Disorders: Third edition (DSM III)*. Washington, DC: American Psychiatric Association.

American Psychiatric Association (1987) *Diagnostic and Statistical Manual of Mental Disorders: Third edition revised (DSM III-R)*. Washington, DC: American Psychiatric Association.

American Psychiatric Association (1994) *Diagnostic and Statistical Manual of Mental Disorders: Fourth Edition (DSM IV)*. Washington, DC: American Psychiatric Association.

Anastasiow, N.J. and Harel, S. (1993) *At-Risk infants: Interventions, Families and Research*. Baltimore: Brookes.

Appleton, P. and Minchom, P. (1991) 'Models of parent partnership and child development centres'. *Child Care, Health and Development 17*, 1, 27–38.

Apter A. and Shah, M.A. (1994) 'Cultural Effects on eating attitudes in Israel sub-populations and hospitalised anorectics.' *Genetic, Social and General Monographs 120*, 1, 83–99.

Arnot, M. (1991) Equality and democracy: a decade of struggle over education. *British Journal of Sociology of Education 12*, 4, 447–466.

Arnot, M. (ed) (1985) *Race and Gender*. Oxford: Open University.

Asher, S.R. and Coie, J.D. (eds) (1990) *Peer Rejection in Childhood*. Cambridge: Cambridge University Press.

Asher, S.R., Hymel, S. and Renshaw, P.P. (1984) 'Loneliness in children'. *Child Development 55*, 1456–1464.

Ashworth, J. (1996) 'Universities in, and for the world.' *Royal Society of Arts Journal 144*, 5466, 36–45.

Association of Metropolitan Authorities (1995) *Reviewing Special Educational Needs*. London: AMA.

Babad, E., Bernieri, F. and Rosenthal, R. (1989) 'When less information is more information: diagnosing teacher expectations from brief samples of behaviour.' *British Journal of Educational Psychology 59*, Part 3, 281–296.

Bacon, D. (1966) *The Duality of Human Existence*. Chicago: Rand McNally.

Bailey, T. (1991) 'Classroom observation: a powerful tool for teachers?' *Support for Learning 6*, 1, 32–36.

Ball, S. (1981) *Beechside Comprehensive*. Cambridge: Cambridge University Press.

Bandura, A. (1986) *Social Foundations of Thought and Action: A Social Cognitive Theory.* Englewood Cliffs, NJ: Prentice-Hall.

Barkley, R. (1990) *AD/HD: A Handbook for Diagnosis and Treatment.* New York: Guildford.

Barrett, H. (1991) The social experience of childminded children. Unpublished PhD thesis, Birkbeck College, University of London.

Bates, J.E. (1986) On the relationship between temperament and behavior problems. In G.A. Kohnstamm (ed) *Temperament Discussed: Temperament and Development in Infancy and Childhood.* Lisse: Swets and Zeitlinger, pp. 181–189.

Baugher-Palmer, R. and Liddle, H. (1996) 'Adolescent drug abuse: contemporary perspectives on etiology and treatment'. In G. Blau and T. Gullotta (eds) *Adolescent Dysfunctional Behavior.* Thousand Oaks, CA: Sage.

Baumrind, D. (1970) 'Socialization and instrumental competence in young children'. *Young Children 26,* 104–119.

Beck, A.T. (1967) *Depression: Clinical, Experimental and Theoretical Aspects.* New York: Harper & Row.

Beck, A.T. (1976) *Cognitive Therapy and the Emotional Disorders.* New York: New American Library.

Becker, W.C. (1971) *Parents are Teachers.* Champagne Illinois, IL: Research Press.

Belsky, J. (1993) 'Etiology of child maltreatment; a developmental ecological analysis'. *Psychological Bulletin 114,* 3, 413–434.

Bennathan, M. and Boxall, M. (1996) *Effective Intervention in Primary Schools: Nurture Groups.* London: David Fulton Publishers.

Bennett, N. (1986) 'Co-operative learning: children do it in groups or do they?' *Educational Child Psychology 4,* 7–18.

Bennett, N. and Dunne, E. (1992) *Managing Classroom Groups.* London: Simon and Schuster.

Berg, L. (1968) *Risinghill: Death of a Comprehensive.* London: Penguin.

Berger, M. (1985) 'Temperament and individual differences'. In M. Rutter and L. Hersov (eds) *Child and Adolescent Psychiatry: Modern Approaches.* Oxford: Blackwell.

Bernard, M.L. and Bernard, J.L. (1983) 'Violent intimacy: the family as a model for love relationships'. *Family Relations 32,* 283–286.

Bettelheim, B. (1955) *Love Is Not Enough.* Illinois: The Free Press.

Bird, H.R. (1966) 'Epidemiology of childhood disorders in a cross cultural context.' *Journal of Child Psychology and Psychiatry 37,* 35–49.

Birenbaum, M. (1994) 'Towards an adaptive assessment – the students' angle.' *Studies in Educational Evaluation 20,* 239–255.

Bishop, D.V.M. (1989) *Test for the Reception of Grammar.* (2nd edn). Manchester: Manchester University Press.

Blackham, G.J. and Silberman, A. (1971) *Modification of Child Behaviour.* Belmont, CA: Wadsworth.

Blakemore, C. (1991) 'Sensitive and vulnerable periods in the development of the visual system.' In G.R. Bock and J. Whelan (eds) *The Childhood Environment and Adult Disease.* Ciba Foundation Symposium, 156. Chichester: John Wiley and Sons, pp.129–147.

Blakemore, C. and Cooper, G.F. (1970) 'Development of the brain depends upon the visual environment.' *Nature 228,* 477–478.

Blau and Gullotta (1996) *Adolescent Dysfunctional Behaviour. Causes, Interventions and Preventions.* London: Sage.

Blau, B. (1996) 'Oppositional defiant disorder'. In G. Blau and T. Gullotta (eds) *Adolescent Dysfunctional Behavior.* Thousand Oaks, CA: Sage.

Bloom, B.S. (1956) *Taxonomy of Educational Objectives, Vol. 1.* London: Longmans.

Bovair, K. and McGlaughlin, C. (1993) *Counselling in Schools.* London: David Fulton Publishers.

Bowe, R. and Ball, S. (1992) *Reforming Education and Changing Schools: Case Studies in Policy Sociology.* London: Routledge.

Bowers, S. and Wells, L. (1988) *Ways and Means: A Problem Solving Approach*. Kingston: Kingston Friends Workshop Group.

Bowlby, J. (1944) 'Forty-four juvenile thieves: their characters and home-life, II'. *International Journal of Psychoanalysis 25*, 107–128.

Bowlby, J. (1994) 'Forty four juvenile thieves; their characters and home life'. *International Journal of Psychoanalysis 25*, 1–57.

BPS (1996) *AD/HD: A Psychological Response to an Evolving Concept*. Leicester: BPS.

Bradley, L. and Bryant, P. (1985) *Children's Reading Problems*. Oxford: Blackwell.

Bremner, J.G. (1994) *Infancy*. (2nd ed). Oxford, UK and Cambridge, MA: Blackwell.

Bridgeland, M. (1971) *Pioneer Work with Maladjusted Children*. Crosby: Staples.

British Institute of Learning Disabilities (1996) *Physical Interventions: A Policy Framework*. Kidderminster: BILD Publications.

Brodzinsky, D.M., Schechter, D.E., Braff, A.M. and Singer, L.M. (1984) 'Psychological and academic adjustment in adopted children.' *Journal of Consulting and Clinical Psychology 52*, 582–590.

Bronfenbrenner, U. (1979) *The Ecology of Human Development: Experiments by Nature and Design*. Cambridge, MA: Harvard University Press.

Brown, G. (1990) Some more equal than others. Some observations on how well the education system accommodates individual differences. The Tenth Vernon-Wall Lecture. Leicester: The British Psychological Society.

Burland, R. (1987) 'The behavioural approach at Chelfham Mill school'. In K. Wheldall (ed) *The Behaviourist in the Classroom*. London: Allen and Unwin.

Burman, E. (1994) *Deconstructing Developmental Psychology*. London: Routledge.

Burn, M. (1956) *Mr Lyward's Answer*. London: Hamish Hamilton.

Butler-Por, N. (1987) *Underachievers in School*. Chichester: Wiley.

Callias, M. (1994) 'Parent training'. In M. Rutter, E. Taylor and L. Hersov (eds) *Child and Adolescent Psychiatry: Modern Approaches*. (3rd ed). Oxford: Blackwell Scientific.

Callias, M. (1995) 'Parent training'. In M. Rutter, E. Taylor and L. Hersov (eds) *Child and Adolescent Psychiatry*. London: Blackwell, pp.918–935.

Campbell, S.B. and Ewing, L.J. (1990) 'Follow-up of hard-to-manage preschoolers: adjustment at age 9 and predictors of continuing symptoms'. *Journal of Child Psychology and Psychiatry 31, 6*, 871–889.

Campbell, S.B., Ewing, L.J., Breaux, A.M. and Szumowski, E.K. (1986) 'Parent-referred problem three-year-olds: follow-up at school entry.' *Journal of Child Psychology and Psychiatry 27, 4*, 473-488.

Campion, J. (1985) *The Child in Context: Family Systems Theory in Educational Psychology*. London: Methuen.

Campion, J. (1992) *Working with Vulnerable Young Children: Early Intervention*. London: Cassell.

Cantor, L. and Cantor, M. (1991) *Assertive Discipline. Revised edition*. Bristol: Behaviour Management Limited.

Caplan, P.J. and Hall-McCorquodale, I. (1985) 'Mother blaming in major clinical journals'. *American Journal of Orthopsychiatry 55*, 345–353.

Carey, W.B. and McDevitt, S.C. (1989) *Clinical and Educational Applications of Temperament Research*. Lisse: Swets and Zeitlinger.

Carey, W.B. and McDevitt, S.C. (1994) *Prevention and Early Intervention: Individual Differences as Risk Factors for the Mental Health of Children: A Festschrift for Stella Chess and Alexander Thomas*. New York: Brunner/Mazel.

Carrigan, T., Connell, B. and Lee, J. (1987) The 'sex-role' framework and the sociology of masculinity. In C. Weiner and M. Arnot (eds) *Gender under Scrutiny*. London: Unwin Hyman.

Cashdan, A. (1976) 'Problems of adjustment and learning'. *Personality and Learning: Block 9*. Milton Keynes: Open University.

Castle, F. and Parsons, C. (1997) 'Disruptive behaviour and exclusions from school: redefining and responding to the problem'. *Emotional and Behavioural Difficulties 2*, 3, 4–11.

Cattell, R.B. (1973) *Personality and Mood by Questionnaire*. San Franciso, CA: Jossey-Bass.

Charlton, T. and David, K. (1990) 'Towards a whole school approach: helping to ensure schools are fit for the future'. *Links 15*, 3, 20–24.

Cheeseman, P. and Watts, P. (1985) *Positive Behaviour Management: A Manual for Teachers*. Beckenham: Croom Helm.

Chess, S. and Thomas, A. (1984) *Origins and Evolution of Behaviour Disorders: From infancy to Early Adult Life*. New York: Brunner/Mazel.

Chisholm, B., Kearney, D., Knight, G., Little, H., Morris, S. and Tweddle, D. (1986) *Preventive Approaches to Disruption: Developing Teaching Skills*. London: Macmillan.

Cleckly, H. (1941) *The Mask of Insanity*. St Louis: CV Mosby.

Clements, J.C. (1987) *Severe Learning Disability and Psychological Handicap*. Chichester: John Wiley and Sons.

Cocker, C. (1995) Special needs in the infant school. *Support for Learning 10*, 2, 75–78.

Cohn, A.H. and Daro, D. (1987) 'Is treatment too late? What ten years of evaluative research tells us'. *Child Abuse and Neglect 11*, 433–442.

Coie, J.D., Dodge, K.A. and Coppotelli, H. (1982) 'Dimensions and types of social status: a cross-age perspective'. *Developmental Psychology 18*, 557–570.

Cole, T. (1986) *Residential Special Education*. Milton Keynes: Open University.

Cole, T. (1989) *Apart or A Part?* Milton Keynes: Open University.

Comings, D. (1990) *Tourette Syndrome and Human Behaviour*. Derarte, CA: Hope Press.

Cooper, M. (1984) 'Self identity and adolescent school refusers and truants'. *Education Review 30*, 229–237.

Cooper, P. (1993a) *Effective Schools for Disaffected Students: Integration and Segregation*. London: Routledge.

Cooper, P. (1993b) 'Learning from the pupil perspective'. *British Journal of Special Education 20*, 4, 129–133.

Cooper, P. (1995) *Helping them to Learn: Curriculum Entitlement for Children with Emotional and Behavioral Difficulties*. Stafford: Nelson.

Cooper, P. (1996b) 'Fight or flight? Are there too few positive images of masculinity in the media?' *Special*. Autumn, 12–13.

Cooper, P. (1997) 'Biology, behaviour and education: ADHD and the bio-psycho-social perspective.' *Educational and Child Psychology 14*, 1, 31–39.

Cooper, P. (ed) (1995) *Helping Them To Learn: Curriculum Entitlement for Children with Emotional and Behavioural Difficulties*. Stoke on Trent: NASEN.

Cooper, P. (ed) (in press) *Pupils with ADHD: Research, Practice, Theory and Opinion*. London: Whurr.

Cooper, P. and Ideus, K. (1995) 'Is attention deficit hyperactivity disorder a Trojan Horse?' *Support for Learning 10*, 1, 29–34.

Cooper, P. and Ideus, K. (1996) *Attention Deficit/Hyperactivity Disorder: A Practical Guide for Teachers*. London: David Fulton Publishers.

Cooper, P. and McIntyre, D. (1996) *Effective Teaching and Learning: Teachers' and Students' Perspectives*. Buckingham: Open University.

Cooper, P. and Upton, G. (1990) 'An ecosystemic approach to emotional and behavioural difficulties in schools'. *Educational Psychology 10*, 302–321.

Cooper, P. and Upton, G. (1991) 'Controlling the urge to control: an ecosystemic approach to problem behaviour in schools'. *Support for Learning 6*, 1, 22–26.

Cooper, P., Smith, C. and Upton, G. (1991) 'Ethnic minority and gender distribution in schools for children with EBD in England and Wales'. *British Journal of Sociology of Education 12*, 1, 77–94.

Cotterell, G. (1985) *Teaching the Non-Reading Dyslexic Child.* Wisbech: Learning Development Aids.

Coupe, J. and Porter, J. (eds) (1986) *The Education of Children with Severe Learning Difficulties: Bridging the Gap Between Theory and Practice.* London: Croom Helm.

Coupe, J., Barber, M. and Murphy, D. (1988) 'Affective communication'. In J. Coupe and J. Goldbart (eds) *Communication Before Speech: Normal Development and Impaired Communication.* London: Croom Helm.

Coupe-O'Kane, J. and Goldbart, J. (eds) (1988) *Communication Before Speech: Development and Assessment.* London: David Fulton Publishers.

Cox, A.D., Packering, C., Pound, A. and Mills, M. (1987) 'The impact of maternal depression in young children'. *Journal of Child Psychology and Psychiatry 28,* 6, 917–928.

Cox, A.D., Pound, A., Mills, M., Puckering, C. and Owen, A.L. (1991) 'Evaluation of a home visiting and befriending scheme for young mothers: Newpin.' *Journal of the Royal Society of Medicine 84,* 217–220.

Cox, C.M. (1926) *Genetic Studies of Genius Vol 2. The Early Mental Traits of 300 Geniuses.* Stanford, CA: Stanford University Press.

Crick, N.R. and Dodge, K.A. (1994) 'A review and reformulation of social information-processing mechanisms in children's social adjustment'. *Psychological Bulletin 115,* 1, 74–101.

Crick, N.R. and Ladd, G. (1991) Children's perceptions of the consequences of aggressive behaviour: do the ends justify the means? *Developmental Psychology 26,* 6, 12–20.

Cripps, C. (1989) *A Hand for Spelling.* Wisbech: Learning Development Aids.

Crittenden, P.M. (1985) 'Maltreated infants: vulnerability and resilience'. *Journal of Child Psychology and Psychiatry 26,* 85–96.

Croll, P. and Moses, D. (1985) *One in Five.* London: Routledge and Kegan Paul.

Cronk, K. (1987) *Teacher–Pupil Conflict in Secondary Schools.* Lewes: Falmer.

Cropley, A.J. (1994) 'Creative intelligence. A concept of true giftedness.' *European Journal of High Ability 5,* 16–23.

Curry, M. and Bromfield, C. (1994) *Circle Time.* Stafford: NASEN.

Dare, C. (1985) 'Psychoanalytic theories of development'. In M. Rutter and L. Hersov (eds) *Child and Adolescent Psychiatry: Modern Approaches.* Oxford: Blackwell.

Darling, N. and Steinberg, L. (1993) 'Parenting style as context: an integrative model'. *Psychological Bulletin 113,* 3, 487–496.

Davie, R., Upton, G. and Varma, V. (eds) (1996) *The Voice of the Child.* London: Chapman.

Davies, J. and Lloyd-Smith, M. (1996) *On the Margins: The Education Experience of 'Problem' Pupils.* London: Routledge.

Davies, L. (1984) *Pupil Power.* London: Falmer.

Davis, C.A. and Brady, M.P. (1993) 'Expanding the utility of behavioral momentum with young children: where we've been, where we need to go.' *Journal of Early Intervention 17,* 2, 211–223.

Dawson, R. (1981) 'The place of four pioneer tenets in modern practice and opinion'. *New Growth 1,* 2, 44–47.

De Haan, R.F. and Havighurst, R.J. (1957) *Educating Gifted Children.* Chicago: Chicago University Press.

De Luca, R.V., Boyes, D.A., Grayston, A.D. and Romano, E. (1995) 'Sexual abuse: effects of group-therapy on pre-adolescent girls'. *Child Abuse Review 4,* 263–277.

De Mink, F. (1995) 'High ability students in higher education.' In M.W. Katzko and R.F. Monks (eds) *Nurturing Talent: Individual Needs and Social Ability Vol.1.* Assen, the Netherlands: Van Gorcum, pp.168–176.

De Shazer, S. (1985) *Keys to Solution.* New York: Norton.

Dearing, Sir Ron (1994) *National Curriculum Revised.* York: National Curriculum Council.

Deci, E.L. and Ryan, R.M. (1983) *Intrinsic Motivation and Human Behaviour.* New York: Plenum Press.

Deem, R., Brehony, K. and Heaths, S. (1994) 'Governors, schools and the miasma of the market place'. *British Educational Research Journal 20*, 4, 535–550.

Deluty, J. (1981) 'Alternative-thinking ability of aggressive, assertive, and submissive children.' *Cognitive Therapy Research 5*, 309–312.

Denton, C. and Postlethwaite, K. (1985) *Able Children: Identifying Them in the Classroom.* Windsor: NFER-Nelson.

Department of Education and Science (1979) *Aspects of Secondary Education. A Report by HMI.* London: HMSO.

DES (1967) *Children and Their Primary Schools* (the Plowden Report). London: HMSO.

DES (1978) *Special Educational Needs* (the Warnock Report). London: HMSO.

DES (1981a) *Education Act.* London: HMSO.

DES (1981b) *Statistics of Education.* London: HMSO.

DES (1989) *Discipline in Schools* (the Elton Report). London: HMSO.

Detweiler, R., Hicks, A. and Hicks, M. (1995) 'The multi-modal diagnosis and treatment of ADHD'. *Therapeutic Care and Education 4*, 2, 4–9.DfE (1992) *Exclusion: A Discussion Paper.* London: HMSO.

DfE (1993) *Press Release on National Exclusions Reporting System.* London: DfE.

DfE (1994) *DfE Circular 9/94: The Education of Children with Emotional and Behavioural Difficulties.* London: DfE.

DfE (1994) *Pupils with Problems* (draft circulars). London: DfE.

DfE (1998) *DfE Circular 10/98: XX.* London: DfE.

Diekstra, R., Kienhorst, C. and de Wilde, E. (1995) 'Suicide and suicidal behaviour among adolescents'. In M. Rutter and D. Smith (eds) *Psychosocial Disorders in Young People.* Chichester: John Wiley and Sons.

Digman, J.M. (1990) 'Personality and structure: emergence of the five factor model.' *Annual Review of Psychology 41*, 417–440.

Dodge, K.A. (1991) 'The structure and function of reactive and proactive aggression.' In D.J. Pepler and K.H. Rubin (eds) *The Development and Treatment of Childhood Aggression.* Hillsdale, NJ: Lawrence Erlbaum Associates, pp.201–218.

Dodge, K.A. (1993) Social-cognitive mechanisms in the development of conduct disorder and depression. *Annual Review of Psychology 44*, 559–584.

Donellan, A., LaVigna, G., Negri-Shoultz, N. and Fassbender, L. (1988) *Progress without Punishment: Effective Approaches for Learners with Behaviour Problems.* New York: Teacher's College Press.

Dunn, J. and McGuire, S. (1992) Sibling and peer relationships in childhood. *Journal of Child Psychology and Psychiatry 33*, 1, 67–107.

Dunn, L.M., Whetton, C. and Pontille, D. (1982) *British Picture Vocabulary Scale.* Windsor: NFER-Nelson.

Earls, F. (1995) 'Oppositional-defiant and conduct disorders'. In M. Rutter, E. Taylor and L. Hersov (eds) *Child and Adolescent Psychiatry.* London: Blackwell, pp.308–329.

Easterbrooks, M.A., Davidson, C.E. and Chazan, R. (1993) 'Psychosocial risk, attachment, and behavior problems among school-aged children.' *Development and Psychopathology 5*, 389–402.

Elander, J. and Rutter, M. (1996) An update of the status of the Rutter Parents' and Teachers' Scales. *Child Psychology and Psychiatry Review 1*, 31–35.

Ellis, A. (1962) *Reason and Emotion in Psychotherapy.* New York: Lyle Stuart.

Ellis, A. (1973) 'Rational–emotive therapy'. In R. Corsini (ed) *Current Psychotherapies.* Itasca, IL: Peacock.

Ellis, T., McWhirter, J., McColgan, D. and Haddow, B. (1976) *William Tyndale: The Teachers' Story.* London: Writers' and Readers' Publishing Co-operative.

Elshout, J. (1990) 'Expertise and giftedness'. *European Journal of High Ability 1*, 197–203.

Emler, N. and Reicher, S. (1995) *Adolescence and Delinquency.* Oxford: Blackwell.

Erikson, E. (1950) *Childhood and Society*. London: Norton.

Eysenck, H.J. and Eysenck, S.B.G. (1975) *Manual of the Eysenck Personality Questionnaire*. London: Hodder and Stoughton.

Farrington, D. (1987) 'Early precursors of frequent offending.' In J.Q. Wilson and G.C. Loury (eds) *From Children to Citizens: Vol. III. Families, Schools and Delinquency Prevention*, 27–51. New York: Springer-Verlag.

Farrington, D. (1990) 'Implications of criminal career research for the prevention of offending'. *Journal of Adolescence 13*, 93–113.

Farrington, D. (1995) 'The early prevention of juvenile delinquency'. *Journal of the Royal Society of Arts 142*, 5454, 22–31.

Farrington, D. (1995) 'Intensive health visiting and the prevention of juvenile crime.' *Health Visitor 68, 3*, 100–102.

Fawcett Society (1995) *Equal Citizenship Briefing Pack*. London: Fawcett Society.

Federal bureau of Investigation (1991) *Uniform Crime Reports for the United States: 1990*. Washington, DC: US Government Printing Office.

Feldhusen, J.F. (1990) Conceptions of creative thinking and creativity training. Presentation at the 1990 International and Research Networking Conference, Buffalo, New York.

Feuerstein, R. (1993) Mediated learning experience. Keynote presentation at MLE Conference, London, Regents College, February.

Finkelhor, D., Hotaling, G.T., Lewis, I.A. and Smith, C. (1990) 'Sexual abuse in a national survey of adult men and women: prevalence, characteristics and risk factors'. *Child Abuse and Neglect 14*, 19–28.

Fisher, R. (1990) *Teaching Children to Think*. Hemel Hemstead: Simon and Schuster.

Fletcher, C., Carron, M. and Williams, W. (1985) *Schools on Trial*. Milton Keynes: Open University.

Ford, J., Mongon, D. and Whalen, M. (1982) *Special Education and Social Control*. London: Routledge and Kegan Paul.

Forehand, R. and Macmahon, R.J. (1981) *Helping the Non-Compliant Child: A Clinician's Guide to Effective Parent Training*. New York: Guilford Press.

Fox, N.A. and Calkins, S.D. (1993) 'Pathways to aggression and social withdrawal: interactions among temperament, attachment, and regulation.' In K.H. Rubin and J.B. Asendorpf (eds) *Social Withdrawal, Inhibition, and Shyness*. Hillsdale, NJ: Lawrence Erlbaum Associates, pp.81–100.

Franklin, B. (ed) (1986) *The Rights of Children*. Oxford: Blackwell.

Fraser, W.I. and Rao, J.M. (1991) 'Recent studies of mentally handicapped young people's behaviour'. *Journal of Child Psychology and Psychiatry 32*, 79–108.

Freeman, J. (1991) *Gifted Children Growing Up*. London: Cassell.

Freeman, J. (1992) Thinking in the head and thinking in the real world. Keynote presentation at the 3rd International Conference of the European Council for High Ability, University of Munich, Germany.

Frith, U. (1980) *Cognitive Processes in Spelling*. Chichester: Wiley.

Gabel, S. and Hsu, L.K.G. (1986) 'Routine laboratory tests in adolescent psychiatric inpatients; their value in making psychiatric diagnosis and in detecting medical disorders'. *Journal of American Academy of Child Psychiatry 25*, 113–119.

Gallagher, J.J. (1985) *Teaching the Able*. Boston: Allyn and Bacon.

Gallagher, J.J. and Gallagher, S.A. (1994) *Teaching the Gifted Child*. Boston: Allyn and Bacon.

Galloway, D. and Goodwin, C. (1987) *The Education of Disturbing Children*. London: Longmans.

Galton, M. and Williamson, J. (1992) *Group Work in the Primary Classroom*. London: Routledge.

Galton, M., Simon, R. and Croll, P. (1980) *Inside the Primary Classroom*. London: Routledge and Kegan Paul.

Galton, Sir F. (1869) *Hereditary Genius*. London: Collins.

Gardner, H. (1983) Child prodigies. Paper presented at the British Association for Science Conference.

Gardner, H. (1990) *Frames of Mind. The Theory of Multiple Intelligences.* New York: Basic Books.

Garner, P. (1995) 'Sense or nonsense? Dilemmas in the SEN code of practice.' *Support for Learning 10, 1,* 3–7.

Gedye, A. (1989) 'Episodic rage and aggression attributed to frontal lobe seizures'. *Journal of Mental Deficiency Research 33,* 369–379.

German, D. (1986) *Test of Word Finding.* Leicester: Taskmaster Limited.

Getzels, J.W. and Jackson, P.W. (1962) *Creativity and Intelligence: Explorations with Gifted Students.* Chichester: John Wiley and Sons.

Gilkerson, L., Gorski, P.A. and Panitz, P. (1990) Hospital-based intervention for preterm infants and their families. In S.J. Meisels and J.P. Shonkoff (eds) *Handbook of Early Child Intervention.* Cambridge: Cambridge University Press, pp.445–468.

Gilligan, C. (1982) *In a Different Voice. Psychological Theory on Women's Development.* Cambridge, MA: Harvard University Press.

Gillis, J.S. (1980) *Child Anxiety Scale Manual.* Champaigne Illinois: Institute for Personality and Ability Testing.

Glover, J. (1998) Eugenics and human rights. Paper presented at the Amnesty International Lectures, Oxford.

Goldbart, J. (1995) 'Opening the communication curriculum to students with PMLDs'. In J. Ware (ed) *Educating Children with Profound and Multiple Learning Difficulties.* London: David Fulton Publishers.

Goldberg, L.R. (1993) 'The structure of phenotypic personality traits'. *American Psychologist 48,* 26–34.

Good, T.L. and Brophy, J.E. (1985) *Educational Psychology. A Realistic Approach.* London: Holt, Rinehart and Winston.

Goodwin, S. and Mahoney, M.J. (1975) 'Modification of aggression through modelling: an experimental probe'. *Journal of Behaviour Therapy and Experimental Psychiatry 6,* 200–202.

Goswami, U. (1994) 'The role of analogies in reading development'. *Support for Learning 9,* 1, 22–26.

Goyette, C.H., Conners, C.K. and Ulrich, R.F. (1978) 'Normative data on revised Conners Parent and Teacher Rating Scales'. *Journal of Abnormal Child Psychology 6,* 221–236.

Graham, P. (1991) *Child Psychiatry: A Developmental Approach.* (2nd edn.) Oxford: Oxford University Press.

Graham, P. and Rutter, M. (1968) 'The reliability and validity of the psychiatric assessment of the child. II. Interview with the parent'. *British Journal of Psychiatry 114,* 581–592.

Graham, P. and Rutter, M. (1985) 'Adolescent disorders'. In M. Rutter and L. Hersov (eds) *Child and Adolescent Psychiatry: Modern Approaches.* Oxford: Blackwell.

Graham, P.J. (1989) Practical aspects of dietary management of hyperkinetic syndrome. In T. Segvolden and T. Archer (eds) *Attention Deficit Disorder.* Hillside, NJ: Erlbaum.

Greenberg, M.T., Speltz, M.L. and DeKleyn, M. (1993) 'The Role of attachment in the early development of disruptive behavior problems.' *Development and Psychopathology, 5,* 191–213.

Greenberg, M.T., Speltz, M.L., DeKleyn, M. and Endriga, M.C. (1991) 'Attachment security in preschoolers with and without externalizing behavior problems: a replication.' *Development and Psychopathology, 3,* 413–430.

Gresham, F.M., Elliott, S.N. and Black, F.L. (1987) 'Teacher-rated social skills of mainstreamed mildly handicapped children'. *School Psychology Review 16,* 78–88.

Gross, J. (1993) *Special Educational Needs in the Primary School.* Buckingham: Open University.

Grych, J.H. and Fincham, F.D. (1992) 'Interventions for children of divorce: toward greater integration of research and action'. *Psychological Bulletin 111,* 3, 434–454.

Gubbay, S.S. (1976) *The Clumsy Child.* London: Saunders.

Guerber, H. (1938) *The Myths of Greece and Rome.* London: Harrap.

Guidubaldi, J., Cleminshaw, H.K., Perry, J.D., Nastasi, B.K. and Lightel, J. (1986) 'The role of selected family environment factors in children's post-divorce adjustment'. *Family Relations 35*, 141–151.

Hall, F. and Hall, C. (1988) *Human Relations in Education*. London: Routledge and Kegan Paul.

Hall, S. (1990) 'Cultural identity and the diaspora.' In J. Rutherford (ed) *Identity: Community, Culture, Difference*. London: Erlbaum.

Hallowell, E. and Ratey, J. (1994) *Drive to Distraction: Recognising and Coping with ADD from Childhood Through Adulthood*. London: Simon and Schuster.

Hamblin, D. (1974) *The Teacher and Counselling*. Oxford: Blackwell.

Hampson, S.E. (1995) 'The construction of personality'. In S.E. Hampson and A.M. Colman (eds) *Individual Differences and Personality*. London: Longman.

Hargreaves, D. (1967) *Social Relations in a Secondary School*. London: Routledge and Kegan Paul.

Hargreaves, D. (1984) *Improving Secondary Schools*. London: ILEA.

Hargreaves, D., Hester, S. and Mellor, F. (1975) *Deviance in Classrooms*. London: Routledge.

Harris, J., Cook, M. and Upton, G. (1995) *Pupils with Severe Learning Disabilities who Present Challenging Behaviours: A Whole School Approach to Assessment and Intervention*. Kidderminster: British Institute of Learning Disabilities.

Harris, N. (1995) *The Law Relating to Schools*. Croyden: Tolley.

Harter, S. (1985) *The Self-Perception Profile for Children*. Denver, CO: University of Denver.

Harter, S. (1990) 'Developmental differences in the nature of self-representations: implications for the understanding and treatment of adaptive behaviour.' *Cognitive Therapy and Research 14*, 2, 113–142.

Hastings, N. (1995) 'Seats of learning?' *Support for Learning 10*, 1, 8–11.

Hayley, J. (1976) *Problem Solving Therapy*. New York: Jossey Bass Publishers.

Hearn, J. and Lawrence, M. (1985) 'Family sculpting: II. Some practical examples'. *Journal of Family Therapy 7*, 113–131.

Hendrick, H. (1987) 'Constructions and reconstructions of British childhood: an interpretive survey, 1800 to the present'. In A. James and A. Prout (eds) *Constructing and Reconstructing Childhood*. London: Falmer.

Henriques, J., Hollway, W., Urwin, C., Venn, C. and Walkerdine, V. (1984) *Changing the Subject: Psychology, Social Regulation and Subjectivity*. London: Methuen.

Henry, G. (1983) 'Difficulties about thinking and learning'. In M. Boston and R. Szur (eds) *Psychotherapy with Severely Deprived Children*. London: Routledge and Kegan Paul.

Herrnstein, R. and Murray, C. (1994) *The Bell Curve: Intelligence and Class Structure in American Life*. New York: The Free Press.

Hetherington, E.M., Cox, M. and Cox, R. (1979) 'Play and social interaction in children following divorce'. *Journal of Social Issues 35*, 26–49.

Hewett, D. and Nind, M. (eds) *Interaction in Action: Reflections on the Use of Intensive Interaction*. London: David Fulton Publishers.

Hickey, K. (1977) *Dyslexia. A Language Training Course for Teachers and Learners*. Wimbledon.

Hinshaw, S. (1994) *Attention Deficit Disorders and Hyperactive Children*. Thousand Oaks, CA: Sage.

HMI (1992) *Making Provision for Pupils in Maintained Schools*. London: HMSO.

Hobson, (1985) 'Piaget: on the ways of knowing in childhood'. In M. Rutter and L. Hersov (eds) *Child and Adolescent Psychiatry: Modern Approaches*. Oxford: Blackwell.

Hoffman, L. (1981) *Foundations of Family Therapy: A Conceptual Framework for Systems Change*. New York: Basic Books.

Hoffman, L. (1981) *Foundations of Family Therapy*. New York: Basic Books.

Holt, J. (1984) *How Children Fail*. Harmondsworth: Penguin.

Howe, M.J.A. (1990) 'Does intelligence exist?' *The Psychologist 11*, 490–493.

Hughes, J.N. (1988) *Cognitive Behavior Therapy with Children in Schools*. Oxford: Pergamon Press.

Hughes, J.N. (1988) *Cognitive Behaviour Therapy with Children in Schools.* New York: Pergamon Press.

Hundiede, (1985) 'The tacit backgrounds of children's judgments'. In J. Wertsch (ed) *Culture, Communication and Cognition.* Cambridge: Cambridge University Press.

Hunter, R.S. and Kilstrom, N. (1979) 'Breaking the cycle in abusive families'. *American Journal of Psychiatry 136,* 1320–1322.

Illich, I. (1973) *Deschooling Society.* London: Penguin.

James, A. and Prout, A. (1990) *Constructing and Reconstructing Childhood.* London: Falmer.

Jenkins, H. (1994) 'Family interviewing; issues of theory and practice'. In M. Rutter, E. Taylor and L. Hersov (eds) *Child and Adolescent Psychiatry: Modern Approaches.* Oxford: Blackwell Science Limited.

Jenkins, R.L. (1966) 'Psychiatric syndromes in children and their relation to family background'. *American Journal of Orthopsychiatry 36,* 450–457.

Jones, D. (1997) 'Assessing and monitoring anxiety in children.' In K.N. Dwivedi and V.P. Varma (eds) *A Handbook of Childhood Anxiety Management.* Arena: Aldershot.

Jordan, R. and Powell, S. (1995) *Understanding and Teaching Children with Autism.* Chichester: John Wiley and Sons.

Jules, V. and Kutnick, P. (in press) Students' perceptions of a good teacher: the gender perspective. *British Journal of Educational Psychology.*

Kagan, J. (1966) 'The generality and dynamics of conceptual tempo.' *Journal of Abnormal Child Psychology 71,* 17–24.

Kagan, J., Snidman, N. and Arcus, D. (1993) 'On the temperamental categories of inhibited and uninhibited children.' In K.H. Rubin and J.B. Asendorpf (eds) *Social Withdrawal, Inhibition, and Shyness.* Hillsdale, NJ: Lawrence Erlbaum Associates, pp.19–28.

Karnes, M.B. and Johnson, L.J. (1991) 'Gifted handicapped'. In N. Colangelo and G.A. Davies (eds) *Handbook of Gifted Education.* Boston: Allyn and Bacon.

Kazdin, A.E., Rodgers, A. and Colbus, D. (1986) 'The Hopelessness Scale for Children: psychometric characteristics and concurrent validity.' *Journal of Consulting and Clinical Psychology 54,* 241–245.

Keddie, N. (1971) 'Classroom knowledge'. In M. Young (ed) *Knowledge and Control.* London: Macmillan.

Kellmer-Pringle, M. (1970) *Able Misfits.* London: Longmans.

Kellmer-Pringle, M. (1973) *The Needs of Children.* London: Longman.

Kelly, G.A. (1955) *The Psychology of Personal Constructs.* New York: Norton.

Kempe, H.C. and Kempe, R. (1984) *Child Abuse.* London: Open Books.

Kendall, P.C. and Braswell, L. (1985) *Cognitive-Behavioural Therapy for Impulsive Children.* New York: Guilford.

Kiernan, C., Jordan, R. and Saunders, C. (1978) *Starting Off.* London: Souvenir Press.

Kiernan, C., Reid, B. and Goldbart, J. (1987) *Foundations of Communication and Language.* Course manual and video. Manchester: Manchester University Press.

King, J.E. (1991) 'Dysconscious racisms: ideology, identity and the miseducation of teachers.' In L. Stone (ed) (1994) *The Education Feminism Reader.* London: Routledge.

Kirk, S.A., McCarthy, J.J. and Kirk, W.D. (1968) *Illinois Test of Psycholinguistic Abilities revised edition.* Urbana, IL.: University Press.

Knight, B.A. (1992) 'The role of the student in mainstreaming'. *Support for Learning 7,* 4, 163–165.

Knox, J. (1992) 'Bullying in school: communicating with the victim'. *Support for Learning 7,* 4, 154–162.

Kolb, D.A. (1984) *Experiential Learning. Experience as a Source of Learning and Development.* New York: Prentice Hall.

Kounin, J.S. (1970) *Discipline and Group Management in Classrooms.* New York: Holt, Rinehart and Winston.

Kovacs, M. (1980–1981) 'Rating scales to assess depression in school-aged children'. *Acta Paedopsychiatrica 46*, 305–315.

Kraupl-Taylor, E. (1966) *Psychopathology.* London: Butterworth.

Kutnick, P. (1988) *Relationships in the Primary School Classroom.* London: Paul Chapman.

Lacey, P. (1991) 'Managing the classroom environment'. In C. Tilstone (ed) *Teaching Pupils with Severe Learning Difficulties: Practical Approaches.* London: David Fulton Publishers.

Lamb, M.E., Thompson, R.A., Gardner, W.P., Charnov, E.L. and Connell, J.P. (1985) *Infant–Mother Attachment: The Origins and Developmental Significance of Individual Differences in Strange Situation Behavior.* Hillsdale, NJ: Lawrence Erlbaum Associates.

Lang, M. and Tisher, M. (1978) *Children's Depression Scale.* Victoria: Australian Council for Educational Research.

Lask, B. and Bryant-Waugh, R. (1992) Early-onset anorexia nervosa and related eating disorders. *Journal of Child Psychology and Psychiatry 33*, 281–301.

Laslett, R. (1983) *Changing Perceptions of Maladjusted Children.* Portishead: Association of Workers for Maladjusted Children.

Lawrence, J., Steed, D. and Young, P. (1982) *Disruptive Pupils, Disruptive Schools?* London: Croom-Helm.

Ledingham, J.E., Younger, J., Schwartzman, A. and Bergeron, G. (1982) 'Agreement among teacher, peer and self-ratings of children's aggression, withdrawal and likeability.' *Journal of Abnormal Child Psychology 10*, 3, 363–372.

Levitas, M. (1974) *Markist Perspectives in the Sociology of Education.* London: Routledge and Kegan Paul.

Lindsay, G. (1998) 'The practice of educational psychology: Ethics, quality and a broader role.' *The Psychology of Education Review 22*, 1, 4–10.

Lloyd-Smith, M. (1984) *Disrupted Schooling.* London: John Murray.

Lovey, L. and Cooper, P. (1997) 'Positive alternatives to school exclusion'. *Emotional and Behavioural Difficulties 2*, 3, 34–45.

Luborsky, L., Diguer, L., Luborsky, E., Singer, B., Dickter, K. and Schmidt, K.A. (1993) 'The efficacy of dynamic psychotherapies: is it true that "Everyone has won and all must have prizes"?' In N.E. Miller, L. Luborsky, J.P. Barber and J.P. Docherty (eds) *Psychodynamic Treatment Research: A Handbook for Clinical practice.* New York: Harper Collins, pp.497–576.

Luton, K., Booth, C., Leadbetter, P., Tee, P., and Wallace, F. (1991) *Positive Strategies for Behavioural Management.* Windsor: NFER-Nelson.

Lyon, C. (1994) *Legal Issues Arising from the Care and Control of Children with Learning Disabilities who also Present Severe Challenging Behaviour: A Guide for Parents and Carers.* London: The Mental Health Foundation.

Mac an Ghail, M. (1995) *The Making of Men: Masculinities, Sexualities and Schooling.* Milton Keynes: Open University Press.

MacKenzie, R. (1970) *State School.* Harmondsworth: Penguin.

Mahoney, M. (1995) 'The cognitive and constructive psychotherapies: contexts and challenges'. In M. Mahoney (ed) *Cognitive and Constructive Psychotherapies: Theory, Research and Practice.* New York: Springer Publishing Co.

Main, M. and Solomon, J. (1990) 'Procedures for identifying infants as disorganized/disoriented during the Ainsworth Strange Situation.' In M.T. Greenberg, D. Cicchetti and E.M. Cummings (eds) *Attachment in the Preschool Years: Theory, Research, and Intervention.* Chicago and London: University of Chicago Press, pp.121–160.

Makins, V. (1991) 'Five steps to peace in the classroom'. *Times Educational Supplement,* 1 November, p.23.

Malinosky-Rummell, R. and Hansen, D.J. (1993) 'Long-term consequences of childhood physical abuse'. *Psychological Bulletin 114*, 1, 68–79.

Maras, P. (1995) 'What's 'e doing 'ere then?' *The Psychologist,* 15–16.

Maras, P. (1996) 'I'd rather have dyslexia: perceptions of EBDs.' *Educational and Child Psychology 13*, 32–43.

Maras, P. and Hall C. (1996) Children and Young People with EBDs: Toward a Preventative Service in Kent. The Final Report of the University of Greenwich Kent EBD Project. London: University of Greenwich.

Maras, P. and Kutnick, P. (1996) Children with EBDs: a social psychological perspective. Strathclyde: British Psychological Society Social Psychology Section Annual Conference.

Maras, P. and Redmayne, T. (1996) *What are EBDs? A Summary Review of Medical, Cognitive, Social and Societal Perspectives.* London: Greenwich University Press.

Maras, P. and Redmayne, T. (1996) LEAs, EPs and EBDs: toward coherence. Keynote Address. The Annual Conference of the Association of Educational Psychologists. Scarborough.

Maras, P. and Redmayne, T. (1997) 'Helicopter children and butterfly brains. ADHD: perceptions, issues and implications.' *Educational and Child Psychology 14*, 1, 39–50.

Maras, P. with Archer, L. (1997) '"Tracy's in the home corner, Darren's playing lego"' or are they? Gender issues and identity in educational psychology. *Feminism and Psychology 7*, 2, 264–274.

Marshall, L.L. and Rose, P. (1988) 'Family of origin violence and courtship violence'. *Journal of Counselling and Development 66*, 414–418.

Maturana, H.R. and Varela, F.J. (1980) *Autopoiesis and Cognition: The Realization of the Living.* Dordrecht: Reidel.

Maturana, H.R. and Varela, F.J. (1987) *The Tree of Knowledge.* Boston: New Science Library.

McGee, R., Silva, P.A. and Williams, S. (1984) 'Perinatal, neurological, environmental and developmental characteristics of seven-year-old children with stable behaviour problems'. *Journal of Child Psychology and Psychiatry 25*, 573–586.

McGoldrick, M. and Gerson, R. (1985) *Genograms in Family Assessment.* New York: Norton Publishers.

McGuire, J. and Richman, N. (1986) 'Screening for behaviour problems in nurseries: the reliability and validity of the Pre-School Behaviour Checklist'. *Journal of Child Psychology and Psychiatry 27*, 7–32.

McKenzie, K. and Crowcroft, N.S. (1996) 'Describing race, ethnicity and culture in medical research.' *British Medical Journal 312*, 1054, 1094.

McLeod, J.D. and Shanahan, M.J. (1993) *American Sociological Review 58*, 3, 351–366.

McManus, M. (1989) *Troublesome Behaviour in the Classroom: A Teacher's Survival Guide.* London: Routledge.

Mednick, S.A., Gabrielli, W.F. and Hutchings, P.B. (1984) 'Genetic influences in criminal convictions: evidence from an adoption court.' *Science 224*, 891–894.

Mehan, H. (1992) 'Understanding inequality in schools: the contribution of imperative studies.' *Sociology of Education 65*, 1–20.

Mehler, J. and Dupoux, E. (1994) *What Infants Know: The New Cognitive Science of Early Development.* Cambridge, MA and Oxford, UK: Blackwell.

Meichenbaum, D. (1993) 'Changing conceptions of cognitive behavior modification: retrospect and prospect'. *Journal of Consulting and Clinical Psychology 61*, 2, 202–204.

Meichenbaum, D. and Goodman, J. (1971) 'Training impulsive children to talk to themselves: a means of developing self-control'. *Journal of Abnormal Psychology 77*, 115–126.

Meisels, S.J. and Shonkoff, J.P. (1990) *Handbook of Early Child Intervention.* Cambridge: Cambridge University Press.

Miedzian, M. (1991) *Boys Will Be Boys: Breaking the Link between Masculinity and Violence.* London: Virago.

Mills, H. (1996) 'Anxiety disorders'. In G. Blau and T. Gullotta (eds) *Adolescent Dysfunctional Behavior.* Thousand Oaks, CA: Sage.

Mirza, H.S. (1992) *Young, Female and Black.* London: Routledge.

Mitchell, D. and Brown, R.L. (1991) *Early Intervention Studies for Young Children with Special Needs.* London: Chapman and Hall.

Mittler, P. (1990) 'Editorial foreword.' In D. Montgomery *Children with Learning Difficulties*. London: Cassell.

Moir, A. and Jessel, D. (1995) *A Mind to Crime*. London: Channel 4 and Michael Joseph.

Molnar, A. and Lindquist, B. (1989) *Changing Problem Behaviour in Schools*. San Fransisco: Jossey-Bass.

Money-Kyrle, R.E. (1968) 'Cognitive development'. *International Journal of Psychoanalysis 49*. Reprinted in D. Meltzer (ed) *The Collected Papers of Roger Money-Kyrle*. Strath Tay: Clunie Press (1978).

Money-Kyrle, R.E. (1971) 'The aim of psychoanalysis'. *International Journal of Psychoanalysis 52*. Reprinted in D. Meltzer (ed) *The Collected Papers of Roger Money-Kyrle*. Strath Tay: Clunie Press (1978).

Mongon, D. and Hart, S. (1989) *Improving Classroom Behaviour. New Directions for Teachers and Pupils*. London: Cassell.

Monks, F.J. (1992) 'Development of gifted children. The issue of identification and programming'. In F.J. Monks and W. Peters (eds) *Talent for the Future*. Assen/Maastricht: Van Gorcum.

Montgomery, D. (1984) *The Evaluation and Enhancement of Teaching Performance*. Maldon: Learning Difficulties Research Project.

Montgomery, D. (1985) *The Special Needs of Able Children in Ordinary Classrooms*. Kingston: Learning Difficulties Research Project.

Montgomery, D. (1989) *Managing Behaviour Problems*. Sevenoaks: Hodder and Stoughton.

Montgomery, D. (1990) *Children with Learning Difficulties*. London: Cassell.

Montgomery, D. (1990) *Children with Learning Difficulties*. London: Cassell.

Montgomery, D. (1993) 'Learner managed learning in teacher education'. In N. Graves (ed) *Learner Managed Learning: Policy, Theory and Practice*. Leeds: HEC/World Education Fellowship, pp.59–70.

Montgomery, D. (1994) 'Enhancing student learning through the development and use of cognitive process strategies'. In K.A. Heller and E.A. Hany (eds) *Competence and Responsibility*. Seattle: Hogrese and Huber.

Montgomery, D. (1995) 'Education for renewal: changing teaching for learning worldwide'. *New Era in Education 76*, 3, 69–77.

Montgomery, D. (1996a) *Educating the Able*. London: Cassell.

Montgomery, D. (1996b) 'Differentiation of the curriculum for the Highly Able'. *High Ability Studies 7*, 1, 25–37.

Montgomery, D (1997a) *Spelling, Remedial Strategies*. London: Cassell.

Montgomery, D. (1997b) *Developmental Spelling: A Handbook*. Maldon: Learning Difficulties Research Project.

Montgomery, D. and Hadfield, N. (1989) *Practical Teacher Appraisal*. London: Kogan Page.

Montgomery, D. and Hadfield, N. (1990) *Appraisal in the Primary Classroom*. Leamington Spa: Scholastic.

Morse, P. (1991) 'Cursive in Kingston-upon-Thames'. *Handwriting Review 6*, 24–26.

Mortimore, P., Sammons, L., Stoll, L. and Ecob, R. (1988) *School Matters*. London: Open Books.

Mueller, E. and Silverman, N. (1989) 'Peer relations in maltreated children'. In D. Cicchetti and V. Carlson (eds) *Child Maltreatment: Theory and Research on the Causes and Consequences of Child Abuse and Neglect*. Cambridge: Cambridge University Press, pp.529–578.

Murphy, G. and Oliver, C. (1988) 'Decreasing undesirable behaviours'. In W. Yule and J. Carr (eds) *Behaviour Modification for People with Mental Handicaps*. (2nd Edition). London: Croom Helm.

Myklebust, H.R. (1973) *The Development and Disorders of Written Language, Volume 2*. London: Grune and Stratton.

National Autistic Society (1991) *Managing Feeding Difficulties in Children with Autism*. London: The National Autistic Society.

Neill, A. (1916) *A Dominie's Log*. London: Herbert Jenkins.

Neill, A. (1972) 'Freedom works'. In P. Adams, L. Berg, N. Berger, M. Duane and R. Ollendorff (eds) *Childrens' Rights*. London: Panther.

Nettlebeck, T. (1990) 'Intelligence does exist'. *The Psychologist 11*, 494–497.

Newcomb, A.F., Bukowski, W.M. and Pattee, L. (1993) 'Children's peer relations: a meta-analytic of popular, rejected, neglected, controversial and average sociometric status'. *Psychological Bulletin 113*, 99–128.

Nicholson, L.J. (1980) *Women and Schooling*. In L. Stone (ed).

Nicol, R., Stretch, D. and Fundudis, T. (1993) *Preschool Children in Troubled Families: Approaches to Intervention and Support*. Chichester: John Wiley and Sons.

Nigg, J. and Hinshaw, S. (1998) 'Parent personality traits and psychopathology associated with anti-social behaviours in childhood ADHD'. *Journal of Child Psychology and Psychiatry 39*, 2, 145–159.

Nind, M. and Hewett, D. (1994) *Access to Communication: Developing the Basics of Communication with People who have Severe Learning Difficulties through Intensive Interaction*. London: David Fulton Publishers.

O'Brien, M. and Dale, D. (1994) 'Family-centred services in the neonatal intensive care unit: a review of the research.' *Journal of Early Intervention 18*, 1, 78–90.

Oakley, A., Hickey, D., Rajan, K. and Rigby, A.S. (1996) 'Social support in pregnancy: does it have long-term effects?' *Journal of Reproductive and Infant Psychology 14*, 7–22.

Oakley, A., Mauthner, M., Rajan, L. and Turner, H. (1995) 'Supporting vulnerable families: an evaluation of Newpin.' *Health Visitor 5*, 188–191.

Ockelford, A. (1994) *Objects of Reference*. Revised edition. London: RNIB.

Offord, D.R. and Fleming, J.E. (1991) 'Epidemiology'. In M. Lewis (ed) *Child and Adolescent Psychiatry: A Comprehensive Text Book*. Baltimore: Williams and Wilkins.

OFSTED (1993) *Education for Disaffected Pupils*. London: HMSO.

OFSTED (1995) *Pupil Referral Units: The First Twelve Inspections*. London: HMSO.

Oliver, C., Murphy, G. and Corbett, J. (1987) 'Self-injurious behaviour in people with mental handicap: a total population study'. *Journal of Mental Deficiency Research 31*, 147–163.

Oppe, T.E. (1979) Child abuse. Keynote presentation at the interdisciplinary conference and course at Kingston Polytechnic, October.

Osgood, C.E. (1953) *Method and Theory in Experimental Psychology*. New York: Oxford University Press.

Phoenix, A. (1991) *Young Mothers?* Cambridge: Polity Press.

Ouvry, C. (1987) *Educating Children with Profound Handicaps*. Kidderminster: British Institute of Mental Handicap.

Ouvry, C. and Saunders, S. (1996) 'Pupils with profound and multiple learning difficulties'. In B. Carpenter, R. Ashdown and K. Bovair (eds) *Enabling Access: Effective Teaching and Learning for Pupils with Learning Difficulties*. London: David Fulton Publishers.

Palazzoli, M.S., Boscolo, L., Ceechin, G. and Prata, G. (1980) 'Hypothesising – circularity – neutrality: three guidelines for the conductor of the session'. *Family Process 19*, 3–12.

Parsons, C., Berne, L., Hailes, J. and Howlett, K. (1994) *Excluding Primary School Children*. London: Family Policy Studies Centre.

Passow, A.H. (1990) 'Needed research and development in teaching high ability children'. *European Journal of High Ability 1*, 15–24.

Patterson, G.R. (1982) *Coercive Family Process*. Eugene, OR: Castalia Publications.

Paul, R. (1990) *Critical Thinking Theory*. Sonoma: Sonoma State University, Centre for Critical Thinking and Moral Critique.

Pellegrini, D.S. (1994) 'Training in interpersonal cognitive problem-solving'. In M. Rutter, E. Taylor and L. Hersov (eds) *Child and Adolescent Psychiatry: Modern Approaches* 3rd edition. Oxford: Blackwell Scientific.

Peters, M.L. and Smith, B. (1986) 'The productive process. An approach to literacy for children with difficulties'. In B. Root (ed) *Resources for Reading. Does Quality Count?* London: UKRA Macmillan, pp.161–171.

Phillips, B.N. (1978) *School Stress and Anxiety: Theory Research and Intervention.* New York: Human Sciences Press.

Porter, R.B. and Cattell, R.B. (1963) *The Children's Personality Questionnaire.* Champaigne, Illionois: Institute for Personality and Ability Testing.

Purkey, S. and Smith, M. (1983) 'Effective schools: a review'. *Elementary School Journal 83*, 4, 427–452.

Puttallaz, M. and Wasserman, A. (1990) Children's entry behaviour. In S.R. Asher and J.D. Coie (eds) *Peer Rejection in Childhood.* Cambridge: Cambridge University Press.

Quinton, D., Rutter, M. and Rowlands, O. (1976) 'An evaluation of an interview assessment of marriage'. *Psychological Medicine 6*, 577–586.

Rabiner, D.L. and Gordon, L.V. (1993) 'The relationship between children's social concerns and their social interaction strategies, differences between rejected and accepted boys.' *Social Development 2*, 2, 83–96.

Radford, J. (1990) *Child Prodigies and Extremely Early Activeness.* New York: The Free Press.

Rawlings, A. (1996) *Ways and Means Today.* Kingston: Kingston Friends Workshop Group.

Reeves, J.C., Werry, J.S., Elkind, G.S. and Zametkin, A. (1987) 'Attention deficit, conduct, oppositional and anxiety disorders in children: II. Clinical characteristics'. *Journal of the American Academy of Child and Adolescent Psychiatry 26*, 144–155.

Rende, R. and Plomin, R. (1993) 'Families at risk for psychopathology: who becomes affected and why?' *Development and Psychopathology 5*, 529–540.

Rennie, E. (1993) 'Behavioural support teaching: points to ponder'. *Support for Learning 8*, 1, 7–10.

Renzulli, J.S. (1977) *The Enrichment Triad. A Model for Developing Defensible Programs for the Gifted and Talented.* Mansfield, CN: Creative Learning Press.

Renzulli, J.S. (1994) *Schools for Talent Development: A Practical Plan for Total School Improvement.* Mansfield, CT: Creative Learning Press.

Renzulli, J.S. (1995) 'New directions for the schoolwide enrichment model'. In M.W. Katzko and F.J. Monks (eds) *Nurturing Talent. Individual Needs and Social Ability.* Assen, the Netherlands: Van Gorcum, pp.162–167.

Resnick, L.B. (1989) *Knowing, Learning and Instruction. Essays in Honour of Robert Glaser.* Hillsdale, NJ: Erlbaum, pp.1–24.

Reynolds, C.R. and Paget, K.D. (1981) 'Factor analysis of the revised Children's Manifest Anxiety Scale for Blacks, Whites, Males and Females with a national and innovative sample'. *Journal of Consulting and Clinical Psychology 49*, 352–359.

Reynolds, C.R. and Richmond, B.O. (1978) 'What I think and feel: a revised measure of children's manifest anxiety'. *Journal of Abnormal Child Psychology 6*, 271–280.

Reynolds, D. and Sullivan, M. (1979) 'Bringing schools back in'. In L. Barton and A. Meighan (eds) *Schools, Pupils and Deviance.* Driffield: Nafferton.

Ridehalgh, N. (1996) A study of the relative effectiveness of three dyslexia teaching programmes. Unpublished MA Thesis, Middlesex University, London.

Robins, L. (1966) *Deviant Children Grow Up 1922–1966.* Baltimore: Williams and Williams.

Rogers, C. (1980) *A Way of Being.* Boston: Houghton Mifflin.

Rogers, W. (1994a) 'Teaching positive behaviour to behaviourally disordered students in primary schools'. *Support for Learning 9*, 4, 166–170.

Rogers, W. (1994b) *Behavioural Recovery: A Whole School Approach for Behaviour Disordered Children.* Melbourne: Australian Council for Educational Research.

Rose, S. (1997) *Lifelines: Biology, Freedom Determinism.* London: Penguin.

Rosser, E. and Harré, R. (1976) 'The meaning of trouble'. In M. Hammersley and P. Woods (eds) *The Process of Schooling.* Milton Keynes: Open University.

Rothbart, M.K. and Derryberry, D. (1981) Development of individual differences in temperament. In M.E. Lamb and A.L. Brown (eds) *Advances in Developmental Psychology, I.* Hillsdale, NJ: Lawrence Erlbaum Associates, pp.37–86.

Rubin, K.H. and Lollis, S.P. (1988) Origins and consequences of social withdrawal. In J. Belsky and T. Nezworski (eds) *Clinical Implications of Attachment.* Hillsdale, NJ: Lawrence Erlbaum Associates, pp.219–252.

Rust, J., Golombok, S. and Trickey, G. (1993) *Wechsler Objective Reading Dimensions Manual.* Sidcup: The Psychological Corporation.

Rutter, M. (1975) *Helping Troubled Children.* Harmondsworth: Penguin.

Rutter, M. (1979) 'Protective factors in children's responses to stress and disadvantage'. In M.W. Kent and J.E. Rolf (eds) *Primary Prevention of Psychopathology: Vol. 3. Social Competence in Children.* Hanover, NH: University Press of New England, pp.49–74.

Rutter, M. (1987) 'Temperament, personality and personality disorder.' *British Journal of Psychiatry 150,* 443–458.

Rutter, M. (1989) 'Attention deficit disorder/hyperkinetic syndrome: conceptual and research issues regarding diagnosis and classification.' In T. Segvolden and T. Archer (eds) *Attention Deficit Disorder.* Hillside, NJ: Erlbaum.

Rutter, M. (1989) 'Pathways from childhood to adult life.' *Journal of Child Psychiatry and Psychology 30, 1,* 23–51.

Rutter, M. (1989) 'Isle of Wight revisited; 25 years of child psychiatric epidemiology'. *Journal of the American Academy of Child and Adolescent Psychiatry 28,* 633–653.

Rutter, M. and Giller, H. (1983) *Juvenile Delinquency: Trends and Perspectives.* Harmondsworth: Penguin.

Rutter, M. and Smith, D. (1995) (eds) *Psychosocial Disorders in Young people.* Chichester: Wiley.

Rutter, M. and Smith, D. (1995) 'Towards causal explanations of time trends in psychosocial disorders'. In M. Rutter and D. Smith (eds) *Psychosocial Disorders in Young People.* Chichester: John Wiley and Sons.

Rutter, M. and Smith, D. (1995) (eds) *Psychosocial Disorders in Young People.* Chichester: John Wiley and Sons.

Rutter, M., Cox, A., Tupling, C., Berger, M. and Yule, W. (1975) 'Attainment and adjustment in two geographical areas.1. Prevalence of Psychiatric disorders'. *British Journal of Psychiatry 126,* 493–509.

Rutter, M., Tizard, J. and Whitmore, K. (1970) (eds) *Education, Health and Behaviour.* London: Longman.

Rutter, M.L., Maughan, M., Mortimore, P. and Ouston, J. (1979) *Fifteen Thousand Hours.* London: Open Books.

Ryan, J. and Thomas, F. (1987) *The Politics of Mental Handicap. Revised edition.* London: Free Association Books.

Ryan, M.L., Connell, J.P. and Deci, E.L. (1985) 'A motivational analysis of self determination and self regulation in education'. In C. Ames and R. Ames (eds) *Research on Motivation in Education: The Classroom Milieu, Vol.2.* New York: Academic Press.

Safran, J.S. and Safran, S.P. (1987) 'Teachers' judgements of problem behaviours.' *Exceptional Children 54, 3,* 240–244.

Sameroff, A.J. (1991) 'The social context of becoming a person.' In M. Woodhead, R. Carr and P. Light (eds) *Becoming a Person.* London: Routledge/The Open University, pp.167–189.

Sameroff, A.J. and Chandler, M. (1975) 'Reproductive risk and the continuum of caretaking casuality'. In F.D. Horowitz (ed) *Review of Child Development Research, No. 4.* Chicago: University of Chicago Press.

Sarason, S.B., Davidson, K.S., Lighthall, F.F., Waite, R.R. and Ruebush, B.K. (1960) *Anxiety in Elementary School Children: A Report of Research.* New York: John Wiley.

Schostak, J. (1982) *Maladjusted Schooling.* Lewes: Falmer.

Schweinhart, L., Weikart, D. and Larner, M. (1986) 'Consequences of three preschool curriculum models through age 15.' *Early Childhood Research Quarterly, 1,* 15–45.

Scott MacDonald, W. (1971) *Battle in the Classroom.* Brighton: Intext.

Seeley, S., Murray, L. and Cooper, P. (1996) 'Postnatal depression: the outcome for mothers and babies of health visitor intervention.' *Health Visitor 69, 4,* 135–138.

Segal, L. (1997) *Slow Motion.* London: Routledge.

Seifer, R., Schiller, M., Sameroff, A.J., Resnick, S. and Riordan, K. (1996) 'Attachment, maternal sensitivity, and infant temperament during the first year of life.' *Developmental Psychology 32, 1,* 12–25.

Seitz, V. and Provence, S. (1990) 'Caregiver-focused models of early intervention.' In S.J. Meisels and J.P. Shonkoff (eds) *Handbook of Early Child Intervention.* Cambridge: Cambridge University Press, pp.400–427.

Sharp, R. and Green, A. (1975) *Education and Social Control.* London: Routledge and Kegan Paul.

Shaw, D.S. and Vondra, J.I. (1993) 'Chronic family adversity and infant attachment security.' *Journal of Child Psychology and Psychiatry 34, 7,* 1205–1215.

Shaw, O. (1965) *Maladjusted Boys.* London: Allen and Unwin.

Silbereisen, R., Robins, L. and Rutter, M. (1995) In M. Rutter and D. Smith (eds) *Psychosocial Disorders in Young People.* Chichester: John Wiley and Sons.

Simeonsson, R.J. and Bailey, D.B. (1990) Family dimensions in early intervention. In S.J. Meisels and J.P. Shonkoff (eds) *Handbook of Early Child Intervention.* Cambridge: Cambridge University Press, pp.428–444.

Simon, B. and Chitty, C. (1993) *Save Our Schools.* London: Lawrence and Wishart.

Simonton, D.K. (1988) *Scientific Genius. A Psychology of Science.* Cambridge: Cambridge University Press.

Skinner, B.F. (1954) *Science and Human Behaviour.* New York: Macmillan.

Slee, R. (1995) *Changing Theories and Practices of Discipline.* London: Falmer.

Smith, C.J. and Laslett, R. (1989) *Effective Classroom Management.* London: Routledge.

Smith, D. (1995) 'Youth crime and conduct disorders: trends, patterns and causal explanations'. In M. Rutter and D. Smith (eds) *Psychosocial Disorders in Young People.* Chichester: John Wiley and Sons.

Smith, D. and Rutter, M. (1995) 'Time trends in psychosocial disorders of youth'. In M. Rutter and D. Smith (eds) *Psychosocial Disorders in Young People.* Chichester: John Wiley and Sons.

Smith, D. and Tomlinson, S. (1989) *The School Effect: A Study of Multi-Racial Comprehensives.* London: Policy Studies Institute.

Smith, D.J. (1995) *The Sleep of Reason: The James Bulger Case.* London: Arrow.

Spender, D. (1983) *Invisible Women. The Schooling Scandal.* London: Writers and Readers.

Spielberger, C.D., Edwards, D.C., Montouri, J. and Lushene, R.E. (1970) *The State-Trait Anxiety Inventory for Children.* Palo Alto, CA: Consulting Psychologists' Press.

Spielberger, C.D., Gorsuch, R.L. and Lushene, R.E. (1970) *Manual for the State–Trait Anxiety Inventory.* Palo Alto, CA: Consulting Psychologists' Press.

Spivack, G., Platt, J.J. and Shure, M.B. (1976) *The Problem Solving Approach to Adjustment.* San Francisco: Jossey-Bass.

Sternberg, R.J. (1986) *Beyond IQ. A Triarchic Theory of Intelligence.* New York: Cambridge University Press.

Stevenson, J., Richman, N. and Graham, P. (1985) 'Behaviour problems and language abilities at three years and behavioural deviance at eight years.' *Journal of Child Psychology and Psychiatry 26, 2,* 215–230.

Stirling, M. (1992) 'How many pupils are excluded?' *British Journal of Special Education 19,* 4, 14–18.

Stott, D.H. (1974) *Bristol Social Adjustment Guides Manual: The Social Adjustment of Children* (5th edition). London: Hodder and Stoughton.

Stott, D.H. (1981) 'Behaviour disturbance and failure to learn: a study of cause and effect'. *Educational Research 23*, 3, 187–193.

Susman, J. (1994) 'Disability, stigma and deviance'. *Social Sciences and Medicine 38*, 15–22.

Sutton, C. (1995) 'Educating parents to cope with difficult children.' *Health Visitor 68*, 7, 284–285.

Tajfel, H. and Turner, J. (1979) An integrative theory of intergroup conflict. In S. Worchel and W.G. Austin (eds) *Psychology of Intergroup Relations*. Chicago: Nelson-Hall.

Tattum, D. (1982) *Disruptive Pupils in Schools and Units*. Chichester: John Wiley and Sons.

Terman, L.M. (1925) *Genetic Studies of Genius. The Mental and Physical Traits of a Thousand Gifted Children Vol. 1*. Stanford, CA: Stanford University Press.

Terman, L.M. (1937) *Genetic Studies of Genius. Twenty Five Years' Follow up of a Superior Group Vol. 3*. Stanford, CA: Stanford University Press.

Terman, L.M. and Merrill, M.A. (1960) *Stanford–Binet Intelligence Scale: Manual for the Third Revision Form L-M*. Boston, MA: Houghton Mifflin Company.

Terman, L.M. and Oden, M.H. (1945) *Genetic Studies of Genius. The Gifted Group at Mid Life. A 35 Year Follow-up. Vol. 5*. Stanford, CA: Stanford University Press.

Terre, L. and Burkhart, B. (1996) 'Problem sexual behaviors in adolescence'. In G. Blau and T. Gullotta (eds) *Adolescent Dysfunctional Behavior*. Thousand Oaks, CA: Sage.

Thomas, A. and Chess, S. (1977) *Temperament and Development*. New York: Brunner Mazel.

Torrance, E.P. (1966) *Torrance Tests of Creative Thinking*. 1st edn. Princeton, NJ: Personnel Press.

Usher, R. and Edwards, R. (1994) *Postmodernism and Education*. London: Routledge.

Van Den Boom, D.C. (1989) 'Neonatal irritability and the development of attachment.' In G.A. Kohnstamm, J.E. Bates and M.K. Rothbart (eds) *Temperament in Childhood*. Chichester: John Wiley and Sons, pp.299–318.

Van der Lely, H.K.J. (1996) 'Specifically language impaired and normally developing children: verbal passive vs. adjectival passive sentence interpretation'. *Lingua 98*, 243–272.

Van der Lely, H.K.J. and Stollwerck, L. (1997) 'Binding theory and grammatical specific language impairment in children'. *Cognition 62*, 245–290.

Van Ijzendoorn, M.H., Dijkstra, J. and Bus, A.G. (1995) 'Attachment, intelligence, and language: a meta-analysis.' *Social Development 4*, 2, 115–128.

Van-Os, J., Castle, D.J., Takei, N., Der, G., Murray, R.M. (1996) 'Psychotic illness in ethnic minorities: clarification from the 1991 census.' *Psychological Medicine 26*, 1, 203–8.

Vernon, A. (1993) *Developmental Assessment and Intervention with Children and Adolescents*. Alexandria, VA: American Counseling Association.

Walkerdine, V. (1990) *Schoolgirl Fictions*. London: Verso.

Ware, J. (1995a) (ed) *Educating Children with Profound and Multiple Learning Difficulties*. London: David Fulton Publishers.

Ware, J. (1995b) 'Using interaction in the education of pupils with PMLDs: (i) creating contingency-sensitive environments'. In J. Ware (ed) *Educating Children with Profound and Multiple Learning Difficulties*. London: David Fulton Publishers.

Ware, J. (1995c) 'Classroom organisation'. In J. Ware (ed) *Educating Children with Profound and Multiple Learning Difficulties*. London: David Fulton Publishers.

Ware, J. (1996) *Creating a Responsive Environment for People with Profound and Multiple Learning Difficulties*. London: David Fulton Publishers.

Watson, J. (1995) 'Using interaction in the education of pupils with PMLDs: (ii) intensive interaction: two case studies'. In J. Ware (ed) *Educating Children with Profound and Multiple Learning Difficulties*. London: David Fulton Publishers.

Watts, J. (1977) *The Countesthorpe Experience*. London: Unwin.

Watzlawick, P., Weakland, J. and Fisch, R. (1974) *Change: Principles of Problem Formation and Resolution*. New York: Norton.

Wechsler, D. (1944) *The Measurement of Adult Intelligence* (3rd edition). Baltimore, MD: Williams and Wilkins.

Wechsler, D. (1992) *Wechsler Intelligence Scale for Children* (3rd edition). London: The Psychological Corporation.

Weiner, G. (1992) 'Equal opportunities, feminism and girls' education: an introduction.' In G. Weiner (ed) *Just a Bunch of Girls*. Milton Keynes: Open University Press.

Werner, E.E. and Smith, R.S. (1982) *Vulnerable but Invincible: A Longitudinal Study of Resilient Children and Youth*. New York: McGraw-Hill.

Wheldall, K. (1987) (ed) *The Behaviourist in the Classroom*. London: Allen and Unwin.

Wheldall, K. (1992) *Discipline in Schools: Psychological Responses to the Elton Reports*. London: Routledge.

Wheldall, K. and Glynn, T. (1989) *Effective Classroom Learning*. London: Blackwell.

Wheldall, K. and Merritt, F. (1984) *BATPACK, Positive Products*. Birmingham: Birmingham University Press.

Wheldall, K. and Merritt, F. (1985) *Positive Teaching: A Behavioural Approach*. London: Unwin.

Wheldall, K. and Merritt, F. (1986) 'Looking for a positive route out of poor class behaviour'. *Special Children 2*, 22–27.

White, M. (1989) 'The externalising of the problem and the re-authoring of lives and relationships'. *Dulwich Centre Newsletter*, 3–21.

White, M. and Epston, D. (1990) *Narrative Means to Therapeutic Ends*. New York/London: Norton.

Wilding, P. (1982) *Professional Power and Social Welfare*. London: Routledge and Kegan Paul.

Wilkinson, C. (1995) *The Drop Out Society: Young People on the Margin*. Leicester: National Youth Agency.

Williams, G. (1997) 'Doubly deprived'. In G. Williams (ed) *Internal Landscapes and Foreign Bodies*. London: Duckworth.

Williams, T.R. and Gilmour, J.D. (1994) 'Annotation: sociometry and peer relationships'. *Journal of Child Psychiatry 35*, 6, 997–1013.

Wills, D. (1960) *Throw Away Thy Rod*. London: Gollancz.

Wilson, M. and Evans, M. (1980) *Education of Disturbed Children*. London: Schools Council/Methuen.

Wolpe, J. (1958) *Psychotherapy by Reciprocal Inhibition*. Stanford, CA: Stanford University Press.

Woodward, L., Taylor, E. and Dowdney, L. (1998) 'The parenting and family functioning of children with hyperactivity'. *Journal of Child Psychology and Psychiatry 39*, 2, 161–169.

Woollett, A., White, D.G. and Lyon, M.L. (1982) 'Studies involving fathers: subject refusal, attrition and sampling bias'. *Current Psychological Reviews 2*, 193–212.

World Health Organisation (1992) *The ICD 10 Classification of Mental and Behavioural Disorders: Clinical Descriptions and Diagnostic Guidelines*. Geneva: World Health Organisation.

Wyman, R. (1986) *Multiply Handicapped Children*. London: Souvenir Press.

Yewchuk, C.R. and Bibby, M.A. (1989) 'The handicapped gifted child: problems of identification and programming'. *Canadian Journal of Education 14*, 1, 102–108.

Yoshikawa, H. (1994) 'Prevention as cumulative protection: effects of early family support and education on chronic delinquency and its risks'. *Psychological Bulletin 115*, 1, 28–54.

Young, M. (ed) (1971) *Knowledge and Control: New Directions for the Sociology of Education*. London: Collier-Macmillan.

Zarkowska, E. and Clements, J. (1994) *Problem Behaviour and People with Severe Learning Disabilities: The S.T.A.R. Approach*. 2nd edition. London: Chapman and Hall.

Zigler, E. and Valentine, J. (1979) *Project Head Start: A Legacy of the War on Poverty*. New York: Free Press.

The Contributors

Dr Rob Ashdown is Headteacher at St Luke's School, Scunthorpe.

Dr Helen Barrett is Senior Lecturer in Developmental Psychology at Thames Valley University.

Dr Paul Cooper is Lecturer in Education in the School of Education, University of Cambridge.

Dr David Jones is Chairman of the Department of Psychology at Birkbeck College, University of London.

Dr Melanie Jones is Lecturer in Psychology at Birkbeck College, University of London.

Dr Vinod Kumar is a Consultant Child and Adolescent Psychiatrist at the Child and Family Therapy Centre, Mansfield.

Peter Lloyd-Bennett is an Educational Psychologist in Northamptonshire.

Dr Pam Maras is Senior Lecturer in Psychology at the University of Greenwich.

Professor Diane Montgomery is Professor of Psychology at Middlesex University.

Dr Rafik Refaat is Lecturer in Child and Adolescent Psychiatry at University College London.

Biddy Youell is a Child and Adolescent Psychotherapist in Buckinghamshire and London, and an academic tutor at the Tavistock Clinic.

Professor Harry Zeitlin is Professor of Child and Adolescent Psychiatry at University College London.

Subject Index

Author Index